PIERRE CARDIN

pierre cardin

The Man Who Became a Label

RICHARD MORAIS

BANTAM PRESS

LONDON · NEW YORK · TORONTO · SYDNEY · AUCKLAND

TRANSWORLD PUBLISHERS LTD
61–63 Uxbridge Road, London W5 5SA

TRANSWORLD PUBLISHERS (AUSTRALIA) PTY LTD
15–23 Helles Avenue, Moorebank, NSW 2170

TRANSWORLD PUBLISHERS (NZ) LTD
Cnr Moselle and Waipareira Aves,
Henderson, Auckland

Published 1991 by Bantam Press
a division of Transworld Publishers Ltd
Copyright © Richard Morais 1991

A catalogue record for this book is available from the British Library
ISBN 0593 018001

Typeset in 11/13 pt Garamond
by Photoprint, Torquay, South Devon

Printed in Great Britain
by Mackays of Chatham, PLC, Chatham, Kent

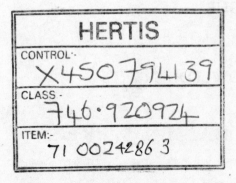

CONTENTS

FOR THAT SPECIAL PERSON, SUSAN.

THE BIGGEST NAME IN THE WORLD $\qquad$ 1

'The office is mine,' he says to me, waving his hands. 'I pay for the location, the people, secretaries. Everything.'

Pause.

'It is the biggest name in the world.'

Pause.

'And I have my theatre. I spend a lot of money on my theatre. It is also to promote the name. I tried to extend my popularity in every field in theatre, culture, music, dance, concert. Everybody knows Pierre Cardin because he sponsors theatre. I'm in food now, and hotels. It's a very big name in every field.'

His voice is extremely nasal, whining. Very much reminiscent of Truman Capote.

'Maybe it's the biggest name in every field – diplomatic people, fashion, industry, dishes, beds.'

Pause.

'It's the most important name in the world. It is number one.'

It is March, 1988, and the conversation is taking place at Pierre Cardin's headquarters in Paris, a conference room at 27 Avenue de Marigny, opposite

PIERRE CARDIN

the Elysée palace. Behind the fashionable address, however, lurk dingy rooms. The walls are smeared with fingerprints; the cheap grey carpet is tattered and threadbare. The conference seats – round foam chairs that look like sawn-off eggs – were designed by Cardin. The seat cushions are filthy, stained with a decade of ashes and coffee spills.

'My name is on everything,' he repeats.

The 69-year-old world-famous couturier, man of culture, man of everything, does not look well. He is not properly shaved and the white stubble gives his appearance a very unsavoury cast. His wispy grey hair needs combing. He is wearing an ill-fitting cashmere jacket and grey slacks, with a purple silk foulard draped from his breast pocket; a paisley tie on a white cotton shirt with thin, grey stripes. The brown loafers are warped, scuffed and badly soiled with what look like salt marks from perspiring feet.

'My standing is higher now than it ever was before,' he says, quivering with excitement. 'We didn't lose our top-level customers, people who buy dresses for 200,000 francs. You will see the [haute-couture] house; it is top-class. There is no building higher. We have all the most important people, not just rich but diplomatic – Madame Chirac, Madame Pompidou, Madame Barre, all these people come to my house to dress.'

He talks very gently now. 'When you grow in different directions you can reach completely different people, not only the very rich, but the different class levels of people.' Pause. 'It is the reason I sometimes sell something very small. I don't like to keep my name only in high class. What is the fortune of the rich people? Some it is fish, some it is cars, some is from food. If you know these respectable people . . . Where does their money come from? Ask the question. Sometimes you are surprised.'

Another man, a public relations officer for the House of Cardin, chimes in. 'He is proud to prove that his money comes from everywhere. From every class of people.'

Cardin continues. 'They don't like you to know where their money comes from. You would be surprised where their money comes from.'

He is fidgeting, constantly turning in his seat, extending his legs, curling them around the base of the chair. He jumps up, waving his long hands, to grab a Pierre Cardin product from a bookshelf. In a flash he returns to his chair, slumps. 'If I give my name to a product it is only to the best product and manufacturer. It's like a queen or a president who goes to a cocktail party to honour the reception.'

He is up again, grabbing items off the bookshelf. He turns. He is swinging a frying pan in the air. 'I am very proud to make that.' He points to his Bleu Marine men's cologne in the phallic-shaped bottle.

'Perfume is what? Perfume is alcohol and some essence. What is it more? What is the difference between the pot and the perfume? I drew them both.'

He is now running his thumb down the black-on-white stripes of the pan. 'Why am I very bad if I sell this, but if I sell this bottle I am very aristocratic?'

Cardin is hopping along past the bookshelf now, really excited. '. . . but if I sell that and that and that I am a very poor man?' He whirls around and taps his temple. 'This is in the mind and isn't reality.'

Suddenly calm, he returns and slides low into his seat. 'Everybody wants to lie with life,' he says quietly, locking his dark, magnetic eyes with mine. 'I don't want to. I like to be myself. I want to be proud of everything. There is nothing dirty. Only the mind can be.'

Some things, apparently, are dirty. What is the sales volume of his companies, I ask. He answers stiffly, 'Je ne sais pas.'

Now the press officer moves in. 'He never counts what he earns because he invests all his money. It is not the point of his life. He needs a lot of money to go on to do the things he wants to do, but he doesn't use it for himself. If he had loved the money for the money he would never have been an adventurer. He would have done nothing. He would have put the money in the bank and earned more money.'

'I accept he puts all the money back into the business,' I say. 'But what amount is that?'

'He has no time to count his money. He has so many things to do.'

'A company that does not know what its income is is in deep trouble.'

'He has never spent more money than he has.'

At this point Cardin leans over to the press officer and says in French, 'I am very economical and I respect cash, but I don't like money for the money.'

He turns back to me. 'It costs a lot to build a name. The name is the most important name, French name, in China . . . Did you see the books?'

He leaps from his chair and dashes to another row of bookshelves where rows and rows of black folders chronicle Cardin's story in the press.

'There are sixteen books on China – we did more. It's incredible. A lot, a lot, a lot – I have some twenty books, maybe. You know it's incredible. Look up number seven. There are sixteen. If I want to pay for all this by advertising, can you imagine how it costs? How much does it cost?'

He is flipping through volume seven, showing German, French, Italian, British and Chinese newspaper clips protected in plastic. He points at some stories in Chinese newspapers showing himself standing on the Great Wall. 'Nobody can buy this. It costs millions and millions and millions. Who can pay? No one. Not even the bank.'

PIERRE CARDIN

He takes down another volume from the bookshelf. 'I pay $20 million when I buy the restaurant Maxim's. It's a lot. But if I want to pay this page of advertising . . . look, a Maxim's dish.' He points at a German trade magazine for tableware. The photographs display chinaware with Maxim's insignia, a stylized M in the belle époque style.

'Look, the front page in the best of Germany. Look, two pages, three, four, five – after that, look, this. All free. Pierre Cardin, Pierre Cardin, Pierre Cardin, Pierre Cardin, Pierre Cardin, Pierre Cardin, Pierre Cardin, Pierre Cardin, Pierre Cardin, Pierre Cardin, Pierre Cardin . . . with all the important people . . . Pierre Cardin, Pierre Cardin, Pierre Cardin, Pierre Cardin, Pierre Cardin.'

Pause. 'Why do people write that?' he asks. 'Because I am Maxim's.'

At this point the press officer whispers to Cardin in French that he is now quite late for his luncheon appointment. He jumps up.

'I am sorry but I have to go to lunch.' He heads for the door, stops and turns. 'You know I sensed it was different . . . I was the first to change the concept, you know, not only perfume.'

His eyes are black and searching and looking for acknowledgment. 'Everything. You know.'

•   •   •   •

Pierre Cardin's organization is utter chaos. One of the most staggeringly unprofessional organizations ever to reach the $1 billion mark. In thirty years no executive working for Pierre Cardin has ever seen a budget or a business plan, or had a traditional MBA-type conference discussing goals and objectives. In fact, Cardin has been known to torpedo executives who tried to organize such a meeting.

Cardin is unreliable. A flake. A man who couldn't manage his way across a room let alone run a multinational corporation. And yet Cardin is a phenomenal success. Consider: worldwide his name sells at wholesale an estimated $1 billion worth of goods. Some 186,000 people work on his label in ninety-four countries. He has 840 licensing agreements. Or that's the best guess. No one at the organization knows for sure what is on the books. Even so, it's certainly more than any other designer has in the world.

Which makes him rich. Very rich. According to the French magazine, *L'Expansion*, Cardin was, with a personal fortune estimated at $310 million, the ninth wealthiest man in France in 1987. A survey in the *Nouvel Observateur* magazine ranked him sixteenth at around $320 million in late 1988. Although both these figures are pure guesswork – he shrouds his organization in a veil of secrecy – it is likely he would be well placed in America's Forbes 400 list.

Forbes magazine estimated he could sell his name for well over a quarter of a billion dollars.

But all that is nothing compared to the sheer number of people around the world who can recognize his name. Or his signature. Who hasn't heard of Pierre Cardin? In 1986, a group of American licensees commissioned The Cambridge Group to study where Pierre Cardin figured in the designer-label line-up in terms of recognition. The results astounded even them. Pierre Cardin (84%) was third behind Calvin Klein (97%) and Christian Dior (88%). Higher than Yves Saint Laurent. Higher than Ralph Lauren. Higher than Bill Blass.

And what goes for America also goes for most other countries around the world. 'We can confirm that Pierre Cardin is one of the best-known names in the world,' says François J. Janet, managing director of Lausanne-based Taroma Inc., a cigarette manufacturer that produced a PC cigarette. 'The recognition normally appears in Monsieur Cardin's personal handwriting. If you show it in Japan or China − even if they can't spell his name photographically they understand the signature like they understand Coca-Cola.' In that sense Calvin Klein and Ralph Lauren are still kiddies.

Cardin's greatest single accomplishment, undoubtedly, has been his contributions to twentieth-century marketing. Almost singlehandedly he revolutionized the selling of clothes. And pans. And ceramic igloos. Pierre Cardin, you see, pioneered the designer label.

The man who pioneered the astronaut and vinyl look is actually terribly suspicious of modern conveniences. Computers are barred from his house. He refuses to use them, say his former employees, out of fear someone could use the machines to discover details of his secretive empire. He has a thing about his accounts; he insists they must be done on old-fashioned graph paper. Once he was observed carrying his worldwide sales figures on an index card in a vest pocket, comfortably nestled against his body. His only help is some half-dozen licensing directors in Paris; a few agents dotted around the world. All of whom he continuously undermines, and most of whom are practically forbidden to talk to each other. 'I'm surprised the Pierre Cardin name is still as good as it is,' says Max Bellest, one of Pierre Cardin's top employees for twenty years.

Pierre Cardin is a designer who has invented his own utterly original method of doing business. It defies conventional business thought. He is a master at producing chaos, a conflagration that burns everything in its path but sometimes spits brilliant business deals from the ashes. His story is about how a sense of the media and self-promotion and hard, hard work can overcome profound ignorance. It is about how touchy-feely intuition and instinct can ultimately blow away MBA strategies. It is the story of a very solitary, very driven man whose only guide-post in the wilderness of business

5

has been an unshakeable belief in himself. Himself above everyone else. The world be damned.

It's a very strange tale. And it boils down to one riddle: How can a man be both a dizzying financial success, and an abysmal failure as a businessman?

And it's not a story he wants told.

A few years ago, Jean Manusardi, a former executive who had been Cardin's top manager for a decade, approached the designer about writing a book. Cardin gave his approval, co-operated, and *Dix Ans Avec Cardin* was born. In 1986 Éditions de Fanval, Manusardi's publisher, showed Cardin the book before going to press. It was an amusing string of anecdotes in good taste. There was nothing overly controversial in it. But at the last moment Cardin withdrew his support without explanation. He instructed his lawyers to block publication; they were unsuccessful. The two parties discussed changes in the book. The book came out. But it was not the end of the story. Cardin went to extraordinary lengths to suppress the book. His loyal press officer, Bernard Danillon de Cazella, called up newspaper editors and told them that Monsieur Cardin did not want this book reviewed. Only one newspaper in France reviewed the book. After selling 2,150 copies the book died. 'The book says nothing Cardin didn't agree with,' says Alexis Ovtchinnikoff, Fanval's publisher. 'I can't understand his attitude. He thinks he is a king.'

Another book story: Dominique Sirop, 35 years old and Hubert de Givenchy's assistant, was writing a book about the house of Paquin, a once grand fashion institution where Pierre Cardin had worked as a young man. Sirop wrote a chapter about an incident that involved Cardin and, as a courtesy, showed it to Cardin's ubiquitous press attaché, Danillon. Danillon ordered it quashed. Sirop sanitized the chapter.

Pierre Cardin has spent years suppressing the real story behind his rise to fame and fortune. A reporter trying to see the public file of magazine clippings on Pierre Cardin at the Musée d'Art et d'Industrie in Saint-Étienne, a town 350 miles from Paris where Cardin grew up, will come across some amazing obstacles. Only the museum's director can show the file. Odd but perhaps understandable in a small town. What was not normal was the receptionist's remark: 'Pierre Cardin does not want this period of his life to be known.'

Occasionally he is seen scuttling from his office on the Faubourg Saint-Honoré to his house a few yards away on the Rue de l'Elysée. People gasp when they realize that this man looking like a wind-swept clochard is the striking Pierre Cardin staring out from magazine articles. But developing a media persona is crucial to his livelihood. Cardin knows that his fortune is primarily built on the fact that consumers buy bits of his celebrityhood when they purchase a signed alarm clock or key chain. That is why he must constantly stay in the public eye.

Doing so is not easy for him. Cardin, in private, is very shy, very discreet. And so, he only plays the media game on his terms, bolstered by a cadre of fanatically loyal employees whose job it is to tidy up after their erratic and unpredictable maître, their genius.

This is his story.

DOWN AND OUT

2

'Rital. Macaroni. Rital. Macaroni.'

In the schoolyard two handsome boys were cornered by taunting children. The two brothers were Italian immigrants. The older, César, was blue-eyed and clear-faced. The younger was intense and reserved, with dark, liquid eyes under long girlish eyelashes. Pierre.

'Macaroni. Macaroni. Macaroni.' The French children continued to chant in the schoolyard air, their faces ruddy with viciousness.

This was 1930s Saint-Étienne, a coal-mining town in south-eastern France, where men, tired and black-faced, were swallowed by and belched from some fifty pits day after day after day. Lanterns clanking, they made their way home through the hillside twists of slate roofs and cobble-stone streets to little, streaked houses. Sheets hung out to dry in light drizzle and inside the halls smelled of wet wool. The men scrubbed. Soon the stringy rabbit, marinated in wine and bay-leaf, would be lifted from the cast-iron pot bubbling on the stove.

Mornings, the Stephanois, as the town's inhabitants are called, walked down the steep streets to the town centre. Just past the grey nineteenth-century stone factories that made parasols and fabrics, little shops sold buttons and wool and lace collars. But during the Depression such luxuries were rarely affordable. The Stephanois instead headed to the church square, where aproned farmers peddled their wares in an open market. Turnips and radishes and potatoes lay on wooden boards alongside stalls with chestnuts and perch. The idle men gathered to talk, spitting out the local patois through the bitter-yellow Gitane cigarettes dangling from their mouths. The women in black wool frocks haggled over the price of goat's cheese . . .

'Rital. Macaroni. Rital. Macaroni.'

'I will take revenge,' Pierre swore in an icy voice to his brother.

Revenge. Revenge for all the indignities his family had suffered. For the degradation, for the immigrant status, for the poverty, for the family's lost fortune.

In sunnier, pre-First World War days, years before Pierre was born, his parents had been fairly well-to-do farmers on the river Piave, 40 kilometres north of Venice. His mother, Maria Montagner, was from a family with genteel pretensions. They bred racing horses in a farm a few kilometres out of San Biagio di Callalta. They owned three houses. And she, a tall, close-mouthed woman, had been a secretary for an opera star for nearly fifteen years. The Montagners were somebody.

At the turn of the century she married Alessandro Cardin, and began bearing children. The Cardins lived just a few kilometres away in a pleasantly faded pink villa in Sant' Andrea di Barbarana. No. 38 Via Manzoni was an elegant farmhouse dignified by stone columns and driveway. In the back was a field and vineyard. Sant' Andrea di Barbarana was a provincial backwater, a hamlet with a few hundred residents some 24 kilometres outside Treviso. It was a dusty little cluster of houses, chicken coops and vineyards sandwiched between country roads crossing the river Piave.

Here Giovanni Cardin, Pierre's paternal grandfather, had been a big success. He was the only farmer in the area who owned the presses and distillery equipment that could reduce the seeds and skins of the grape into that fiery Italian schnapps known as grappa. Owning a local monopoly, Giovanni picked up a nice little income converting his neighbours' wine sediment into the local fire-water in the fall. And he had other ploys to keep his family well-fed with risotto and funghi. He had on his property some deep, cool pits which he had converted into underground warehouses. He sent Alessandro and his other sons to the Dolomite mountains to cut large chunks of ice which were then hauled by horse and cart to his underground storage cells. In the summer Giovanni picked up additional cash selling ice to hospitals. He was, by all accounts, an innovative businessman and would have been very wealthy had he not had so many dependants. Giovanni, according to town records, was the patriarch of some forty-five Cardin offspring.

But disaster struck in 1914. Some of the most important battles of the First World War were fought in the Cardin's backyard. In the Treviso area alone 10,555 local men died amongst the charred farms and craters full of mustard gas. Near Giovanni's town, on the crumbling frame of a burnt-out barn, an anonymous Italian soldier scrawled in charcoal, 'Better to live one day as a lion than 100 years as a sheep.'

And young men from other nations died there too. In 1915 the first Americans to die in the war fell in this corner of the country. On a memorial to Edward McKey, a fellow American soldier, Ernest Hemingway wrote: 'Desire and all the sweet pulsing aches and gentle hurtings that were you, are gone into sullen dark.'

In October 1917, the Italian army collapsed at Caporetto under the steady advance of the Austrian–German army. Alessandro was a foot soldier in the 72nd infantry regiment, a division of the Second Army that buckled under at Caporetto. Weary and desperate, he and his comrades retreated to Tagliamento and then on to the right bank of the River Piave. In the chaos of the Italian retreat he made his way home. It was bedlam. Disbanded units were collapsing in a stream of confused and panicky soldiers; lost riflemen desperately searched for their companies. The ramrod-stern officers tried to regain control and regroup the infantrymen for a new front-line assault. The background noise was a steady barrage of pounding shells and screaming horses leaking their innards into the dust. The moaning of men and clanking of gas masks was mixed with the sulphur smell of gunpowder.

In all this Alessandro Cardin found his village in late November 1917. It was empty. His father, his wife, his children had been evacuated just three days before. His father, the old patriarch Giovanni, had received the orders to evacuate. At first he refused. He had been born there, he protested. He had worked there all his life; he was willing to die there. Told that Sant' Andrea was going to be bombed to smithereens, Giovanni finally gave in. As best he could he quickly fortified his home. Being shelled was one danger; looters were another. Finally, with his family, including six grandchildren and his daughter-in-law, Maria Montagner, the old man joined the thousands of evacuees who, with dogs, copper pans and carts, created a trail of misery south. A train was to take them to safety.

In vain, Alessandro searched for his family. He finally ran into the major who had ordered them to leave. The news was unbearable; having missed his family by only a few days Alessandro was overcome by a profound despair. With fatherly murmurings the major helped restore

11

his courage and put him back in touch with his unit. Alessandro served another year.

Giovanni, in the meantime, had led the family to Reggio, in Calabria, a region of southern Italy that saddles the tip of the boot. The Cardins were eventually put on a boat to Catania in Sicily, where in the Albergo Malta, on the Via Antenea, the family waited out the war. It was grim. At the foot of Mt Etna, amongst the harsh, severe southerners living in low-slung Moorish houses, the family suffered their refugee status. Giovanni received a daily allowance of 1.75 lira for each child dependent on him.

Luckily it did not last long. A year after the Cardins had fled their village, on 11 November 1918, the war ended. In December they returned to Sant' Andrea. It was scarcely recognizable. Three-quarters of the town's houses were destroyed, along with the vineyards and whatever population had stayed behind. Crumbling walls and charred bricks spewed into roads pockmarked by craters.

Trembling, Giovanni walked to his farm. 'In forty-five minutes they had razed everything to the ground,' said César Cardin. 'All my grandfather's property was destroyed, all his wine cellars, everything.' The life they had once known was over.

Alessandro's unit was demobilized, and he too soon joined his family in what was left of Sant' Andrea. In the next four years Alessandro and Maria had two more sons, the second of whom was Pietro-Costante Cardin, born 2 July 1922. Piero, as the family called him, was the youngest of eleven children.

With the family vineyard destroyed, Alessandro was trying to scrape together a living as a 'carrettiere', a carter. He delivered wine; bought and sold gravel, transported by horse from the banks of the Piave to the builders. Alessandro and his eldest son were away for days as they travelled from town to town, sometimes even to Venice. But there was little building going on. Farming, which had never really appealed to Alessandro, could not sustain his family. With few prospects for work he fell into a deep depression.

Relief was to come from France. A small village between Grenoble and Lyon had also been badly hit by the war. On the surface it showed no scars. La Tour-du-Pin was a quaint little town wrapped around a hill, complete with church tower and cobblestone square. Gossip was brought up to date at the Café Charperire at Place Prunnelle. Small factories churned out bolts of fabric. On Sundays the soccer teams competed in the fields. The town's local river often flooded, sending rats into houses well armed with fat tabbies. It was a modestly prosperous community of a few thousand residents. Yet it had one serious problem. There were no men. Casualties of the war.

This severely hampered the factory, Dickson, Walrave & Cie, which made canvas coverings for trucks in neighbouring Saint-Clair de la Tour. To find cheap, reliable labour the factory, founded by a Scottish family in 1844, resorted to a Dickensian workhouse scheme. Young girls of poor Italian families were rounded up and enticed to work at the factory. Once there they were in effect imprisoned in 'La maison d'accueil' – the House of Welcome – which was a self-contained hostel run by severe nuns in black habits.

The girls' cots and their basic education – something they would never have received in Italy – were deducted from their pay. In black uniforms they were forced to attend the chapel built into a room of the huge draughty old house. It was not a pleasant life. They were allowed to cross the road to the factory for work and to play under the great pine trees on the pension grounds. Other than that they were prisoners of the beady-eyed nuns. Those who wanted to go into town to meet a fiancé first had to receive written permission from their parents in Italy. It often took months before the chaperoned excursion happened. That's if it happened at all. 'It was like a jail,' recalled Calpurnia Perrier, one of the girls who worked there at the time. 'Many girls tried to escape,' commented another, Elda Zabotti. In earlier days, troops had opened fire on such unruly women. In the 1920s, however, they were simply sent back to Italy.

The Cardins were drawn into this industrial prison. When a new supply of workers was needed the factory took out ads in local Italian papers and then sent nuns and girls to round up prospects in the company car. The very poor were enticed. Girls were offered a bonus of ten francs for every year they stayed, and a special medal if they stayed for fifteen years. If they married and had children each child was rewarded with fifty francs and the mother received a present. And of course the girls could improve themselves with a little education, all under the strict tutelage of the nuns. To the girls in the war-shattered district on the River Piave it was difficult to turn down. Piero's three older sisters – Teresa, Palmira and Alba – were sent to La maison d'accueil in Saint-Clair de la Tour in 1924. They toiled away in uniforms for nearly two years, bent for hours over the tough canvas as they manned the looms, the air around them filled with canvas fibres and roaring machines. The endless monotony of their lives was offset by the occasional quiet moment under the large pine trees. Here young girls fantasized about marriage and freedom while black ravens cawed from the branches overhead.

In Sant' Andrea di Barbarana, meanwhile, the ravaged economy was producing a new blight on the land: Mussolini's Black Shirts. Piero's eldest brother, André, was corralled by the local fascists and pressured to become a party member. He refused, as his father Alessandro had ordered him to. The mood grew ugly, and soon the fascists were force-feeding reluctant villagers castor oil. Doubled up in pain they made their way home, spurts of diarrhoea weakening them for days. Alessandro feared for his son.

Two French soldiers Alessandro had fought alongside in the war offered a way out. These veterans found work for him in a factory in Firminy, a little town some 12 kilometres outside Saint-Etienne and some 95 kilometres from Saint-Clair de la Tour. In January 1926, Cardin moved his whole family to Firminy. Many years later, Giuseppe 'Tino' Cardin, Pierre's cousin, recalled: 'Alessandro never really liked agriculture, anyway. The Cardins have always been nomads.'

The ties with Italy were severed. The Italian Cardin (Kardeen), became the French Cardin. And Piero, of course, became Pierre. In Italy, meanwhile, the old patriarch, Giovanni Cardin, died at the age of 76, two years after Alessandro and his family left. But the family stayed only a short time in Firminy. The French veterans found work for Alessandro in a large, speciality steel foundry and machine-tool plant that used the abundant coal of Saint-Etienne to stoke up its stoves. Alessandro had traded in the open plains of northern Italy for this red-brick factory lit naturally only by a single round window high up near the roof. He had trouble adjusting to factory life. In Italy he had been his own man. He had had status and vineyards and horses and carts and a large farmhouse. Now he was reduced to an immigrant, anonymously toiling in a grim, blackened factory. Within the year he gave up his work at the Firminy steel works and moved his family to La Tour-du-Pin so that he could work with his daughters at the Dickson, Walrave canvas plant. The Mother Superior, at the daughters' behest, had asked the factory management to give Alessandro a job.

In early 1927 the family settled in a little cul-de-sac called Impasse du Petit-Martinet. Neat two-storey houses painted green and white lined either side of the lane that opened out into a field. This was a lane where wooden benches supported grizzled women knobbly with arthritis. Children played in the dust and the air smelled of rotting apples and wormy wood. At the end of the lane a small factory made fabrics, and the machinery's clanking filled the air.

Practically the whole Cardin family went to work at the Dickson, Walrave factory across from the company stables in Saint-Clair de la Tour. The old hands Teresa (aged 20), Palmira (19) and Alba (22) returned as weavers. Pierre's eldest brother, André (26), threw his grit and muscle into work as a cutter. But even the younger Cardins had to work in the factory. Already Carlo (15) and Amelia (14) toiled full-time as weavers alongside their older sisters. César (7) and Pierre (4) alone escaped the child labour to play in the dust at Impasse du Petit-Martinet. Even though each family member who had reached adolescence was now indentured to put food on the table, the tight-knit family started to disintegrate. Rita (23) had married and stayed in Italy, and Giovanna or Janine in French (24) had moved to Avignon after the family's first stop in Firminy. One boy, Erminio, was adopted by a childless but well-to-do uncle and was being educated in Italy.

The Italian immigrant families in La Tour-du-Pin filled up on café au lait and bread. They ate pasta and polenta and, if they were lucky enough to have a yard, a chicken every now and then. In the apple-ripe autumn, pipe-smoking farmers in cloth caps and bandannas took large scythes to the wheat fields. Afterwards the children gathered the remaining wheat stubble as feed for the scrawny chickens pecking in the dust.

Clothes and fabric were part of Pierre Cardin's life from an early age. Elda Zabotti, a 14-year-old neighbour of the Cardins' in the Impasse du Petit-Martinet, also worked at the canvas plant. For hours little Elda pressed her nose against her window to watch the older Cardin sisters stitching together clothes on the kitchen table. Their mother quietly inspected their work. She was a fierce perfectionist and the scene filled little Elda Zabotti with awe. Every member of the Cardin family could make his or her own clothes.

A place of special wonder for young Pierre was the little chugging fabric factory at the end of the lane. La Tour-du-Pin and Saint-Clair de la Tour had several such factories and a local friend, Andrée, was the daughter of one factory owner. Together the two children entered the warehouse and unrolled miles of white, pink and blue tulle. They hid giggling under a sky of rich, rainbow-colored cloth. Pierre yanked the bolts until the material flew around them. He played at dressmaking, draping Andrée with her father's cloth.

Pierre began kindergarten at the local public school, with 'Liberté, Egalité, Fraternité' engraved into the stone façade above the entrance – lofty ideals that did not apply to the struggling immigrant family. Lessons at the school's small wooden tables and scratchy blackboard were relieved only by break in the little fenced-in play-court. Under the line of oak trees girls played hopscotch. Cardin, wide-eyed, watched the older boys in the gym swinging and sweating on the parallel bars. 'He was slim, shy and very distant,' recalled Zabotti of the five-year-old Pierre. 'He wouldn't play with the other children.'

The Cardins stayed only two years in La Tour-du-Pin before they moved again. This time Alessandro bundled up the family to move to La Ricamarie, a small town 6.5 kilometres from Firminy and just 2 kilometres from Saint-Etienne, another one of the little villages that dot the south-east of France, where little shabby houses crowded around a town hall with flaking shutters. A few months later they moved again, this time to the Solaure district of Saint-Etienne. 'My father was always used to being the patron. It was very hard for him to work for other people,' remembered César Cardin. 'He kept on quitting his job and moving us because he would hear of a better paying factory.'

PIERRE CARDIN

But moving to Saint-Etienne brought a period of relative stability. The family moved a few times within the town, on each occasion to a slightly nicer house only a block or two away. The family maintained their dignity by always moving into newly-built houses. Around 1935, some five years after moving into the corner house at 28 Rue du 10 Août, the Cardins took over a house eventually known as 77 Rue Gabriel Péri. The small, low-slung house had a garden where the patron relaxed by growing the odd tomato or courgette. Although he continued to switch jobs as work opportunities presented themselves, the family remained settled in Saint-Etienne. Pierre's older brothers and sisters all found spouses there and slowly started leaving home to start their own families.

Pierre's love of clothes stayed with him. In 1930, when he was eight, an inspector tracking children came to his local school to give some simple vocational tests. Pierre had been told by teachers he was 'undisciplined, a bad, solitary pupil'. (His brother only remembered him as a good student.)

'Your name, your age, and tell me what you want to do with your life.'

'Cardin, Pierre . . . eight years. I want to be a couturier.'

'You know what that is?'

He did, roughly. Pierre was a boy who played with dolls. At a very young age he had begun making dresses for them, cutting a hole in pale-blue silk, lashing it with a ribbon, and then cutting out holes for the arms. When he was a little older he was sent to a vocational school in Lyon, 35 miles away. In the damp and still dark morning Pierre boarded the 'Red Coach' which took him to a school in Lyon. He was taught some basic accounting and shorthand secretarial skills. But he also took drawing lessons from which he learned the rudimentary skills for designing.

He was very much his mother's boy. The two were bound fiercely together. 'When he was six years old he caught some type of pneumonia,' recalled César Cardin. 'Because of that our mother always protected him. He was the cherished kid.'

Maria Montagner was, like her youngest son, quiet and reserved. 'Pierre and his mother shared shyness,' said his brother. 'Pierre has always been shy – in the sense of being rather remote and reserved.' But his mother was also a severe perfectionist, a woman who liked to stay in control of all work done in her house. Her frugality, too, was an extension of that – each centime won was carefully counted. Remaining in control and watching the cash were two characteristics absorbed by the youngest son who always remained close at her side.

But she was not all business. Maria Montagner's eyes flashed with passion when she pined for Italy, for the once glorious life so full of potential. Pierre Cardin heard again and again about the travelling opera star for whom she had done secretarial work. 'She would have liked to have had some kind of career like that opera singer's,' recalled César Cardin. 'She often mentioned this as the great disappointment of her life.' Pierre was fired by her ambition: artistic work was the ultimate fulfilment in life.

Pierre's father – poor, hard-working Alessandro – elicited mixed responses from his children. While his mother had a reputation for tight-fistedness, César remembered his father as a generous man, someone who 'would give you the shirt off his back' and who enjoyed a glass of wine. But Alessandro was absent from the family a great deal because of his long, grimy hours on the factory floor. Later, on one of the few occasions he publicly mentioned his father, Pierre Cardin would recall him as depressed and distant: 'The only things I recollect him saying to me were, "Go shine your shoes," and "Is there a hanky in your pocket?" ' In another rare interview Pierre said: 'My father did nothing in France. He vegetated.'

Both Maria and Alessandro suffered deeply the indignities of being Italian immigrants. They were second-class citizens. Their Piave Italian was unintelligible to the equally severe Stephanois French. When they could they travelled back to San Biagio for a life-renewing visit, but soon they were back, locked into their dreary, isolated life. Saint-Etienne was populated heavily by crude coal-working families whose lack of education often bubbled to the surface in bigotry. 'We were the Arabs of the 1920s,' remembered César. 'My family never did anything wrong. We've always been honest. But we were rejected.' And that, too, left burn marks on the young Pierre. 'I will take revenge for our parents,' Pierre swore to his brother. 'One day I'll take revenge for what these people have done to them. I'll have them bend their knees before me.'

It was not an empty pledge. At the age of fourteen he became a French citizen. That same year he responded to a help wanted ad and began working during the summer months at a tailor's shop in Saint-Etienne run by Monsieur Vernay. In those days a single wool suit sat in a tailor's shop window, backed by a brown velvet curtain hanging from a brass bar. Inside, irons were heated on coal-burning stoves while a nearly blind tailor stitched through his bifocals. At Vernay, however, Pierre was asked to do some menial tasks and run messages. He showed up at Vernay's with his mother. According to César Cardin he told the tailor that he hadn't come to run errands but to learn a career. And then he quit.

Luckily Pierre was immediately hired at the best tailor in Saint-Etienne, at Chez Bompuis. There he formally began his tailor's apprenticeship, learning how to cut and sew. Among the cardboard boxes stuffed with needles and buttons, the great, flashing tailor's scissors, Pierre began his career. The plump bourgeois women of Saint-Etienne, pulled together with whalebone corsets and carrying lizard purses, descended from their granite town houses to pick up their husband's suits at Chez Bompuis. A wedding, or a christening, required a little something new.

Pierre received a fine education in tailoring. A cutter and his wife took a particular liking to him, teaching him the tailor's skills and even a bar or two on the piano. Once sickly, pale and shy, the now adolescent boy was beautiful, doe-eyed and driven by curiosity. He craved perpetual motion. On top of his work and school Pierre piled demanding hobbies. In the 1930s the Fascist-inspired idolatry of youth and firm, adolescent bodies began its sweep of Europe. In poppy-dotted fields rows upon rows of fresh young girls did knee bends in perfect unison. In the male-dominated gym, meanwhile, shirtless young men in white shorts wrestled each other over medicine balls. Cardin had always been attracted to the gym. Now he found himself at home in the steamy rooms where young men pulled themselves up the smooth, steel rings and hemp ropes till sweat dripped from taut pectorals and onto the wooden floor. He also began living out his mother's craving for the theatre. Like many shy people he came to life on stage. It was a way to step beyond restrictions. He signed up with a comedy troupe that performed at the local public school. In amateur productions full of overly stylized stage voices he assumed the role of the adolescent whenever he could. He never became a professional actor, but in some sense he has always remained one.

'When he wanted something, he really wanted it,' recalled his brother. 'He wanted to fight his way through life.' Pierre was impulsive. He never walked. Instead he half-ran from school to work, from work to gym, from gym to theatre. He brought that feverish half-run pace into adulthood.

It came swiftly, with the start of the Second World War and the fall of France. On 10 May 1940, Germany invaded the Netherlands and Belgium. Within a few days Holland had collapsed. On 15 May France's Ninth Army could contain the Germans no longer and the French people witnessed the terrifying onslaught of modern mechanized warfare. The beribboned French officers on chestnut horses watched in horror as German forces crossed the river Meuse and marched relentlessly into France. In two main lines Nazi tanks and motorcyclists, under cover of low-flying German planes armed with machine-guns and bombs, drove as far as Laon, within striking distance of Paris. But instead of continuing their advance straight into Paris the German forces unexpectedly veered toward the French coast in an effort to cut off French and British troops in the northern sector.

Uncounted hordes of refugees choked all roads in Northern France. In Paris the premier, Paul Reynaud, reshuffled his cabinet, appointing the 84-year-old First World War hero, Marshal Henri Philippe Pétain, as vice-premier. On

1 June German planes bombed Marseille and industrial targets in the Rhône Valley, preparing for a drive to the heart of France. Two days later Paris was hit as some 200 German planes dropped more than a thousand explosive and incendiary bombs on the city. Meanwhile, in the north, British troops were being evacuated from Dunkerque after German forces had encircled them.

On 5 June the Germans began their second push, this time toward Paris. By the 11th Premier Reynaud and his war cabinet had evacuated Paris for Tours. Two days later the French general commanding the Paris defences informed the Germans that the defending army was retreating. At 7 the next morning German motorcyclists entered the city, followed by cameramen, announcers and radio technicians. The Nazi propagandists stationed at Place de la Concorde recorded the march of German troops down the French boulevards for the deliriously happy Germans glued to their radios. It was a sunny day. Swastikas flew from the Arc de Triomphe and the Eiffel Tower. Parisians watched or sobbed quietly on the curbs. The Reign of Terror was beginning.

Again the French cabinet was forced to flee, this time to Bordeaux. On 16 June the cabinet voted 13–11 to ask the Germans for an armistice. Premier Reynaud immediately resigned and Marshal Pétain, in favour of surrendering, was asked to form a government. As he worked on the terms of surrender, fighting still continued. A German column had pushed south of Besançon and then on to Lyon, only 56 kilometres from Saint-Etienne.

With the Germans threatening to overrun Saint-Etienne, many refugees packed up dining-room suites and porcelain basins into overloaded Citroëns and fled deeper into Southern France. They pressed frantically to the border, a panicked stream of mattresses and engraved dowry chests. But the Cardins were not among them. Instead, they sat it out in Saint-Etienne. Perhaps they had fled just too many times before – from poverty, from war, from Italy, from Black Shirts, from factories, from xenophobes. They were to be refugees no more.

The panic subsided. On 22 June the Pétain government signed an armistice agreement with Hitler. Within six weeks the battle for France was over. Pétain had agreed to 'forbid French citizens to fight against Germany' and to pay for the occupying force. As part of the agreement a line was drawn across France. North of this border was the German occupation zone, south was the domain of the emasculated French government. The dividing line ran from Geneva in the east across France to just south of Tours, then straight down to the Spanish border at Saint-Jean-Pied-de-Port.

Not all Frenchmen surrendered. In London, General Charles de Gaulle asked all French people to support his continuing war with Germany. He said that the agreement was not only a capitulation but a 'submission to slavery'. Pétain immediately stripped de Gaulle of his military rank.

PIERRE CARDIN

On 2 July 1940, Pierre Cardin's eighteenth birthday, the Pétain government moved to Vichy. The fashionable spa town was chosen partly for its abundant hotels, which were requisitioned by the government. On 9 July, in this once peaceful town, the French parliament drew up a new constitution. France now had an authoritarian government; Pétain was its Chief of State.

Meanwhile in Saint-Etienne, 145 kilometres to the south, young Pierre Cardin had packed a small suitcase. Although his parents had stopped fleeing long before, Pierre was just beginning his great escape to the boulevards of Paris. His parents were shocked when he told them of his dream to become a star in the glittering capital. He was so young, they argued, so quiet. But all pleadings ended when they saw the resolve in their youngest son's dark-liquid eyes. 'They knew I was driven by an irresistible call,' Cardin would remember. They let him go.

Cardin tied a cardboard suitcase to his bicycle and started cycling to Paris some 480 kilometres to the north. He ate apples. He was free in some of the most glorious landscape in France. The N7 was a road that climbed granite rock faces and pine-lined gorges. Leafy oak and silver birch cast shade over trout brooks. Then the country levelled. In the right seasons gentle pear and apple orchards were tended by teenage boys in blue cotton shorts and braces. A farmer and his skinny horse pulled farm equipment while, above, a solitary hawk circled in the hot-air streams.

But the beauty was soon cut short. The N7 became choked with Citroëns and Mercedes loaded with fleeing people, some trying to unite with families in the occupied zone, others, in the opposite direction, desperately trying to reach contacts in Morocco for safe passage to America. Wealthy Parisians clutched their sable wraps and jewels. Three generations of peasants made their way on foot with all they could carry. At Moulins, 55 kilometres north of Vichy and a border town marking the German occupation zone, the red and white barricade of the demarcation was plastered with 'Halt'. Cardin got in line with the other bicyclists. Past them a line of cars stretched, waiting their turn as two German soldiers checked papers and an SS officer watched from the side.

Cardin was arrested. The Germans locked him in a railway station waiting-room for hours. They finally released him after taking his money. His only choice was to make his way back the way he had come with his battered suitcase and bicycle. But his vision held as he cycled back to the nearest town, Vichy. As his bicycle rattled down the town boulevards, the sun was brilliant and the fashionable little milliners' shops and teak-panelled tea-rooms sparkled. Elegant hotels the colour of eggshell commanded the corners. And then there were the parks 'à l'anglaise' that lined the river bank – little gravel walks through Norwegian pines and chestnut trees.

Pierre had never seen such a glamorous place and he fell in love with it.

Vichy bustled. The old Roman spa had been very fashionable at the turn of the century, when Europeans rushed to sample its hot, foul-smelling waters that gushed from taps in the town's focal point, the parc ancien. Women in ostrich hats and military men on the prowl tried to cure their gout and kidney stones and hepatitis and migraines with waters rich in sodium and potassium. But they had since been kicked out, their hotels confiscated by the Pétain government that had swelled Vichy's population by tens of thousands of additional citizens.

Cardin immediately began looking for work. He walked through the parc ancien, where hotels and waters and casino all met. He noticed a tailor's shop on the Rue Royale corner. Chez Manby commanded a trapezoid-shaped building facing the park. It had a wide-open glass shop-front that revealed busy saleswomen climbing stairs to the floor above. Customers were being fitted; ambassadors were eyeing themselves in mirrors. It was the best store in Vichy.

The shy boy found the manageress and asked for a job. His frail good looks — the brown wavy hair and dark deep eyes under girlish eyelashes — appealed to her.

'What can you do?' she asked.

'Sew.'

'Good. Come tomorrow and we'll see if it's true.'

He had work and he found a room near by.

Cardin has never shown very much interest in politics. To him it is an inconvenience that occasionally interferes with his work. Ironic, then, that he found himself front row and centre before a political drama at its most vivid. Only 150 yards across the park, through the chestnut trees and the galerias covered by white lattice-work, the aged Marshal Pétain lived in room number 35 at the Hotel du Parc. A few doors over his cabinet held office. Behind that was the American embassy, keeping an eye on the German embassy only four blocks away. In many parts of Vichy France, civil servants and officers had to swear allegiance to Pétain. Their outstretched hands shot into the air in the fascist salute; SS officers watched carefully from the sides.

But to Cardin Vichy was merely fashionable. Manby's clients were such important people, even if they were mostly fascists and collaborationists, that to the provincial boy it seemed like the height of prestige to work there. 'All the important personalities of Vichy, including politicians and diplomats, used to dress there,' he would later say. When Pierre's closest brother, César, a foot-soldier who had witnessed the scuttling of the French Navy, spent one day of this three-day leave with him, Pierre was so proud of his new life that he even introduced César to his boss.

Manby's was primarily a men's tailor, although it did carry some women's suits. Women's wartime suits were on the severe side. 'Those suits were extremely solid and masculine,' recalled Cardin. 'Every dart, every seam had its immutable place and the revers were severely classic.' But that hardly marred the town's elegance. The privileged wives of ambassadors – white-gloved women with lace collars and fox stoles – sipped afternoon tea and splurged on little bags of Vichy pastilles, mint toffees. Because of petrol rationing they went home by vélo-taxi, a sort of bicycle rickshaw pedalled by a driver with a chauffeur's cap. Meanwhile, the townspeople lost weight in food queues that stretched for blocks.

No matter. Cardin continued his education as a tailor. He became accomplished in the art of cutting, fitting and sewing; at the time apprentice sewers and tailors earned about 1,200 francs a month. And he had protection, too. Blanche Popinat, Manby's directrice, warmed to the hard-working adolescent. She was the first of the strong women with whom he would surround himself.

But the war would not leave him alone. In 1942 the Vichy government began forcing skilled workers, particularly those involved in metallurgy, to work in German factories. The deportations were met with massive resistance, and on 16 February 1943 the government instituted the Service du Travail Obligatoire (STO), whereby all French males were forced into compulsory labour service. More than 630,000 Frenchmen were drafted for German factories.

The STO was a serious blunder on the part of Pétain's government. The idea was so horrific to the young Frenchmen and their families that they preferred risking severe punishment and fled into the woods instead. From this army of men in hiding the ranks of the French Resistance began to swell.

Cardin, now twenty, was among those called up to work for the STO. According to his brother César, like many others, he fled to the woods. For about three months he was on the run, hiding in rambling woods of oak. At solitary farms, a curl of smoke rising from a chimney, young men like himself begged for food from brave farmers. One day he picked up a sharp object and started scraping his leg. He scraped and scraped until the skin and flesh were in shreds and the white of bone shone through the wound. Then he hobbled back into town. He was forced to register and take a medical exam. César Cardin said that Pierre continued to rub his wound for weeks till the sceptical doctors were convinced that he could not be sent to Germany. He believed Pierre maintained the wound by rubbing it with wood.

The strategy worked. The STO assigned him a job in France. Because he had picked up some secretarial skills while at school in Lyon, he was sent to work at the French Red Cross. The Red Cross was a beam of light in France's dismal war. At the Gare de l'Est in Paris, while gendarmes randomly checked luggage for black market goods, Red Cross workers ladled out hot bouillon and comfort to political and war prisoners, STO draftees, crammed in trains bound for Frankfurt. The Red Cross headquarters, of course, were in Vichy, and at Vichy's white-pillared Grand Casino the Red Cross often raised money for war prisoners. A favourite method was auctioning rabbits to the meat-starved wealthy. On banks of tables some fifty blooded rabbits were spread out while the auctioneer's sing-song voice pushed up the bidding.

Pierre began as a general office boy in the Vichy headquarters but was soon transferred to the personnel division, where he learned some basic administration. He had a high school certificate. Ever ambitious, however, he now studied accountancy at night. As he recalled, 'I hadn't done any studies like all my co-workers at the Red Cross. All of them were graduates. Every single employee had some degree, like in law. I didn't. I really had a very primary education.'

His education in clothes, however, was well advanced. Marie Epstein worked with Pierre in the same Red Cross department. 'He was a very kind young man,' she recalled. 'Already he had some talent for dressmaking, and in his small hotel room he made outfits and jackets for his female co-workers.'

Then, in 1944, Paris beckoned again. The Allied invasion had reversed the tide of the war, and on 25 August General Jacques Leclerc and his troops entered Paris. At first there was delirium: dancing in the streets; long days of hugging and kissing anyone in reach. Then the retribution began. Women who had taken German lovers were dragged into the streets, punched and pummelled, their heads publicly sheared like sheep. Other more serious collaborators were shot or hanged.

Pierre was now determined to get to Paris, but his personnel job required him to help wind up the Red Cross operations, sending some 800 employees back to their homes. Stuck in Vichy, he met with a stroke of good luck. Accustomed to eating at a small hotel in a back street, on a bitterly cold November day he came into the restaurant and took off his navy-blue overcoat and pale-blue scarf. He always sat in the same place. Now that he was resolved to make his move to Paris he began noticing another regular customer who often sat across from him. The old lady, quite tiny, read Tarot cards and tea-leaves. Soon they struck up a conversation.

What happened next is a bit of a mystery. The mature Pierre Cardin, playing to the press, likes to tell differing versions. In one, he claims that the clairvoyant predicted for him 'fame and fortune in the four corners of the earth'.

PIERRE CARDIN

In another, less exciting but probably more accurate, the ever-ambitious young man told the woman his dream was to work for a fashion house in Paris and flatly asked her if she knew anyone who could help him. She did. From the old lady Cardin obtained the name of a tailor who was connected with the great couture house, Paquin.

Finally the moment arrived. One morning in late November, Cardin climbed aboard a French Red Cross truck. As a security he had talked his way into a position at the Red Cross's Paris office in the Rue de Berri. In his pocket, however, was his burning hope – the address of a man working in haute couture.

His truck rolled into Paris's Gare de Lyon late on a Saturday. Finally he was there. Vichy was beautiful, but Paris . . . Everywhere in the night were the twinkling lights that spoke of millions of people. An exotic minaret arose majestically from the station's intricately carved stone roofs. Men, wrapped against the winter wind, dashed under turn-of-the-century lampposts, were lit up and then disappeared anonymously into the inky night. The odd wood-burning 'gazogene' car, with its tanks soldered onto its back, rattled through the streets. And on the Seine barges moaned eerily. That night Pierre slept at a small hotel on the Rue Vivienne in the second arrondissement.

Exactly what happened next again remains a mystery. Later in life Pierre recalled this story with many colourful variations. (In particular, the timing and precise connections between Monsieur Waltener and Maison Paquin have never been clarified.) As he has told it, however, the next morning he awoke early, alive with the possibilities of Paris. He quickly headed for the Faubourg Saint-Honoré, and the address that was in his pocket. It was a cold November. Snow started falling. At 9 a.m. on Sunday morning the street was deserted, and to the young provincial the dark and shuttered blocks of stores appeared to stretch for ever. As the snow fell Cardin clutched his light rayon coat closer. The only sign of life was the thud of his wooden-soled shoes echoing back at him, and he was starting to become despondent.

When the Rue Saint-Honoré turned into the Rue du Faubourg Saint-Honoré, Cardin noticed the Lanvin boutique. His heart quickened. He thought he had found the house he was looking for. Peering in at the boutique he soon realized his error. But finally someone else in Paris was up. A man was walking down the street in his direction. Cardin stopped him.

'Excuse me, sir, can you tell me if number 82 is far from here?'

'Who are you looking for at number 82?'

24

Cardin immediately became suspicious. He was uncomfortable telling the man the truth.

'I have a friend who lives at 82.'

'What's his name?'

'Monsieur Waltener.'

The man roared with laughter. 'I am Monsieur Waltener.'

Cardin started working at Paquin the next day.

A PROVINCIAL AT DIOR

3

It was 4.20 in the afternoon on 26 August 1944 when General Charles de Gaulle marched his provisional government across the Seine to Notre Dame. Paris had been liberated just the day before by the highly-strung, cane-carrying, General Jacques Leclerc, and now de Gaulle was greeted by throngs of Parisians waving flags and handkerchiefs, saluting, sobbing. A 70-year-old woman stood atop a ladder twelve feet above the pavement and teenage boys scampered up street lamps. Young mothers thrust their babies at soldiers to be kissed.

A machine-gun concealed in the rooftops and pointed at the crowd opened fire with a splattering of pavement stone. The crowd screamed, stampeded, scattered, piled three or four deep behind curbs. The Maquis and soldiers returned fire. Officers tried to hustle de Gaulle through the doors of Notre Dame, but he shook them off and slowly, unfalteringly, walked into the cathedral. A few steps down Notre Dame's centre aisle and another hail of fire opened up. Three snipers with machine-pistols had hidden themselves in the organ pipes, from which moaned a Te Deum. While the bullets poured over him – flashes and shards of flying flagstone and pew – de Gaulle walked slowly and steadily. By some miracle he was not hit.

It was his first public appearance as head of the new French government.

PIERRE CARDIN

Sixteen months later, on 30 December 1945, he gave the nation a brief New Year's message. 'In 1945 France was able to win victory in war,' his voice crackled over the wireless into heatless homes. 'In 1946 France will be able to earn her living.' Meanwhile, across town in parliament, politicians were locked in chambers trying to approve a budget for the following year. At one minute to midnight, following pre-war custom, the parliamentary clocks were stopped as the debate raged into the early hours of 1946. Senators shifted their behinds on red velvet cushions as colleagues gave speeches shaking with emotion. On 1 January, at 2.45 a.m., a budget was passed by 544 votes to 31. Fixed expenditures were budgeted at 487 billion francs while revenue estimates only amounted to 311 billion francs. France was running a large and growing deficit.

On 4 January, the same goateed senators in sack suits were hammering out the details of France's future, in the shape of a new constitution for the embryonic Fourth Republic. This, it was decided, should include roles for a president and prime minister, and reduce the voting age to twenty. But such niceties papered over the nation's immediate difficulties. That same day, in the grimy factories of Paris and Lille where oily men with wheelbarrows of scrap-metal trundled to warehouses, spontaneous strikes erupted over the reintroduction of bread rationing. The man in the street had run out of patience. He was subsisting on just 300 grams of bread a week.

The trouble was just beginning. In black-market restaurants tucked away in the medieval alleys of the Quartier Latin, the privileged treated themselves to a steak and cauliflower, crêpes Suzette and wine for about $10, a sum equivalent to about half a week's wage for a young actress. But suddenly a wine ration came into force as the government discovered in January that it had but two months of supplies left. The very same restaurants were already struggling with a power shortage. By 10 p.m. the sad-eyed waiters in white aprons were forced to recap the Pernod and shutter down. Non-priority industries were even worse off, with electricity flowing for just three days a week. Concierges had to hurry to scrub their building's stone steps before the lights were cut off. Household currents were switched off for twenty hours over every four-day period. This was a life tyrannized by coupons. Not even the Métro could be counted on.

Paris was then hit by the meat crisis. During the war women queued around the block waiting their turn at the *boucherie* sparsely stocked with grey, curling beef tongues and soft pink platters of sheep brains. In very poor neighbourhoods spindly-legged children wobbled from malnutrition while their parents cooked rutabaga, a turnip formerly fed to cattle, over ten-gallon cans welded together and fuelled by tiny balls of wet newspaper. Ersatz coffee was made from acorns and chick-peas.

But compared to buzz-bombed London, Paris fared well. To anyone with a bit of money the city was comfortably stocked. Secretly, slabs of boiling beef and pork sausages were available, and such treats often parted the White Russian matriarch from the family pearl and sapphire choker. Paris became the largest rural town, awakened at dawn by the explosion of roosters kept in rooftop pens, garrets and backyards. Old women and little boys illegally snipped grass from the public park for rabbits kept in bathtubs. Eggs (40 cents each) and butter ($10 a pound) changed hands in a flourishing black market.

In January 1946, however, the French government clamped down with price controls on wholesale meat. In protest Paris butchers sold off their stocks and refused to reorder from the wholesalers. The city ran out of meat in mid-January. General de Gaulle returned from holiday on 14 January to an emergency cabinet meeting. The next day shops were forced to reopen, new prices were fixed, and butchers had to register their meat. Gendarmes arrested the president of the Paris Butchers' Union and charged him with attempting to cause an illegal rise in meat prices. The populace, meanwhile, was solaced with a weekly ration of 150 grams of frozen meat.

But the damage was done. The city was out of control; de Gaulle resigned and silently retreated to a hunting lodge in a forest near Marly.

The new socialist premier, Félix Gouin, backed by his coalition partners the communists and the MRP (Christian Democrats), painted a glum picture of France during his inaugural speech of 29 January. Normally cheerful, Gouin soberly urged the people to eat even less meat, even less bread and wine. Normal revenue sources covered only 37 per cent of the 1945 expenditure of 532 billion francs, he revealed. He expected a deficit in 1946 of 309 billion francs. Most of the populace, however, never learned the contents of his speech: the printers' union had just begun an all-out strike. Paris's thirty-four newspapers never appeared that day.

Then it began to snow. Hard. It was one of the worst winters on record, and in March young men in coarse knickers skied through the narrow back streets of Montmartre under leaden, swirling clouds.

Paris needed to have some fun.

•   •   •   •

Couturier Maggy Rouff opened the season in her gold and blue salon on 2 October 1944, not two months after Paris was liberated. Her airy salon was stuffed with madly behatted American and French reporters, who had cycled through the Bois de Boulogne for the occasion and now demurely sat cross-legged, showing off their silk stockings, while they took notes on ladylike little pads. Four years of lean rations and daily bicycle rides had toned bodies and slimmed legs.

With coupons, black-market bolts and scavenging, the great fashion houses had scraped together the first post-war collection. That season the designer Alix Grès, the classicist with a fetish for turbans, made a culotte dress for bicycling, a sort of billowy, pasha trouser of silk Jersey. Jean Patou cobbled together a balloon skirt, pleated with horse-hair. And Jacques Fath produced a plaid, square-shouldered dress, lashed together with a large belt. But it was all for show. A light-hearted celebration. None of the houses had enough fabric to satisfy a customer's order.

'The women of Paris are still very smart,' wrote Al Newman admiringly, *Newsweek*'s war correspondent, in a dispatch two weeks after the city was liberated. 'They dress fit to kill and make up thickly but on the whole artistically. The supplies of cosmetics and perfumes are still abundant but your correspondent, no connoisseur, still isn't sucker enough to believe the stuff in the Chanel No. 5 bottle smells the same as it did in 1940. It just doesn't. One other scrap of information about the women in Paris: the current hair style is an extremely unflattering pile-up at the front, sometimes to a height greater than the length of the face.'

The salacious 1930s, when women were fitted for satin nightgowns, died when Tiger tanks rolled down the Champs-Élysées. What followed were ugly days and the clothes reflected them. The German women in Paris were known as the souris grises, the grey mice. In reaction wartime Parisians mastered the Zazou look. It started with clunky wooden or cork-soled platform shoes, an inch high in the front, three inches at the back. Sometimes the heels were made of glass (readily available in occupied Paris) and jazzed up with glass petal decorations. Skirts were short, loose wraps, because of the scarcity of material and because they were convenient for bicycles (the only means of transport). Shoulders were heavily padded and mannish, on dresses often made of synthetic plaids, corduroy, rayon, or man-made fibranne. Whatever came to hand. One wartime fabric was made of wood fibres: when it rained, Parisians joked, the termites came out.

The hair, meanwhile, was piled high on the forehead in a cockatoo-like mop, and then fastened down the back of the head in a mane. The effect was topped off with an overpowering hat. Women teetered under great floppy hats or papal-like bicycle bonnets which sometimes added another foot to their height. Since material was a scarce luxury, hats were garnished with feathers, ribbon, artificial flowers, tulle, veiling, wood shavings and even newspaper. The occasional yard of real wool on the black market had been dropped by the RAF, a reminder of a life before occupation.

The Zazou look, from its platform shoes to the minaret hats, turned the petite Frenchwoman into an Amazonian — a monsterish look that, in retrospect, seemed as if it was meant to out-intimidate the city's brutal occupying force.

The first post-war collection was simply more of the same. The designer Lucien Lelong in his Avenue Matignon salon produced one of the prettiest numbers of the season, a little black cocktail dress. That Paris couture was still even operating was largely thanks to him. Besides running his own house, Lelong was also president of the Chambre Syndicale de la Couture Parisienne during the war. This was a syndicate of some twenty couturiers, a sort of élite guild that set the rules and regulations of the business. During the early years of the war the Germans had tried to move the couture houses to Vienna, and it was Lelong who conspired to keep the work in Paris. After a tough haggle Lelong was also able to replace the clothes rationing for haute couture with a point system based on pre-war figures. The amounts were still insufficient, and Lelong devised a way to cook the books. Clients brought in old clothes, which were exchanged for points towards a bolt of the man-made textile, fibranne. He hyped the points. But it was very touch and go. In 1940 the Germans raided the Chambre Syndicale offices and found a few English-speaking method books and a Union Jack. The Germans piled up the contraband and placed a placard on top of it. In neat Germanic script the Chambre staff was informed, 'It is German you should have studied.'

Some of the houses were secretly criticized for their wartime survival tactics. Jacques Fath, for example, was considered one of the top designers in Paris on the eve of the Second World War. Briefly taken prisoner in 1940, he then returned to his Paris apartment with his wife. The foppish Fath managed to get through the war by dressing the BOF – the war's new rich: wives of the black-market dealers – in 'beurre, oeufs et fromages'. If the wartime couturier pined for his elegant, educated clientele of the 1930s, he never showed it. The BOF pulled wads of notes out of crocodile bags and piled expensive furs on top of their simple dresses.

Cristobal Balenciaga was another designer who serviced the BOF during the war. The son of a fisherman, war haunted the shy Spanish tailor. The Spanish Civil War had forced him to emigrate to Paris in 1937. His collections just prior to the world war were hailed as masterpieces of colour, cut and line, and foreshadowed the reputation he was to build. Fashionable women snapped them up and waddled home with his trademark white-and-blue boxes. He was a classicist whose only indulgence apart from his atelier was antique shopping. Proud seventeenth-century Spanish chairs stood elegantly around his boutique. He spent the war dressing the thick-waisted butchers' wives, as the white paint of his salons yellowed and the white satin curtains grew dingy.

The designer Elsa Schiaparelli, on the other hand, spent most of the war in New York. Her daughter married an American and Schiaparelli became a nurse's aid at the American Red Cross. But a skeletal staff managed to keep her

PIERRE CARDIN

21 Place Vendôme shop open. The salons were in need of paint and heat, the vendeuses were pinched and worried. But they were still selling gaily-striped turbans, and that first season Schiaparelli was represented by an embroidered cocktail jacket over a wool dress.

In sunnier pre-war days the Italian-born Schiaparelli was a fiery fashion leader. In the 1920s she had looked for design work but was told she would be better off planting potatoes. She did not agree, and in 1928 a knitted pullover sweater in black and white wool, with a trompe-l'oeil bow-tie at the neck, wound up in French *Vogue*. Her career was launched. In the early days her range went from day blouses that buttoned at the hem to simple black evening dresses. But she soon found her natural voice. 'She branched out to glorify the hard elegance of the ugly woman. Her daring nonsense – fish-shaped buttons, monkey hats, fox-head gloves, skunk coats, lobster prints, bold colours – plus a true sense of hard chic made her exactly right for those last, frivolous, extravagant days before the Second World War,' observed the fashion editor, Bettina Ballard. 'To be shocking was the snobbism of the moment, and she was a leader in this art. Looking at a shrunken Peruvian head, her reaction was, "How very, very pretty" and her influence was great enough to have made shrunken heads fashionable if she cared to.'

Schiap, as she was known, had an idée fixe about buttons. The wackier the better. Beautiful garments were often held together with buttons in the shape of bullets, cars, cupids, rabbit paws, drums, clowns and signs of the Zodiac, to name just a few. Accessories? There was her famous befrilled lamb-chop hat, then came an inkpot hat, and even a Salvador Dali-designed high-heeled-shoe hat. Handbags went the same mad way. They came shaped as milk cows or apples made in vivid red suede. Necklaces looked like a string of aspirin or metal insects mounted on clear plastic. Clients dying to be risqué flocked to her Place Vendôme boutique, with its Dali-made sofa in the shape of lips and the giant stuffed pink bear.

Schiaparelli's colour sense was equally dramatic. Linen in turquoise was trimmed with grape velvet; olive was combined with a dark red; black dresses matched with fire-red stockings or fleecy lime-green coats. But her trademark was a bright magenta known as 'shocking pink'. Schiap also experimented with fabrics, pioneering man-made materials that looked like cellophane or a crinkly fabric known as 'treebark'. One year Paris was swathed in a material of newsprint modelled on a collage of her own press clips.

By the Second World War Schiap had radically changed the way designers were viewed. She shoe-horned the demure turn-of-the-century dressmaker into the outlandish 'artiste' of the 1930s by employing famous Surrealists to design for her. Sadly, she was never to regain her pre-war stature.

In London, Captain Edward Molyneux designed wartime ready-to-wear for the British government. The captain was a First World War British officer who became a Paris-based designer in the intervening years. He was a darling of the 'train bleu' Riviera set and helped craft the slinky satin silhouette which became the trademark of the 1930s. But in the autumn of 1944 his skeleton staff could barely stitch together an uninspired black wool dress and wide skirt.

Robert Piguet produced a dress with muff fur pockets draped like an apron that first season. Before the war he had carved out a nice business. He was a Swiss-trained banker who had fled from his humdrum life and opened his own Paris fashion house in 1933. Piguet was not a designer but did handsomely buying the designs of freelancers which he then produced as sumptuous dresses in his boutique. His dress-making techniques were actually quite basic. Even so, his house had gained a good deal of recognition because he had a strong editorial eye and a belief that elegance lay in simplicity. The word was he made very chic air-raid costumes during the war.

Conspicuously absent from that October 1944 fashion collection was Coco Chanel, the queen of pre-war fashion. Her list of fashion accomplishments – her suit and pants, her bob, pearls and perfume – was confiscated from her by her sordid wartime activities. Two weeks after General de Gaulle's triumphant march through the city she was arrested. At 8 a.m. two young men wearing sport shirts and sandals, with revolvers tucked into their belts, stormed her rooms at the Ritz Hotel. Terrified but imperial as ever Chanel was escorted past the hotel staff, through the lobby, and into a waiting car. The Resistance had embarked on their *épuration*, the bloody and feverish purge of suspected Nazi sympathizers.

Chanel had closed her boutiques in 1939 and fled to the south of France, but she returned to Paris in August 1940 and discovered that the Germans had requisitioned the Ritz. That it was a Nazi headquarter didn't seem to bother her. She moved back in and spent the war making love to a much younger German intelligence officer, Hans Gunther von Dincklage. According to her biographer, Chanel had a bizarre notion that she was going to convince Churchill to stop the war earlier by asking him to agree to secret Anglo–German talks. She appealed to her friend Rittmeister Theodor Momm, who was the German administrator of the French textile industry, and he put her in contact with Obergruppenführer Walter Schellenberg of the SS, chief of all Germany's foreign spies. Coco went to Berlin, Schellenberg liked the idea, and 'Operation Modelhut' was born. Needless to say, nothing came of her grandiose plans, and Schellenberg, Himmler's right-hand man, eventually went to jail for war crimes.

Chanel, however, was released by the French Resistance shortly after she was arrested in 1944. A powerful figure must have been protecting her. She did not show any clothes in October 1944 but fled to Switzerland, where she remained until it was safe to return to the Paris fashion scene ten years later.

Finally there was the house of Paquin. They opened in 1891 when Madame Paquin's husband, fresh from a killing on the Bourse, set his wife up in her own couture house. She became well known for updating mournful nineteenth-century black town coats with vivid red silk linings or fiery embroidery. In the teens, while Diaghilev's Ballet Russe stormed Paris, she turned to exotic Chinoiserie opera cloaks and Chantilly lace butterfly-wing headdresses with bird-of-paradise antennae. Socialites and actresses snatched up her evening gowns and Tango dresses. Her tailored clothes also gained a following. She favoured soft, pale wool felt, decorated with finely traced scrolling braids and inserts of Irish crochet lace. Smartly tailored suits were often trimmed with fur. Soon fur became the trademark of the Paquin house and her coats were usually piped with sable, fox, chinchilla or monkey.

Paquin made a reputation for herself by making clothes active women of the twentieth century could wear. She helped end Victorian-style restrictive dressing – a Western version of Chinese foot-binding achieved through wire and whalebone corsets and impossibly narrow skirts which made the simple matter of walking a difficulty. Fashionable women in the nineteenth century were forced by etiquette to change their clothes some half-dozen times a day. What a woman wore during the day at home, for example, had to be different from the dress she wore while calling on friends for afternoon tea. But in 1913 Paquin created the day dress that could be worn into the evening. Keeping in mind Parisians who travelled by Métro, she rebelled against the narrow skirts of the early 1900s and cut suits her clients could comfortably strut in. And she knew how to market her services shrewdly. Clients wrote to her itemizing the social events they were attending in the coming season; she returned with a complete wardrobe. It was all done with such ease. As a Paris guidebook of 1906 explained, 'No haughty seclusion, no barred doors, at the Maison Paquin. Madame was probably met at the door by Monsieur Paquin himself, and to be met by Paquin was a treat.'

From a business standpoint, too, the house had an illustrious past. Paquin was the first Paris couturier to expand internationally, opening up a branch in London in 1898, followed by Buenos Aires, Madrid, and fur shops in New York. She was the first to parade her models at the trend-setting races at Longchamp and Chantilly. In 1910 she sent a dozen of her models to tour the major cities in the Americas.

Tragedy, however, turned the fortunes of the house. Shortly after the First World War Monsieur Paquin died, and without his companionship Madame wilted. She gave up her role as house designer and in the early 1930s retired. The house continued but the mood and reputation changed. Even so it was still one of Paris's great fashion institutions and in the 1940s the respected Spanish designer, Antonio del Castillo, was providing lustre to the house. A smattering of Paris's rich, determined to remain upbeat during the war, held little weekend parties at country estates, where full dress was de rigueur. For them Castillo built a technically complicated, much talked-about line with the armholes of the sleeves beginning at the waist.

Maison Paquin was located at 3 Rue de la Paix, next door to Madame Grés and near Schiaparelli. In the elegant Place Vendôme cyclists pedalled through the square where ornate street lamps wore iron crowns. Along the perimeter of the square, under stately stone arcades, mustachioed dandies tried to sell pear-shaped diamond necklaces at the old French jeweller, Chaumet et Cie. On the floors above, maids aired rugs over clawed and twisted iron porches inlaid with brass. And on the other side of the square harried diplomats impatiently searched for their drivers as they came out of the Ritz Hotel.

The Place Vendôme tapered into Rue de la Paix. Immediately on the left the house of Paquin commanded a massive six-storey stone building which was so deep it stretched back an entire block to an employees' entrance on Rue Volney. At its peak it was the biggest couture house in Paris, with some 2,700 employees bustling through the doors. By the end of the war, however, only some 250 employees were at work.

Imagine: in the ground-floor sale-room saleswomen, modishly attired in red plaid, flattered clients clutching white kid-skin gloves. The directrice effortlessly glided up and down stairs, lightly clucking with customers over the electricity shortage. As soon as the customer turned her head, however, the directrice was back to barking sharp rebukes at fitters kneeling over tweed hems and porcupined pin cushions.

The house of Paquin was fully integrated. Everything needed to run a garment business was at hand: from storerooms with bolts of rare cloth to the finished gown leaving the sale-room in a neatly tied box. Upstairs, accountants pencilled wage details into eight-column graph pads; buyers searched for rare swatches of taffeta. A client might be in the furrier's department, trying on the latest chinchilla rabbit muff. Another client's face might disappear under a velvet hat that collapsed over her brow like a bad soufflé.

Off the hospital-like corridors near the back entrance on Rue Volney, the heart of the couture house beat. It was in these workshops that Castillo's sketches took material shape. On long tables bolts of fibranne were cut with exaggerated Alice-in-Wonderland scissors. Castillo's assistants, like doctors, stomped officiously through the corridors in white lab coats to rooms where young apprentices and old women bent over embroideries. On cloth stretched over wooden frames such nimble-fingered women sewed pearl and lace and glass bangles on what was to be the sleeve of a jacket. In other rooms shoulder padding was stitched into thick woollen coats, while Castillo and assistants hovered around a model, readjusting a tuck.

One such workshop was run by Monsieur Serge. In the back, on a high stool amongst rows of sewers and cutters working together the invisible seams of fur and velvet, an anonymous provincial tailor bent feverishly over his work. Pierre Cardin was the first tailor in Monsieur Serge's workshop.

'There was nothing I wouldn't do in order to get a job there,' Cardin once quietly said.

•   •   •   •

Jean Cocteau was on the hillside of Rochecorbon in Touraine on 26 August 1945. He recalled an earlier visit. The sky was pale, the Loire river slowly rolled through the brush that tumbled down hills to the river bank. His car stopped. And there he found what he was looking for: castle, wash-house, orchard, watering cans, a woodpile. It was perfect.

Perfect to stage his come-back. Paris's famous enfant terrible had scraped through the war his own unique way – part hero, part collaborator. His open homosexuality, an article attacking racism, and his play *Les Parents Terribles* (alluding to incest) made him a target for the moralistic Vichyites. He was openly cursed in the street. In 1940 he wrote an extremely brave call to artists to rally against the oppressive regime. And yet in 1943 he wrote a *Salute to Arno Breker*, one of Hitler's favourite sculptors who had been sent to Paris in a Nazi–Vichy exchange. A decade of on-again, off-again opium addiction had also taken its toll on the quality of his work.

His salvation was a beautiful, little-known actor, sandy-haired and muscular, whom Cocteau had met in 1937. The young man was Jean Marais, an extremely hard-working talent who would eventually become one of France's greatest actors. Cocteau and Marais became close, and it was to this rock of hope that Cocteau clung through the war. Marais was opposed to drugs; he encouraged Cocteau to wean himself off his opium habit.

When the war ended Cocteau was making undignified excuses for not having joined the Resistance. He was suffering from a tormenting skin ailment that made him flake with revolting regularity, and he had produced nothing of real literary value for quite some time. A string of books and articles highly critical of him were being published. Marais, who did not want to be a mere actor but a film star, showed his friend the way to a come-back. Cocteau had already turned his hand to all the arts from poetry to painting, but in 1942 the 53-year-old began his film apprenticeship (he had earlier made one film, *The*

Blood of a Poet). He wrote the dialogue for a B movie, *Le Baron Fantôme*, a ghost story to distract Frenchmen from their Occupied plight. Then came *L'Eternel Retour*, a modern-day Tristan and Isolde directed by Jean Delannoy. The role of Tristan was written as a vehicle for Jean Marais. By then Cocteau's confidence had grown and at the end of the war he was ready to take on a project that he could completely call his own.

It was *La Belle et la Bête*. Cocteau fell in love with Beauty and the Beast, the eighteenth-century fairy tale written by Madame Leprince de Beaumont. He marshalled together a wonderfully strong cast. Jean Marais played the dual role of Beast and Prince Charming. The lovely Josette Day, another Cocteau favourite, was Beauty; the star Mila Parély was one of the sisters. Georges Auric was sent off to compose the score, and for the costumes and set Cocteau relied on his long-time friend, Christian Bérard.

Christian 'Bébé' Bérard, the son of a funeral-parlour family, was a member of Cocteau's pre-war set: extremely talented artists who shared several strong bonds, including a gift of the gab, a penchant for opium, and usually homosexuality. At first glance Bérard repulsed: his rotund body was covered by oily, smeared suits and torn shirts; pieces of food were often decaying in his flowing red beard. But he was a respected painter, and Paris's privileged women rushed to have a little something of Bérard's in their salons. The Vicomtesse de Noailles owned many of his early paintings; Comtesse Marie-Blanche de Polignac had a dining-room of Bérard frescoes; in Marie-Louise Bousquet's salon, where Bérard had electrified his audience with sketches and witticisms, hung a portrait he had painted of her. He was better known for the sets he designed for the theatre and ballet. He brought to life everything from Molière to Giraudoux. He designed, created fabrics, decorated interiors. Parisians inhaled his influence like some rich, rare bouquet. He was 'lionized, quoted, flattered, spoiled, loved, and aped'. On a wide expanse of white tablecloth at some Comtesse's dinner, Bérard often entertained by sketching whomever he had seen that day, and whatever they were wearing.

He was particularly friendly with the couture world. Bébé Bérard loved visiting Elsa Schiaparelli, who was cut from the same mad cloth. He often entered her salon with his filthy white poodle Jacinthe swept up in his arms. He headed to the Magnum-sized bottle of Shocking Pink, Schiap's best-selling perfume, and liberally doused his long greasy beard until the scent trickled into his torn shirt. (Although his trousers were unravelling, his shoes torn apart, friends claimed he never really smelled.) Seated in the front row of Schiap's fashion show Bérard soon could not contain himself. His corpulent enthusiasm got the better of him and, at the twirl of one of Schiap's more outrageous numbers, he bellowed out 'C'est divin! C'est divin!'

PIERRE CARDIN

Opium eventually destroyed Bérard's heart. Before the war he had drifted into fashion illustration as the only way he could finance his voracious appetite for opium, gold Fabergé boxes and the many friends who lived off him. His potential as a fine artist gave way to commercial illustrations for *Vogue* and *Harper's Bazaar*, whose pages filled up with his sad Renaissance heads of long, lanky hair and floppy hats. His opium habit, however, often got the better of him. Half-way through the sketches Bérard would disappear. While magazine editors frantically looked for him, Bérard was safe in rooms piled high with dirty clothes. With trembling, sweating hands he would take out a key from his baggy pants, lock the door and pull down the shades. His bulky body moved quietly and quickly. He unlocked a suitcase, took out a small jar, a long-stemmed pipe and an alcohol lamp. He stuck a long stick into the jar which came out with a blob of black, honey-like substance at the end. And then Bérard – sweating, trembling, hyperventilating – slowly cooked the opium on the alcohol burner. When it was prepared, he lay down on the cot and smoked, finally slipping into a pink peace as the sickly, sweet smell curled to the ceiling.

Bérard was known to pass out in the ladies' room at the legendary nightspot, Maxim's de Paris. Yet to sum him up simply as an illustrator with an opium habit was to do him a grave injustice. He was much, much more. He was a motivator – a witty inspirer of creative ideas for all of Paris's fashion designers. 'Bébé Bérard was like someone from the age of Charlemagne,' recalled Diana Vreeland in her autobiography. 'He was the friend of everyone in Paris with talent.'

In 1945 Bérard was working on the costumes for *La Belle et la Bête*. He tapped another friend, the costume-maker Marcel Escoffier, for help. The two men produced lavish designs that borrowed from Vermeer and from Gustave Doré's original illustrations for the book. The trick was to achieve lushness in post-war France, to finance a fairy-tale vision in a stringent economy. 'Perhaps this is the way to stimulate the imagination which sleeps quietly enough in contact with wealth,' said Cocteau.

Just some six months after Pierre Cardin had arrived in Paris, Escoffier and Cocteau chose the house of Paquin to execute the designs. The irrepressible Bérard began to work. He took over the elegant workrooms of Paquin while ancient women specializing in embroidery looked on in amazement. Bérard was surrounded by tulle and ostrich feathers, smeared with charcoal, covered with perspiration and ink spots, his beard singed by fire and his shirt hanging out. Paquin's designer, Antonio del Castillo, occasionally entered, gave some advice, departed.

Under the direction of Escoffier the Paquin employees scrounged for material. Scraps of lace appeared. Velvet. 'Bérard dared to do what no-one else would have done,' recalled Jean Marais. 'One day he couldn't find the material he wanted for a particular dress of Beauty's. He looked up and saw the curtains on the windows and he said, "This is the fabric I want." So we took the curtains down and we made Beauty's most beautiful dress out of it.' Embroiderers began stitching bangles and glitter on fabric stretched taut over a wooden frame. Bolts were cut, feathers and black beads assembled. Slowly the costumes took shape. 'Bérard and Escoffier made costumes out of nothing but a few rags,' wrote Jean Cocteau in his diary.

At a crucial point, when a fitting had to be done, Jean Marais happened to be in Switzerland. One of the principals – Escoffier or Bérard – saw a beautiful dark-eyed boy in the workshop where the costumes were being stitched. They asked him to come down to the showroom to try on the costume in Marais' absence. It was Monsieur Serge's workshop and the boy was Pierre Cardin. Bérard and Cocteau set to work fitting the costumes on him. 'I was so overjoyed I used to dream about it at night,' said Cardin. 'Monsieur Bérard, Monsieur Cocteau, Monsieur Escoffier – all those people who were working on the movie – became so aware of my enthusiasm for the work.'

The men were attracted to Cardin's unbridled, childlike enthusiasm and asked him to work on the costumes. With almost religious fervour Cardin began on the Prince's costume and that of the prince's father and the spectacular outfit of the Beast. He became obsessed with the Beast's costume, spending hours working the fabrics to perfection. He alone worked on it, jealously protecting it from other Paquin workers. No-one else was allowed to sew a stitch on it. (This version of events, which is how Cardin tells the story, has its sceptics. The story certainly has become richer, more embellished over the years. Some of his later profiles state that he designed the costumes, which is certainly not true. But even the fact that he was the stand-in for Marais is questioned. 'Anyone who knows what Jean Marais looks like and how well built he was, well . . . I don't think Monsieur Cardin corresponds to the same type of body at all,' said a knowledgeable source. 'Jean Marais' costumes were made in Monsieur Serge's workshop, where Pierre Cardin was the first tailor. He may have cut and stitched Jean Marais' costumes. And you know, in a workshop it often occurs that a sleeve needs to be tried on. And when there's no male model, which was the case since Paquin only made women's clothes, they would ask any young man there to see how the sleeve was hanging. And that was it. There was nothing more to it.' Mila Parély, the actress who played one of the sisters, defended Cardin. 'If he says so, then it's true.')

Whether he was an anonymous sewer or the principal interpreter of the Beast's costume may be disputed, but he was there. 'He was very young, very good-looking, absolutely adorable,' recalled Parély. 'He was not like so many people you meet now, who are pushy. He was shy, but he was so enthusiastic and marvelled at everything. He was just charming.' Confirmed Jean Marais: 'I do recall Pierre Cardin as he was in 1945. He was one of Marcel Escoffier's best friends. Cardin helped with the fittings, but he didn't make any of the designs. Christian Bérard did it all.'

On 29 August the costumes from Paquin arrived on the film set. At the hotel dressers and fitters fussed around Marais as he was fitted for Prince Charming and the Beast. 'The Beast is perfect,' gasped Cocteau. And it was. The Beast's two sides − prince and wild animal − were there in the costumes. The face painfully covered in horsehair was contrasted with the regally elegant black-velvet suit and cape. Hideously tufted paws graciously disappeared in hunting gloves of glittering golden embroidery. Fangs and lace. The costumes were rich. No sign whatsoever that they had been made in a blighted city. No sign that sheets without patches were hard to find; that the meat strike coincided precisely with the time when they needed a deer carcass; that old cameras jammed, lenses warped, electricity failed or was cut off. No sign even that Cocteau himself was living off food packages sent by a friend in California.

On the set, in the yard chickens pecked at the feet of Beauty's mean sisters. They hung laundry, gossiped, the white, white sheets snapped in the light like a twentieth-century experiment in chiaroscuro. 'I remember one of my costumes, a famous one, where the blue velvet was absolutely extraordinary. The scene where we hang the sheets, I wore a vivid red skirt. And the sheets, Cocteau didn't just hang them. He wet them, and not all of them. That's why it looks like a painting. They showed such extraordinary care,' said Parély. Of course, the film was black and white and yet somehow the rich red and blue velvet costumes came through on the celluloid. 'In all my working years, in all the fields I've ever worked in, I've never seen such attention paid to detail,' said Parély, now in her seventies.

La Belle et la Bête was first screened on 30 May 1946, in Saint-Maurice. Marlene Dietrich appeared and took her seat next to Cocteau. He took her hand, crushed it. No-one expected the pain of Jean Marais' Beast. It was all so surreal, or Cocteau's peculiar brand of 'realism of the unreal'. Hands miraculously came out of the castle wall to hold candelabra; wild swans hissed at the feet of the dying Beast; strands of pearls turned to rope before the audience's eyes. But most beautiful were the costumes. They turned the film into an international hit, a cult classic. And Cardin was a part of it.

'What Pierre had was incredible luck. Talent? Sure, but he also had tremendous luck to be immediately in the midst of these marvellous people − Cocteau and Bébé Bérard,' said Parély. 'At the time we didn't know what he would become. He was just an enthusiastic boy.'

•   •   •   •

As Cocteau's film was released, the long-dormant couture industry twitched alive. Lucien Lelong's assistant, Pierre Balmain, left his maître in 1945 to create his own house. It was an instant success. Balmain's friends Gertrude Stein and Alice B. Toklas lent a dose of intellectual meatiness to the house, and that opening year he showed a long bell-shaped skirt with small waists – a look that foreshadowed Christian Dior's fashion revolution. 'The opening was a knockout,' said Erik Mortensen, the designer who took over after Balmain died. 'Remember, people still needed coupons to buy bread, gas and sugar. There was an electricity shortage. There was no fabric. Designers had to create with bits and pieces left over from before the war, somehow weaving them together to make something. His opening was like the first breath in a free country.'

The same year, Madame Mallet Carven opened a boutique and couture house. An architect by training and just five feet tall, Madame Carven noticed that couture clothes were always designed for the 5 feet 8 inch models, while most women were considerably smaller. Rather than adjusting the clothes, she decided to design dresses specifically made for petite women. Again an immediate success. (As usual the ubiquitous Bérard was in the midst of the action. His ratty little dog urinated over Madame Carven's shoes while they lunched in a Left Bank café.)

Then there was Marcel Boussac, the cotton king. Boussac was the rich and powerful, square-jawed head of the cotton industry board. He also owned Maison Philippe et Gaston, a once-snobbish dress shop that was hard hit by the war. It was reduced to selling furs. Boussac wanted to restructure Maison Gaston and was looking for a designer who could instil the old house with new life. A director of Gaston turned to a childhood friend at Chez Lelong for help. His name was Christian Dior.

Dior was the son of a well-to-do chemicals and fertilizer manufacturer from Granville. At the age of twenty-one, and with the backing of a family resigned to his eccentric artistic bent, Dior opened an art gallery in Paris. He stuffed it with modern art and soon it was thriving. Max Jacob, Jean Cocteau and Christian Bérard supported the young gallery owner. But the 1929 crash wiped out the Dior family fortune. The art market withered. Penniless, Dior moved into a flat with a friend who made his living selling sketches to designers. Dior too began to illustrate, and it wasn't long before his network of artistic friends had made some important fashion introductions for him. The Swiss-born couturier Robert Piguet – prim little moustache and reedy elegance – relied entirely on freelance designers for his collection. Dior became a contributor; by 1938 he was on staff. But the war intervened, of course, and Dior wound up in the country planting turnips. By the end of 1941 he made it back to Paris to find his position at Piguet had been filled. That was when Lucien Lelong took him on board.

Six years later, Dior was not just a designer but well educated in the technique of dress-making. Lelong's other assistant, Pierre Balmain, had struck out on his own with enormous success and a twinge of ambition began to stir in Dior's double-breasted chest. That was when, in 1946, Marcel Boussac opened the door. The pudgy Dior, so superstitious he couldn't move without the advice of clairvoyants, finally met Boussac after carefully studying Maison Gaston's prospects. A resurrected Gaston was bound to fail, Dior told him. Too musty, too set in its ways. He then told the beefy, scowling Boussac what *would* work: a new fashion establishment. All around life was beginning anew, said Dior, and it was now time for a fresh trend in fashion. He wanted a house where every single thing would be new, from the make-up to the staff, from the furniture to the spirit. The 41-year-old wanted to herald a new era. Boussac bought it. He put his powerful financial clout at Dior's disposal and Dior gave notice to Lucien Lelong. Dior, along with Balmain and Carven, filled out the new post-war ranks.

Meanwhile, the 23-year-old Pierre Cardin was having an uncharacteristic slump. Once the thrill of *La Belle et la Bête* was over he grew tired of Paquin. Ambition was tugging. He was stuck in the back, an anonymous tailor mounting sleeves. Around him were white-haired men and women numb from decades of repetition. 'I can't possibly stick around in a studio,' he told himself.

Through working with Escoffier and Bérard, Cardin had had some useful introductions. One was to the manageress of the house of Elsa Schiaparelli. In 1946 Pierre joined the Place Vendôme boutique as a cutter in the tailored-suits atelier. It was, however, more of the same. Different place, same anonymity. He stayed all of two months, then he dashed off again. 'I was more interested in theatre and film,' he decided. Cardin went back to the reliable Marcel Escoffier and asked to become his assistant. This, too, was not to his liking. Costume-making for eighteenth-century drawing-room comedies at the Comédie-Française or some inane, overacted film farce was a seasonal business. There were long periods of inactivity which produced almost a physical pain in the hyper-active young tailor. He made three attempts to get hired by Cristobal Balenciaga who was, in his eyes, the embodiment of a couturier. Balenciaga was reclusive, brilliant, odd, but each effort to slip into the secret fold was rebuffed.

It was during this uncharacteristic lull in Cardin's career that he fell, once again, upon some good fortune. His hunger for hard work always created good luck. This time Escoffier and Bérard introduced him to an assistant designer at Lucien Lelong.

The designer was Christian Dior; the timing was perfect. Dior was feverishly putting his new house together and on the look-out for the best talent he could find. Cardin designed, cut and made a coat and suit for Dior, who immediately recognized the tailor's superb technical abilities. He offered Cardin a position as head of a coat and suit studio in the new house. 'I will open my house in six months,' Dior said. 'If you think you can wait, I'll hire you.'

Dior, in the meantime, had fallen in love with 30 Avenue Montaigne, an extremely elegant stone mansion. He wanted the house designed in a 1910 version of Louis XVI. First came the 'Helleu' salon, all in white and pearl-grey. In the corners sat quintias palms, from the ceiling hung crystal chandeliers. Christian Bérard came by to inspect the boutique. He suggested covering the walls with toile de Jouy and scattering Dior-inscribed hatboxes on the tops of cabinets and wardrobes and in odd corners. It was the perfect touch. It softened the elegant formality.

At 8 a.m. on 18 November 1946, said Cardin, he was standing on the door step of 30 Ave. Montaigne. He was there an hour before Dior and the rest arrived. Cardin and the other forty-seven original employees set to work. They had till 12 February 1947 to produce a complete collection.

Dior's concept was simple, logical. The world had been in uniform since 1939. Fashion highlights came in the yellow serge boiler suits and fire-resistant turbans of the British Royal Ordnance factories, or the Parisians' 'mode martiale' and ridiculous Zazou look. Enough. Dior wanted to put an end to wartime misery. He wanted rounded shoulders, feminine busts, willowy waists ending in a spreading skirt – all built on the best pre-war construction techniques. The style accentuated the female body by means of boned underwear and stiffened fabrics which hugged the body. The tight-fitting corset built into the dress was sculpted with a hot iron and a brand-new mysterious substance – paper-stiff nylon. The sophisticated long-line bustier was made as part of the dress, and lined with two pieces of tulle placed in opposite directions to one another, a technique invented by Dior's famous technician, Madame Marguerite Carré. First came a sheaf of tulle, then a sheer organza that came from the Swiss company, Abraham, and then, to prevent the tulle from scratching and making ladders in stockings, a very fine silk pongée was added to line the skirt. Each of Dior's dresses rested architecturally upon foundations. Darts were forbidden and a hot iron was used to shape the fabric, bringing sculpture back into fashion. 'A well cut dress is one with few cuts,' Dior told his employees.

He also rediscovered fabrics. During the war Japanese silks and the finest Scottish wools were out, of course. The richest fabrics tended to be crêpe romain or crêpe georgette, muslin and clinging jersey. And they were limited to scraps of cloth at best. But Dior was only going to use the best materials – taffeta, faille, duchesse satin and wool taffeta. And yards of it. One of his first dresses used as much as eighty yards of pleated white faille, a glossy silk with a cross-wise rib effect.

When Dior finished his designs, known as the Corolle line, his employees went feverishly to work. His chief technician, the perfectionist Madame Marguerite Carré, distributed the designs to all the various studios for production. Dior's own studio, formally a boudoir, disappeared under fabric and the designer was forced to work on the landing, and then on the stairs. A key technician collapsed under the stress and was replaced by an assistant. There were only six mannequins for the ninety models, and one of them, a petite English girl, fainted into Dior's arms, sliding through his grasp until he was left holding only her falsies.

Cardin was the foreman of the coat and suit studio. It was crammed with technicians and stuffed dummies wobbling on wooden bases. In starched white shirt, grey suit and polka-dot tie Cardin cut fabric on long tables; next to him young girls sewed with foot-pedalled Singers. The return to long-forgotten dress techniques created problems for most of the staff and Madame Marguerite threaded her way through the crowded studio answering questions. Rulers and chalk squares and measuring tapes disappeared under fabric. Young men in thick glasses stitched sleeves while their backs pressed against cupboards moaning under bolts.

Cardin was asked to produce an outfit called the 'Bar' dress. It was deceptively simple: a two-piece suit with a fitted, pale pink shantung jacket over a black-wool crêpe skirt which fanned out half-way down the calf. By then the fashion world was a-twitter. The day before the opening, in a Paris bistro, Bébé Bérard started to draw on a wine-spotted table-cloth what he had seen at 30 Avenue Montaigne. 'You'll see,' he said to the group of fashion freaks gathered around him and looking over his shoulder at the sketches. 'Christian Dior is going to change the whole fashion look when he opens tomorrow. He's making huge pleated skirts like those the Marseilles fishwives wear, long, like this, and with tiny bodices and tiny hats.'

On 12 February 1947, Dior gave his fashion show. It was bitterly cold. Coal was in short supply; the French newspapers were shut down by a strike. But the fashion world could not have cared less. A crush of frantic people pushed at the grey-canopied entrance of Avenue Montaigne. Sandwiched into Dior's pearl-grey salon were the international fashion press and cognoscenti. Above the rows of little gold chairs was a mantel-mirror decorated with a baroque garland of real flowers. 'I was conscious of an electric tension that I had never before felt in couture,' recalled *Vogue* editor Bettina Ballard. 'People who were not yet seated waved their cards in a frenzy of fear that something might cheat them of their rights.'

Rita Hayworth was in the front row on the fake Louis XVI couch, a cigarette in one hand, leather clasp-purse on her lap. She peered haughtily through tear-shaped sunglasses. Next to her was the Begum Aga Khan, softer-looking with a plain wool dress and mink stole draped over her knees to keep warm. Countess Greffulhe was never to be outdone. She liked to be seen bejewelled and beveiled, wearing on her head a cloth appendage the size of a small bathtub. She wore a black fur coat with gigantic silk ruffles, and wrapped around her throat was a white ermine-like stole that was so long and wide it fell to the floor like a bed-sheet. Richard Avedon, the photographer, nervously touched his glasses while he sat buttocks-to-buttocks with the aged fashion gnome, Carmel Snow, *Harper's Bazaar* editor-in-chief. Lesser mortals squeezed out space on the staircase, stood against walls and knocked askew gilt-edge frames. The air hummed with excitement. Feet jiggled. Painted lips took hard little puffs on Camels.

One of the first dresses to come out was the Cardin-made 'Bar' dress, with a sprig of lily, Dior's lucky flower, attached to the lapel. The model wore a bowl-shaped straw hat, black gloves, a single short strand of large pearls, and white high-heeled shoes. More models emerged, wrapped elegantly in hollow-waisted, rounded-hipped coats of black wool, or cocky with a green velvet chignon hat perched to one side of the head. The tempo was fast. Models provocatively swirled their pleated skirts in the packed room, knocking over ashtrays with the flare. The audience perched at the edge of their seats. After the initial shock the room began to buzz. As the wedding gown, the traditional finale of couture shows, rounded out the programme the audience was clapping and shouting madly. Dior came out for his bow. He was trembling.

'It's very good, what little Christian's doing,' the Countess Greffulhe noted grandly.

'It's quite a revolution, dear Christian. Your dresses have such a new look,' said Carmel Snow.

Dior collapsed in tears. Everyone was running around hysterical, hugging. Even Bébé Bérard's dog was there, and Bérard tied a tiny side-slanted hat on its head. Georges Geoffroy, a celebrated decorator of the time, made flowery speeches about design and Dior's genius. 'There was such emotion,' said Thelma Sweetinburgh, there for *Vogue*. 'They put on quite a show.'

The New Look was born. The war, still so tangible, was buried by the satiny opulence of the New Look which, ironically, was not really that original. Many, most notably Balenciaga, had dabbled with it in the late 1930s. But Dior's timing was perfect. And the deceptively simple Cardin-made 'Bar' dress, the show's best-seller, became the prototype for the look that seemed to quench the thirst for happier, more frivolous days. That was all the New Look was ever really about. And Cardin was in the midst of it.

The outside world went wild. Some lavished praise, others abuse. In Paris indignant women picketed the Avenue Montaigne house. Immediately after the February collection Dior went on a tour of the USA. An engineer in Texas threatened to kick him out of the state; in Chicago housewives threatened to burn him. 'I was in college in 1947 and found the new clothes ridiculous. So did most of the girls I knew. We all laughed together over such French frivolity,' said James Brady, the journalist who later became publisher of *Women's Wear Daily* and *Harper's Bazaar*. 'Within a few months the girls were wearing their own, cheaper versions of Dior's "ridiculous" New Look.'

What was all the excitement about? The length of the skirt was shocking. The extravagant use of rare materials – during a period of brittle post-war economies – was considered decadent. The furore was international in scope, not just limited to Paris. In the ensuing months of 1947 the London *Times* was crammed with hysterical letters. 'To try to change fashion so drastically at such a period is surely the most anti-social move to have been made for some time,' fumed Jill Craigie from Hampstead. Sir Stafford Cripps, President of the Board of Trade, thumped his pulpit over the undesirable and drastic changes in fashion which jeopardized cloth-starved manufacturers. 'Sir Stafford Cripps cannot halt the world march of fashion. He has the choice of encouraging our manufacturers to keep up with fashion or of forcing England to trail behind, an isolated pocket of dowdiness,' retorted Anne Scott-James, London editor for *Harper's Bazaar*. That got reader John Pollock, comfortably ensconced in his rooms at the Athenaeum, terribly upset. 'If the market in America demands long skirts, let them be made for it. But let English legs be untrammelled.'

The debate raged. The public hysteria propelled Dior onto the front pages of every newspaper in the world. It did not take long before his was an international household name, recognized like Stalin or Gandhi. It was the birth of the designer as pop star, and the publicity, of course, translated into a fortune for the house of Dior. 'Better to be slated on three columns on the front page than congratulated in two lines on the inside pages,' Dior said.

Dior emerged as a fashion force. Meanwhile Cardin, although shy, was being noticed. Jacques Rouët, the business brain behind Dior, recalled that from the beginning Cardin stood out.

November 25th is the day of Ste Catherine, the patron saint of the couture world. Traditionally it was a day off for all the couture employees, a day spent celebrating all that was good at the house. Awards were given to veterans; poems composed and performed; vin rouge poured into the cups of giggly seamstresses. Women employees 25 years old and not yet married were crowned 'Catherinettes' with specially made hats of green and yellow – the colours of hope – built up with satin and paper, flowers and ostrich feathers. At Maison Dior each foreman of a studio had a party in his atelier, followed by a skit. Dior and Rouët made the rounds, starting at 9 a.m., until some four hours later they had visited all the studios. Of course these occasions were tailor-made for the compulsive worker who once had thespian aspirations. 'Cardin's imagination was so overflowing that his show was always the greatest,' said Rouët.

The young tailor was also noticed for his ambition. Much to the annoyance of his employees, Dior often wanted a new dress at the last possible moment. 'If I cannot have this dress the collection has no meaning,' Dior complained, thumping the floor with the gold-tipped cane he instructed with. 'Besides, there is still one night left.' Near to tears with fatigue, most seamstresses and tailors could not hide their dismay. They had already been working 18 hours a day for weeks. And yet one of the most likely to volunteer for the overnight job was Pierre Cardin. He liked nothing better than a work binge. 'A perfectionist, he spent the whole night doing and undoing,' remembered Carré on one occasion. The next morning he emerged bleary-eyed, stale but victorious. 'He looked like Jesus Christ,' she said.

But the happy days at Christian Dior were short-lived. In 1948 Pierre's mother died. And then he found himself, in his own account of the matter, embroiled in a scandal.

Couturiers, of course, made money on their paying customers, but they also earned a fee from manufacturers and store buyers. Professionals were required to pay a deposit, known as a caution, before they entered a couturier's show. Against this caution manufacturers ordered models from the couturier. The outfits were delivered to an American manufacturer several weeks after the show and he immediately flew them to New York. In his factory the seams were opened and the garment dissected in a sort of fashion autopsy. On the basis of the autopsy, a pattern of the garment was made for mass production and the factory moved into high gear. By mass-producing and substituting cheaper cloth, buttons, linings and trim, the price of a $1,000 dress was reduced to, say, $100. The manufacturer then slapped his label on the garment and rushed it to the stores.

Often the manufacturers were owned or contracted by the great stores like Saks Fifth Avenue or Macy's. Many clothes merchants were not even this honest. They preferred to bypass the caution system altogether. It amounted to industrial espionage: stealing the couturiers' ideas while not even buying a token dress from the artists who underwent the pressures of creating original lines twice a year. Photographers were not allowed into the shows during the 1940s, so unethical manufacturers hired illustrators to view the collections. They sat for two hours on the fake Louis XVI chairs, fixedly watching the 175 models twirl by. As each mannequin did her 40-second strut down the catwalk the illustrator jotted down notes. Back at his hotel he then expanded his notes into a hundred or so remarkably accurate sketches of the collection. The sketches were used as a basis for producing copies.

Copying was an aspect of the couture business that made poor Christian Dior quite faint. And now, at his house in 1948, a new, uglier wrinkle in copying had appeared. An employee on the take, probably quite high up, was leaking the Dior designs to manufacturers even before the fashion shows. It was very sordid. Rouët called in the police. They arrived at Cardin's studio one day and interrogated him at length in front of the other Dior employees. Then the workers in his studio were questioned.

'There was this sketch leak,' said Cardin, 'and they suspected that I might have acted in a dishonest way.'

'He was never suspected of anything,' said Rouët. 'There were rumours, people gossiped, but they found where the leak was taking place and prosecuted someone from another studio. We never accused him of anything.'

Though he was innocent, it was enough for the tongue-clicking vendeuses and seamstresses to suspect that Cardin was the thief. It was unbearable. He handed in his resignation. He was going to start his own business.

CARDIN SOLO

4

Over green copper roofs the winter sky lightened. Then, as now, the city seemed to jolt awake. Parisians briskly marched to work under the Rue de Rivoli archway lined with shops opening for the day's business. The shivering manageress of a tiny parfumerie rolled up the rattling iron grille; next door, dapper salesmen dusted counter-tops at Hilditch & Key, the shirtmaker. On her way to work a secretary, her clasp-purse under an arm, pulled apart a croissant as if she were quartering a chicken. A gendarme rooted in his nose with a nicotine-stained finger.

At Place de la Concorde, cars and motorbikes and bicycles raced around the 3,300-year-old pink-granite obelisk taken from the Temple of Luxor. A Deux Chevaux driver, jerky with too many cups of coffee, cut off a motorbike and it spilled onto the cobblestones. Cars screeched, pedestrians stopped to stare. The biker rubbed his corduroy knee and then jumped on the running-board of the Deux Chevaux trying to drive away. He banged on the canvas roof. Cursed 'Salaud'.

Some of the rush-hour pedestrians turned down Rue Saint-Florentin. On the left was the elegant boutique of Jean Patou, the façade discreetly graced with a marble plaque and gold lettering. On the next block, across the Rue Saint-

PIERRE CARDIN

Honoré, Rue Saint-Florentin turned into the less fashionable Rue Richepance. Three months after he handed in his resignation at Maison Dior, Cardin opened a theatre- and movie-costume business at No. 10 Rue Richepance. A partner and backer was the ever-reliable Marcel Escoffier. Fate played into their hands: a costume-maker, Monsieur Pascaud, had just gone bust and the two men took over his small atelier. Cardin had once again returned to his two childhood loves of fashion and theatre.

Au Nain Bleu, a toy store, stood on the corner of Rue Richepance and Rue Saint-Honoré. It was Paris's equivalent to London's Hamley's or New York's F.A.O. Schwarz, and in its windows Christmas trees were usually crowded by rosy-cheeked Pierrots, blue Victorian doll's houses and models of the Orient Express. Children pressed foreheads against the glass frosted with paper snow-flakes, and pined for the heap of plump-bellied bears with paws in honey-pots. Its saleswomen often lunched under one of the red awnings of a Rue Richepance brasserie, where the dainty French spent two hours devouring a steaming plate of choucroute.

The façade of No. 10 was quite elegant. The rows of windows on the seven-storey building were framed by stone angels and garlands. The entrance was a dark passageway with a mosaic floor. The poor lighting barely illuminated the mosaic of brown and yellow daisies, obscured by generations of urban grit and dust. To the left was a glass door, some bells, two steps. The tiny, tatty handkerchief-sized entrance and plaques ran immediately into the sharp curve of the iron balustrade and twisting staircase. The walls were mouse-brown and flaking. But to Cardin it was beautiful. He bounded up the five flights of steep stairs to his atelier. Panting slightly, he removed a clunky brass key from his pocket and unlocked the wooden door to his rooms. They were few and small. But they were his.

It was early 1949. Cardin trumpeted his opening, staging a press conference at the elegant Hôtel George V. No world was farther from his modest fifth-floor walk-up. Today the George V looks very much as it did then. In front of the hotel's blue awnings, drivers leaned against black-fendered Citroëns. Bellhops in trim grey and red-collared uniforms delivered calling cards and walked coiffed, liver-coloured terriers. Next to Chinese vases whiskered men sat in cherry-wood chairs and waited for their mistresses. The George V symbolized everything that Cardin wanted to be a part of. It was redolent of old money: red-velvet chairs that uttered sighs when sat upon; packages from Jean Patou left with the concierge; silver-blue tapestries of courtly medieval love, slightly faded. The lobby had that curious feel that most institutions strove for: it was humming with activity and yet embalmed in an atmosphere of effort-less serenity.

In some small reception room off corridors of glass and marble the press gathered. Christian Dior, by the winter of 1949, was the pope of couture. He, too, was at the George V, fully endorsing his former assistant. It is likely that the sweet and plump Dior felt terrible about the circumstances of Cardin's departure. He was also certain of his former protégé's talent, and now he wanted the press to know about him. It was no small thing. If the great Dior said a former assistant was talented, all the press jotted down his oracle and kept an eye on the young man.

The first day the 27-year-old opened his doors, Dior sent him 144 red roses. They did not even fit into his three Rue Richepance rooms. But Dior's powerful patronage did not stop there. Shortly after he opened shop, Comte Etienne de Beaumont sent out invitations to his 'Bal des Rois'. Dior, fashion's new star, was of course invited. The balding couturier gave Cardin one of his first orders, a costume for Beaumont's ball of kings. Dior and his former assistant decided on a lion, the King of the Animals, and in March 1949 Cardin knelt at the feet of his former maître, fussing over tassels and tucks. Anyone who expected Cardin to produce a recognizable lion was to be disappointed; he had far too much imagination. Dior's lion was red, created by a multi-coloured ribbon cape.

During this time Maison Dior was often asked to make ball costumes, and when demand overextended his staff Dior always sent the overflow to Cardin. Costumes? Wasn't that an obscure and unprofitable business? Not at all. Cardin's timing was exquisite.

• • • •

Paris went ball-mad just prior to the war – frantic play at the edge of a volcano. In 1939 there were garden and cocktail parties every day, and a ball or some such every night during all June and most of July. One of the most successful balls of that season was at the Hôtel Salé, a seventeenth-century palace in the Marais quarter of Paris. The invitations asked ladies to appear in white ball gowns and tiaras, gentlemen in white tie and decorations. Only Bébé Bérard did not follow the dress code to the letter: instead of medals he appeared with a row of garters across his chest. 'I went home at six with my white tulle Piguet dress splashed with champagne and smudged at the hem with eighteenth-century dust that came out of the parquet floors,' recalled Bettina Ballard.

It all began again in the 1950s when a waterfall of engraved, swirling invitations poured into mail-bags. This time the frenzied partying was used to smother the scars of war, the manic tinkling of martini glasses fuelling the pitch of gay chatter. 'We had to live again,' said André Ostier, the society photographer of the day. 'There was the glamour of society before the war. One

wanted to . . . we didn't know life was going to change so much. One wanted
to get back to the past.'

Costume balls were an easy way to mask trauma. Between 15 May, when
wealthy Parisians returned to Paris from the Riviera, and 1 August, when they
left for their country estates, the capital was the stage for a hysterical burst of
balls and charities.

In July 1950, the Princess Dolly Radziwill-Tvede and Baroness de Cabrol
held a benefit for abandoned children at the 300-year-old mansion of Prince
Czartoryska. Le tout Paris was there twirling in the Ile Saint-Louis mansion by
the banks of the Seine. The outer courtyard was covered, transforming it into
a dance-floor, while the outer walls were draped in velvet. Voilà, a breezy party
on the banks of the Seine had a cosy inside feel. Windows were made to look
like opera boxes. At least the 6,000-franc ($17 in 1950) admission fee went to a
worthy cause. Couturier Pierre Balmain swilled champagne and looked arch; the
Duke and Duchess of Windsor waltzed to one of the four orchestras. Till 5 a.m.

Slightly more decadent was the mythological-themed costume ball of the
milliner Gilbert Orcel, given in March 1949 just as Cardin opened shop. With
gold trident in hand and his tubby belly peeking out of his scant Neptune
costume, Orcel greeted his guests at midnight with some 200 bottles of
champagne. It started self-consciously, but by dawn the laurel-crowned royalty
in golden sandals were chatting up film starlets clad as fruit-carrying nymphs.
One guest was covered in a veil of stars, a Jean Cocteau-designed costume. Only
Orson Welles was not in toga. He wore a tuxedo.

But the crowning costume ball of the day was that of the Mexican silver-mine
millionaire, Don Carlos de Beistegui y Iturbi. In 1951 de Beistegui threw a
housewarming party at his Venetian Palazzo Labia which he had just renovated
for, the papers reported, $6.25 million. In the eighteenth century, according to
legend, the Labias threw their guests' gold tableware into the canals so that the
sounds of dishwashing would not disturb the festivities. De Beistegui surpassed
even the Labias' extravagance.

Months before the ball, social climbers clamoured for invitations to the party
that cost de Beistegui $200,000. Some 3,000 glitterati were invited and yet
more invitations magically appeared for $500 each on the black market in Rome
and Paris. They were snatched up. A widow wrote to de Beistegui, 'My deep sor-
row at my husband's death can only be eased by an invitation to your party.'

Finally the great day approached. The lagoon in Venice filled with sleek
yachts, while celebrity-chasing journalists staked out perches for 80,000 lire
in the windows of nearby palazzi. Harried concierges on the Grand Canal
scrabbled to house the celebrities. Hotels like the Danieli were jammed with
seven Rothschilds; the Maharanee of Hyderabad; Kings Peter of Yugoslavia

and Michael of Rumania; French film directors Jean Renoir and René Clair; dancer Serge Lifar and photographer Cecil Beaton. But not everyone accepted their invitation. The Duke and Duchess of Windsor and Winston Churchill politely declined.

By 10 p.m. the floodlit canal was choked with gondolas and motorboats. The wheelchair-bound Aga Khan came as a Venetian domino and Orson Welles bellied up as Othello. Barbara Hutton arrived in a $15,000 Mozart-like get up, while Gene Tierney spent only $16 on her peasant costume (including the vegetables). The designer Jacques Fath, meanwhile, minced around as the Sun King in a white satin, gold-fringed coat and towering ostrich-feather head-dress. Shortly before midnight a flurry of trumpets ushered the guests into the great hall, where de Beistegui formally unleashed them on the period tableaux, acrobats, ballets, two live bands, champagne, lobsters, minuets, sambas and rumbas. It lasted till dawn. The very pleased 5 foot 6 inch de Beistegui, in his scarlet robes and eighteenth-century wig, was walking tall. Undoubtedly the platform shoes that elevated him sixteen inches helped.

As a precaution against a communist revolt the Palazzo Labia was encircled by 1,000 gun-toting carabinieri and fifty policemen, forced by de Beistegui to go under cover in eighteenth-century costumes and wigs. But nothing happened. For the *hoi polloi* in the square outside the Labia palace de Beistegui provided free music, a Punch and Judy show, and a greased pole with 35,000 lire and a bottle of wine tied to the top. The Venetians had to pay for their drinks.

By the time the last guest had paddled away at dawn, Mrs Louis Arpels, wife of the jeweller, had danced in the streets with an open-shirted Venetian; Salvador Dalì had trotted amongst the pigeons in fluorescent pink socks; and seventeen Venetians were fished out of the canal. It was a great bash.

•   •   •   •

Dior pulled Cardin aside and gave him a lecture. 'Pierrot,' he whispered, 'don't sell at a low price. Make it expensive. Talent should be paid for.' Cardin, fond of cash, did just that. He once said he charged up to 1.2 million francs ($35,000 in 1951) for a suit. For the same price one could buy a house, and yet the ultra-wealthy of the day seemed to think such costumes worth the investment. The Chilean millionaire Arturo Lopez, for example, wore a Chinese outfit to de Beistegui's ball at a reported cost of $55,000.

'Those were incredible years for designers,' said Cardin. 'There seemed to be a ball every night, and each one was more splendid than the last. Women thought nothing of spending $2,000 for a dress. And what dresses. They glittered with sequins and spun-gold thread.'

PIERRE CARDIN

The costume orders kept on coming. For de Beistegui's Venetian ball alone Pierre Cardin made some thirty outfits. Business was brisk. His dozen or so workers had to be doubled; the next ball season he needed in excess of thirty. 'Customers snaked around the corner to my boutique,' he said, 'and it was not difficult to sell $50,000 worth of business in one day.'

Cardin's staff trundled up the five flights of stairs. In the three fifth-floor rooms, each some 17 feet by 12 feet, ostrich plumes and spears and felt and saffron-coloured bolts piled pell-mell against long work-tables. Racks of harlequin suits and tin armour were lit up by large windows that looked on to Rue Richepance and a pigeon-spattered roof. On the tables were spools of silver-coloured thread and wool yarn, scraps of calf leather and ashtrays, pin-cushions, irons and thimbles. There were order books, heavy pencils and chalk.

Cardin had to take rooms on the sixth floor, up a sharp, twisting staircase to another set of brown, flaking doors off a corridor. The rooms looked on to a courtyard. Across the way sagging gutters and pipes ran past flaky, unhinged wooden shutters on bathrooms and kitchens. His rooms were crushed under the teetering dummies and racks of plumed head-dresses and visored helmets and long viewing mirrors. Before long he took rooms on the seventh floor as well. The seventh floor was as high as he could go at Rue Richepance. Above was only sky, a sky he could see through the seventh-floor skylight. (Today he still nostalgically owns a few rooms on the seventh floor of Rue Richepance. He houses one of his principal technicians in them.)

During the early years that Cardin was in business, François Lesage, a young embroiderer who supplied Paris's couturiers, realizing that Dior's former assistant was going to become a fashion force to be reckoned with, extended him financial protection by charging him 750 francs for any embroidery he wanted, no matter how elaborate and time-consuming the assignment. But Lesage, the consummate professional, was not impressed by Cardin's business. 'It was a bordello,' he recalled. 'Rolls of fabric falling all over the atelier. People you had appointments with were engaged and couldn't be found. It was totally unprofessional.'

But the disorder never prevented Cardin from getting work. From the beginning he had a small roster of important clients, many of whom had come from Dior. He made costumes for, among others, the extravagant de Beistegui and Etienne de Beaumont; Madame Arturo Lopez-Willshaw and Madame de Casteja, reigning 1950s socialites; and Paul-Louis Weiller, an air force commandant and wealthy industrialist who leased his Rue de la Faisanderie mansion to the Duke and Duchess of Windsor. 'Initially there was no reason for me to become successful,' Cardin once recalled in a moment of humility. 'I mean my cultural education, my background, is rather elementary.' And yet he was in the swim of it.

•   •   •   •

From the beginning Cardin quietly turned his hand to making small collections of coats and suits. The ball seasons were intense and profitable, but they were followed by lags. Cardin, restless, paced. 'It kills me, doing nothing,' he said. He whipped together some fifty coats and suits for the press. Rue Richepance might not have been very chic, but it was conveniently located on the journalists' and buyers' circuit.

In 1951 he made a black silk coat-dress with wasp waist and swishing skirt, and the same nipped waist on a black wool coat. The following year Cardin made a very successful lipstick-red pleated coat which the model wore with a pillbox hat. Nathalie Mont-Servan, a young reporter at *Women's Wear Daily*, tramped up the stairs to Cardin's rooms on one of those early sunny spring afternoons. 'He had a few coats, as he was originally a suit and coat specialist,' she said. 'They were very round and tight weaves. Very sculpted.'

'At that time it was difficult not to imitate Balenciaga or Dior,' admitted Cardin. The fashion world was taking its leads from the two chief designers, and Cardin's suits and coats were no exception. Dior and Balenciaga were squaring off. By 1949 Dior's New Look had slimmed down. It was a period when the length of the hem was front-page news. It crystallized into eleven inches from the ground in formal wear, rising to fourteen inches for country clothes. Waists were still tiny and made even more so by wasp corsets, coloured cummerbunds and belts.

Dior kept on moving. In 1951 he did away with the intensely bifurcated waist. The New Look was so copied that the fashion cognoscenti were starting to sniff at its vulgarity. In 1954, in deference to the H-bomb, Dior launched his H line, also known as the 'French Bean' look or the 'Flat Look'. It had an elongated torso from bust to hip-bone, looser than the severely architected look of 1947. In the spring of 1955 he produced his A look, with narrow shoulders crowning the triangular A shape. But all Dior's new lines were very disciplined, very refined variations of a silhouette that roughly followed the natural curves of the body. 'Dior's New Look stayed a dominant fashion for ten years. Other clothes ideas were shown and worn – many of them smartly; but it is a fashion fact that, for ten years, if a woman was in this New Look silhouette, she could feel that she was in fashion.' That was the summation of a group of fashion editors twenty years later.

Equally respected was the mysterious Cristobal Balenciaga. Painfully shy, he never gave interviews and was rarely seen. He had so little interest in publicity, he refused even to attend his own couture shows; silence and reverence pervaded his house. For those who simply died for fashion his salon was a monastery, Balenciaga God. (He was actually very human. He liked to tidy up his dog's bottom with a clean linen handkerchief after it had had a kerbside poop.)

Balenciaga, more than Dior, was a fashion prophet, foreshadowing trends some ten years before they became the mainstream. The silhouette of his 1930s clothes was already the New Look. While Dior was establishing the New Look, Balenciaga was playing with the chemise dresses that became prominent in the late 1950s and early 1960s. Already in 1950, turning Dior's look upside down, Balenciaga made a loose, smock-like jacket over a strict skirt. In 1951, hinting at the chemise or sack dress, he produced a brown lace middy. It was much to Dior's chagrin that most fashion cognoscenti considered Balenciaga the true visionary. It was Dior, however, who had the golden touch of timing.

Cardin was simply one of the little boys lost somewhere among the Titans. He continued to produce respected, clean-cut suits and coats. One of the mannequins for his first show was the breathtaking Bettina Graziani. With sensuous lips and perfect bone structure, Bettina was one of the top models in Paris during the 1950s. She was the inspiration of Jacques Fath, and in 1952 a newcomer, Hubert de Givenchy, designed a blouse which was widely copied and later became known as the 'Bettina'. 'Cardin was not well known except that he was Dior's young assistant who had opened his own house,' recalled Bettina. Thelma Sweetinburgh, who covered fashion for *Vogue*, said 'His workrooms didn't impress me at the time. Being very busy at *Vogue* I only went as a favour to a friend.' But both were struck by Cardin when they met him. 'He was very thin, very romantic-looking, and very charming,' said Bettina.

For Bettina Cardin made a suit of shantung jacket with a black velvet collar. She says she paid for it although she was given a discount. It was customary for designers to give their couture clothes to beautiful celebrities who could show off the gowns in the right society. A 'mannequin du monde' received a 'prix jeune fille' – that is to say, she was given a dress to wear and keep. At that time Bettina was starting to run with café society, which was constantly on the move. A changing cast of glitterati jumped from Acapulco to Paris, from Rome to Capri, sometimes with a little skiing in St Moritz. Besides Bettina and the playboy Aly Khan, the café society of the day also included the Duke and Duchess of Windsor. It was a superb advertisement for Cardin that Bettina should wear one of his creations.

Cardin's great coup of those Rue Richepance days was to convince Carmel Snow, editor of *Harper's Bazaar*, to climb the five flights to his rooms. She did so for two seasons. Snow was a little gnome with a tight, monkey-like face, a white pillbox hat invariably perched atop. She looked like someone's country aunt and habitually fell asleep at the shows. Her appearance, however, belied her abilities: even when she fell asleep, said her former colleagues, she instinctively awoke when the only important model of a 120-piece collection came down the runway. 'She was the single most imposing fashion figure in Paris, her small frame dwarfing the rest of the fashion press with an authority that seemed to bristle from her bones. She had an infallible instinct for ferreting out the writer, the dancer, or the artist on the verge of success and featuring them in her magazine,' said her *Vogue* competitor Bettina Ballard. It was Carmel Snow who named Dior's New Look, and she had understood and pushed Balenciaga's genius from his first pre-war collection.

There were other newcomers to the fashion scene besides Cardin. Hubert de Givenchy, a former law student, had been around the boulevards; he had worked for Fath, Piguet, Lelong, Schiaparelli, before starting his own business in 1952. The International Wool Secretariat's young designer contest was uncovering talent in unknowns like Karl Lagerfeld. In 1953 a 17-year-old from Oran, Algeria, won the contest with designs for an asymmetrically-draped, one-sleeved cocktail dress. Tall, with nervous blue eyes under large glasses, he was Yves Saint Laurent. Michel de Brunhoff, director of *Vogue*, saw the young man's portfolio and was astounded by the similarity between this teenager's designs and those of Dior's upcoming A line. He called up Dior. 'You must take him on,' he said. Dior did and Yves Saint Laurent became the master's first assistant designer.

Chanel was back. On 5 February 1954, the 71-year-old showed her first collection in fifteen years. She never appeared herself but sat hidden between mirrors at the top of the Rue Cambon staircase. Journalists sat in gilt chairs, handbags collapsed at their feet. Cigarettes flared, spiral notebooks opened, pencils poised for sketching, for judgement. The collection shocked. It was as if the war, and the innovations of Dior and Balenciaga, had never happened. 'It was awful,' said Sweetinburgh. The Parisian press called it a 'melancholy retrospective' and 'ghosts of the 1930s gowns'. The headline of *Combat*, an extremely respected paper, screamed: 'Out in the sticks with Chanel.' The British and Americans were no kinder. 'A fiasco', announced the *Daily Mail*. That night Chanel turned to her fitter and admitted she had lost her touch.

The next day Chanel was on the floor of her salon, feverishly cutting, fitting her next collection. She was obsessed; people thought she was a little mad. But it took just a year before she was back on top, dictating, her crisp signature suits gobbled up by American women. Wrote *Vogue*: 'If the simplicity of her line is not new . . . its influence is unmistakeable.'

PIERRE CARDIN

'Balenciaga? He dresses women to look like old Spaniards,' Chanel snapped. 'Dior? To look like armchairs. He puts covers over them.'

●   ●   ●   ●

Cardin was straining under the lack of space at Rue Richepance. He wanted to break out, to arrive. And that's when he became aware of space available at 118 Rue du Faubourg Saint-Honoré, the Fifth Avenue of the French fashion scene.

The house at 118 Faubourg Saint-Honoré belonged to the Comte d'Harcourt. 'As the aristocrats have always done,' said Nathalie Mont-Servan, 'the façade was rented out and they lived in the back, over the courtyard.' It was by far the most lovely house on the block. The stone was a soft golden ochre, the colour of afternoon sun in Corsica. The monotony of the four-storey façade was broken half-way up by a moulding of angels around a snarling, malevolent satyr. On the ground floor, on either side of the courtyard entrance, were shops. The doors immediately on the left and right of the entrance passage led into the salons that were available, and inside a spiral staircase led to wide, open rooms with parquet floors, where baronial ceilings were illuminated by natural light from a string of five windows. Back in the courtyard, past the entrance to the salons, was the apartment of the gardien from which one could hear and smell mushrooms and onions browning in a pan. Across the cobblestone courtyard neat steps led up to the elegant home of the Comte d'Harcourt. It was magnificent. The Hôtel Bristol, a favourite hotel of famous fashion journalists, was just a stone's throw away.

Cardin moved from Rue Richepance to his new fashionable salon in 1953. At first he had the ground floor and shops plus an additional room upstairs. Eventually he took all three floors and attic. In this building, redolent of old money, he could comfortably welcome the same guests that stayed at Hôtel George V.

It was an expensive move. Cardin has repeatedly claimed that throughout his career he was 100 per cent self-financed, which by and large he has been. He was earning well in the early 1950s. It was, after all, the time when extravagantly rich women went mad: the American Mrs Biddle brought her jewellery casket to Paris and ordered dresses to match the colour of her gems; the Spanish Madame Anchorena spent 28 million francs a year ordering the same model in different shades, as well as fur coats and hats to match the ensemble. Even so, journalists and former employees have always suspected that Cardin needed additional help to catapult himself from the Rue Richepance rooms to the Comte d'Harcourt mansion.

During the end of the 1940s Cardin moved to an apartment at Rue de Monttessuy. It was an elegant street and far from the Solaure district of Saint-Etienne. Rue de Monttessuy ran into the Parc du Champ-de-Mars with its Eiffel Tower centrepiece. The sky above the street was dominated by the ribbed steel girders of the tower's giraffe-like neck. It was a polite neighbourhood. Red geraniums lightened up the odd window-box and wrought-iron balcony; bakers sold warm slivers of tarte tatin.

In the same building, upstairs from Cardin, lived Daniel Pérou, a gentle, well-educated if not particularly bright homosexual. (In an interview Cardin once claimed, oddly, that René Gruau, the famous artist behind Dior's publicity, also lived in the same building. 'I never lived on Rue de Monttessuy,' said Gruau when asked about this.) Pérou was from a good family with a rapidly dwindling fortune. (Friends of his said that within Paris's city limits he had owned a farm with grazing cows, but that his fortune was depleted by the end of his life.) It was soon obvious that Daniel Pérou adored the reed-thin couturier with the brown wavy hair and thick farmer's ankles and wrists. It was to Pérou, observers speculated, that Cardin turned for help. Along with Escoffier, he was rumoured to be a silent minority partner at Rue Richepance. Once the move to Faubourg Saint-Honoré was completed, however, Pérou became increasingly visible as a general director of the house. Some of Cardin's former employees believed that it was Pérou who provided additional financing and, in exchange, was made director and general manager.

At the age of 31 Cardin had his own elegant maison. But there were problems. The Comte d'Harcourt's servants were always sneaking out to photograph the models in the courtyard. And there was another problem. 'As part of his purchase agreement Cardin was obliged to continue an ultra-conservative men's furnishings shop that for many years had occupied the ground floor,' stated his 1965 biography. 'Unwilling to associate himself with traditional men's shirts and ties, he divided the floor into two boutiques: one he called "Adam", the other, "Eve".'

In "Eve" of course he featured his women's suits and coats − the lovely thick collars on cherry-red wool 1950s coats. In "Adam", however, he began displaying men's clothes more to his taste. He even tried his hand at designing some men's items: waistcoats, ties and sweaters. Fashionable young men were soon coming by to pick up square-ended bow ties made up in knobbly tweed, doe-skin, and exotic brocades. He even made a beautiful nineteenth-century smoking jacket in wool, and installed new shirt cuffs, woven-silk waistcoats and flashy sweaters.

He was on to something. A merchandising manager from Chicago's Marshall Field showed up at the boutique. He spotted a sweater he liked. It was a long mohair sweater, with three buttons and a piece across the waist. It came in dark green, maroon and blue and he snapped up a few. They were taken back to Marshall Field and copied.

All along, however, Cardin was rehearsing his début as a fully-fledged member of the Chambre Syndicale, with a place among the top couturiers. In 1954 he made a bubble dress, a dress that ballooned, and a chemise-like dress with a criss-cross front. In 1955 he made a very pretty and prim pink coat.

Already in the mid-1950s Cardin designs were worn in the street, even though few had heard of him. Sydney Gittler was a chief buyer for Macy's and Ohrbach's. Nicknamed the 'Coat and Suit King' by John Fairchild of *Women's Wear Daily*, Gittler ran stitch-for-stitch departments in his New York stores – coats were 'bought in Paris, but made in America'. In other words, he was a copyist with an eye and intuition that was unrivalled. 'On a rainy Saturday in January there wasn't anything going on and I asked if there was anything to see,' recalled Gittler. 'Someone said there's a new tailor who left Dior over on the Faubourg Saint-Honoré. Someone showed me his clothes, and then I saw a red-pleated coat with a little white cuff and collar – the prettiest coat I'd seen that season.'

Gittler bought it for Macy's and took it back to New York. He had it copied in silk, wool, taffeta and alpaca. He knew he was the only one with the coat and he made sure it stayed that way. He waited till March to advertise – so that no-one could copy it till the next season – but then he made a big splash, running full-page ads four Sundays in a row.

One reason Gittler was attracted to the Cardin coat was its price. As a copyist, Gittler said, he generally had to pay about $450 for each couture coat, sometimes as much as $1,000. A coat from the relatively unknown Cardin, however, cost only around $250. 'The coat was sensational. It became the Ford of New York,' said Gittler, using the trade term for a runaway success. 'By the fall everyone had copied it and it was selling in all the New York stores. Two years later it appeared in Sears as a house coat.'

While still relatively unknown, Cardin held a fundamental grasp and broad vision of the business. He was way beyond tunnel-vision dressmaking. A young man, Jean-Guy Vermont, had just started his own embroidery house in 1955. A few years later he was commissioned by Cardin to make some tunics, a transparent smock heavy with embroidery. Vermont made fifteen of them, which was a large order. The next season Vermont caught up with Cardin.

'What do you think of the tunic we did?' Cardin asked Vermont.

'They were fantastic. I am very pleased we worked together so well.'

'So am I,' continued Cardin. 'I am planning to make plenty again this season.'

'Fine,' said Vermont. 'But, Monsieur Cardin, if you could also agree in making some little things, like collars with little motifs, that would help. Because these tunics are very rich and they didn't sell that well.' (To stay in business Vermont needed reorders, and that was why he was pushing smaller items that had a likelier chance of selling.)

Cardin looked hard at Vermont. 'Let me tell you something, Monsieur Vermont,' Cardin said. 'I don't mind if it doesn't sell. I don't need it to sell. What I want is to be noticed, to be photographed. I want people to speak about my talent.'

•   •   •   •

Into the 118 Faubourg Saint-Honoré boutique walked a young man, still a teenager. It was the mid 1950s. André Oliver was a clean-scrubbed, polite boy from a comfortable middle-class family from Toulon. He had just finished design and fine art courses and was looking for a job. He had dark pretty eyes, a sultry sort of prettiness. Cardin hired him.

André Oliver fell for Cardin. Cardin was drawn to Oliver and took great delight in teaching the eager young man the tricks of dressmaking – the importance of knowing the technical details, like cutting and sewing. Oliver was bright, a good learner. He was Cardin's wide-eyed assistant. It was the same open curiosity that Cardin had, that he never lost. 'He was completely taken with Pierre,' said a friend of theirs. 'André was Pierre's Pygmalion.'

Cardin, very old-fashioned and discreet about his private life, occasionally told friends of ill-fated relationships with women. 'When I started at Cardin, Pierre told us about an affair he had with a girl when he was serving in the Red Cross,' said Roland de Vassal, his photographer during the 1950s and 1960s. 'He showed us letters the girl had sent him, and he didn't understand why she had stopped writing to him.' Cardin's brother, César, was told of another girlfriend. 'He fell in love with a young woman and wanted to marry her,' said César, 'but she caught some disease that affected her spine and died. He was very disappointed and told me, "I know I'll never get married now." He never told me her name. He was still at Paquin at the time.'

The moment Cardin arrived in Paris in 1944 he was surrounded by some of the most interesting and colourful artists of the day, many of whom were homosexuals. Jean Cocteau wrote frankly about his sexual life. 'Homosexuals recognize each other – the way Jews do,' he wrote in *Le Livre Blanc*. Cocteau had deep, long-lasting love relationships; but in one period of despondency, when he was briefly incapable of attachments, he often spent his Sundays at a Turkish bath, hidden in a secret compartment behind a one-way mirror. 'Standing in

61

the tub, they looked at themselves (looked at me) and began with that special Parisian grimace which exposes the gums; then they would rub one shoulder, pick up the soap, and work it into a lather. The soaping turned into a caress. Suddenly their eyes left the world, their heads snapped back, and their bodies spat like furious animals.' Behind the mirror Cocteau masturbated.

Was Cardin seduced by Cocteau and his set? No, said Mila Parély, the actress who was not only Jean Cocteau's friend but also very close to Pierre Cardin. 'I don't think he was seduced by Cocteau. Not for one second. When I lived with Cocteau young men were throwing themselves at him. When you are seventeen or eighteen it's a choice. I think people are born homosexuals. All my friends were homosexuals and there was always something there in their lives.' Jean Cocteau would probably have agreed. 'As far back as I can remember, even at the age when the mind does not yet influence the senses, I find traces of my love for boys,' he wrote.

'If I had been a man, I too would have been a homosexual,' said Parély. 'Especially in the couture business. I loathe those women. They are dreadful, the ones who wear the clothes. With a man so sensitive as Pierre, such a creator, it would have been terrible.' She added: 'Thank God Pierre is a homosexual. His work has been his wife. He's married to his work. It's much more important.'

MOREAU AND THE PAPARAZZI   5

On New Year's Eve 1957, terror struck Algeria. In the village of Mac-Mahon twenty-one innocent spectators at a football match were blasted into the stands when a bomb was thrown. At Touggart, a village on the fringe of the desert in the south, tit-for-tat grenades were thrown under the tables at French and Muslim cafés. A bomb in Mecheria killed or injured nine people; in the capital, Algiers, three bombs exploded. Meanwhile, in Paris, accounts were settled; six Muslim Algerians were murdered in café attacks as they sipped mint tea and worked their worry beads.

The revolt in Algeria erupted in 1954, only a few months after France's war in Indo-China ended. But Algeria was different from France's Asian colony: by legal dictum Algeria was an integral part of France, and a million European colons lived there, many families for several generations. Yet the native Algerians, mostly Muslim, were unimpressed and wanted their independence. They formed the FLN (the National Liberation Front) which in 1954 began an armed revolt, using the hit-and-run terrorist tactics of the Maquis.

In 1956 the Socialist Guy Mollet became premier. At first he leaned towards a negotiated settlement; but angry and militant colons changed his mind, and a year later he drafted into the war half a million troops, the largest French expeditionary force since the Crusades. The conflict grew more bitter, more bloody. Teenage Muslims locked in cells never survived their 'questioning'; young French farmers drafted into the war and relaxing in a café looked down after the smoke cleared and saw bloody stumps where once they had legs. Inhuman atrocities were inflicted by both sides.

Governments paid the price for not being able to end the war. Mollet's administration fell in May 1957, the next government by April 1958. It took a month after that to patch together another coalition little different from the one preceding it. On 13 May, when the new premier, Pierre Pflimlin, was to present his cabinet before the National Assembly, French extremist leaders organized a thundering demonstration in Algiers. It turned into a riot. The colon leaders stormed the government building and proclaimed a revolutionary government in Algeria.

France was on the brink of civil war. In the latter half of May French–Algerian troops were rumoured to be planning a paratroop attack on Paris, co-ordinated with army units in the provinces. On the 24th rebels seized Corsica in a successful coup. Premier Pflimlin was unable to get the insurrection in hand. The country teetered.

Waiting in the wings was the old war-horse and brilliant political strategist, Charles de Gaulle. This was war and the towering man with moustache and military gait relished it. De Gaulle flew into Paris from his country estate as Communist-dominated labour unions decided to go on strike and rumours swirled of insurrection in Toulouse, Pau and Perpignan. Senators openly called on de Gaulle to save the nation from civil war.

De Gaulle made his conditions: he would, for a limited period, be given extraordinary powers; he would be given a mandate to prepare a referendum on constitutional changes. By 1 June he had been voted into power by 329 to 224 votes. It was the last time the Fourth Republic met. No one mourned its demise. De Gaulle's proposed new constitution strengthened the executive branch, but kept the drafting of legislature in the hands of parliament. A strengthened prime minister became the head of government, displacing the former weaker premier. Most important, the National Assembly's right to overthrow governments was sharply curtailed. The referendum went to the ballot in September 1958. Almost 80 per cent of the voting population was in favour. France's antiquated, institutionalized weakness was dead. Even the most cynical Frenchmen began to have new hope.

Algeria? Pure cunning. Charles de Gaulle, called in by the right wing to keep Algeria French, at first gave lip service to his constituents. 'In Algeria there are only full-fledged French citizens,' he declared on 4 June 1958. By 3 October he had back-pedalled: 'Algeria's future will have a dual basis: its own character and its close ties with France.' In July 1962, De Gaulle signed a declaration granting Algeria its independence.

'[Power] was given him so that he could keep Algeria French,' wrote the French historian Robert Aron in 1966. 'Later, the question would be raised as to whether that was indeed de Gaulle's true intention, or whether it was a pretext that allowed him to return to power and reform the regime.'

•   •   •   •

'The chemise has arrived,' shrieked Carmel Snow in 1957. She was referring to the loose-waisted sack dress Balenciaga had been dabbling in since 1950. In 1955 the newcomer Hubert de Givenchy made a dress that was pure chemise – beige soft wool, short sleeves, collarless neck. But it took Christian Dior's chemise line of 1957 to produce Carmel Snow's dictum. France was entering a new, uncharted era. The New Look was based on a pre-war sense of elegance, now something else was required. The answer was the distinctly modern look of the chemise, and from 1957 to 1967 its line dominated fashion.

That same year, in the autumn/winter collections held in July, two newcomers became fully-fledged members of the Chambre Syndicale. One was Guy Laroche. The other was Pierre Cardin.

Cardin presented a 120-piece collection of suits, gowns, coats and evening dresses. It went well. His silk and muslin evening gowns were applauded by the white-glove set. He leaned towards crisp fabrics. His big success was a variation of the sack dress with a looped back and draping. 'Another designer specializing in youthful styles is Pierre Cardin, who has a small, beautifully made collection of two main themes,' wrote a fashion correspondent for the London *Times* in August, 'Short jackets over short straight skirts were high-buttoning in the front, and at the back folds of the fabric dropped in a deep oval curve to the edge.' What *The Times* said was not important; that *The Times* mentioned him at all, however, was very significant.

Cardin's career leaped forward just two months later through an event that was beyond his control. On 24 October tragedy hit the fashion world: Christian Dior died. Fashion's kindly first statesman had one weakness: food. 'He gorged himself as if he would never see another meal,' said Sweetinburgh. Only his food was richer than the solid silver tub he bathed in or the red velvet bedroom he retired to. Dior's chef was famous for inventing a moulded vanilla ice-cream swimming with hot fudge inside.

He died at the Italian spa Montecatini, where he was taking a cure. The circumstances of his death, at the age of 52, remain cloudy. Officially he had a stroke, but rumours swirled. The story fashion journalists circulated most among themselves was sad. Allegedly Dior's Montecatini diet was too much; he broke down and began gorging himself, choking to death, they said, on morsels caught in his throat. In whatever shape his demise came, it was clearly not his astrologer's fault. She had warned him against taking the cure.

It was a very undignified end to a very dignified man. Roland de Vassal, the photographer Pierre Cardin had used since 1953, first heard of Dior's death at 7 a.m. He immediately got on the phone to Cardin, who became hysterical. 'Pierre turned upside down,' said de Vassal.

The funeral was incredible. Every church in Paris seemed to ring its bells. The traffic of black cars and black veils jammed into a ferocious knot. Couturiers wept. According to John Fairchild, chairman of *Women's Wear Daily*, Pierre Cardin fainted dead away at the funeral. Maison Dior, overwhelmed, sent a jungle of flowers to be laid at the Arc de Triomphe.

No sooner was poor Dior buried than the fashion press went wild speculating on who was going to fill his shoes. A few months before his death, he had paid his last tribute to Cardin. At a large dinner party he said that as long as there was bright new talent like Cardin, Paris would remain the centre of haute couture. 'Take up the torch,' Dior said publicly. 'It can be yours.'

The message was received by the press. In November 1957, the *Sunday News* in New York profiled 'Les Boys' – the four up-and-coming young men who were coming into their own. At Dior, of course, there was the teenager prone to headaches, Yves Saint Laurent; Givenchy, the former lead designer for Schiaparelli, was respected; the colour-keen newcomer Guy Laroche had a chance; and lastly there was Pierre Cardin.

Cardin was in the majors. That was about the time the photographer Cecil Beaton met him. He had the 'pallor of a convolvulus' and was 'seething with inner combustion', observed Beaton. 'When he speaks of his work his eyes blaze, his saliva runs dry, and his voice assumes enough volume to crack the Edwardian plasterwork on his ceiling.'

The press was now following Cardin's moves very closely. And 1958 was going to be his big year. The 1958 collections were a runaway hit. With Dior gone, Cardin was now becoming his own man, self-assured and leaning towards avant-garde designs. 'Dior taught me everything I knew,' he said, 'except how to make a Cardin.' That year he came out with a widely copied 'mushroom collar' which looked like a wavy wool halo around the neck. He pioneered huge cape-shape collars, often fluted or cartridge-pleated, on slender 1950s coats. His technique of double-layered collars was swiftly seized on by manufacturers and many women began wearing a Cardin invention without realizing it. He was one of the forward-looking designers pushing the chemise, the elegant loose-fitting sack. There were ideas bursting out of his work: bucket hats, wide shoulders, figure-concealing cuts and short skirts.

Through the explosion of tailoring details was one message: Cardin was predicting a lurch away from elegant, old-ladyish day dresses to a swinging younger image. That year he made a short loose top of mohair and paired it with tight lurex ski-pants. The chemise went just so far in heralding a new era. Cardin was going farther; he was pushing at the edge. 'The couturier', he explained, 'should, through a dress, express the customs and civilization of an era.'

The press frothed at the mouth. The highly respected Eugenia Sheppard, critic for the *New York Herald Tribune*, called his collection ' the gayest', the 'loveliest' she had seen in a long time. 'The clothes look young and spontaneous. Cardin cuts as well as he thinks.' *The New York Times* was equally impressed. Pierre Cardin was 'the fashion designer on everyone's lips' and 'the battle for seats was such that it might have been the World Series at Yankee Stadium'. His 1957 showing was an immediate success, it noted, 'but it took his current collection to put him in the front ranks of Paris designers'. *The Times*, in its arch, utilitarian descriptions spent time on his use of colour. 'Colours were unusually varied and included many blues, red, orange, apricot shades, raspberry, lilac, and light green.'

Cardin's hard work had paid off. That he was and is probably one of the best technicians in the couture business was the sum of his experiences as a tailor's apprentice in Vichy and Saint-Etienne; as an intimate of Christian Dior; as an experimenter in novel cuts. Apart from Balenciaga, Cardin was the only designer who could make a dress from the first pencilled sketch, through mock-up, cutting, stitching, fitting and finishing down, to the last buttonhole.

Cardin's clothes rapidly became known for their novel cut and construction. He was, for example, a master at the spiral and bias cut, a complicated technique of cutting diagonally across the grain of the cloth. It made the material move with the body, was easy for the couturier to drape, and made the clothes appear very elegant. But the bias cut was so technically difficult it was also impossible to copy and mass-produce. His architectural bent also made him a unique specialist in panels and pleats and cowl draping. His spring fashion of 1959 established a look that became very popular throughout the 1960s: three-quarter length sleeves and collarless jackets paired with stiletto heels and pouffe hats. Some hats looked like giant felt bell-jars. One collarless coat was a marvel of construction, its silhouette identically matching the bell-jar hat, but with tucked folds that ran from the bosom to the below-the-knee hem. They looked like Alice-in-Wonderland pockets, with an opening three feet long.

Of course, Cardin was not alone. Yves Saint Laurent was also fighting for the limelight. In October 1957 Christian Dior had walked into Jacques Rouët's office. 'I've made up my mind. There are thirty models in my latest collection that are based on Saint Laurent's designs. He is an exceptional talent. He's been working beside me for eighteen months. I want the papers to know all about him; I want him to be recognized; I want justice to be done.'

'But he's not yet twenty,' said the incredulous Rouët. 'Wait just a little longer.'

'No,' Dior answered. 'I won't wait. I want it done by next time.'

A few days later, of course, Dior was dead. Yves Saint Laurent, whom Dior had nicknamed his 'dauphin', was immediately promoted to head designer for the House of Dior. At 21 he was already the head of the largest maison de couture in all of France.

Saint Laurent's first collection, in January 1958, was the Trapeze line, named after the shape of the silhouette. The acclaim and hysteria rivalled anything Christian Dior had received. The audience jumped over the little gold chairs, screaming. There was wild, wild emotion and kisses and tears. Like royalty, Saint Laurent appeared on the Avenue Montaigne balcony waving to a huge crowd chanting his name.

His second collection in 1958 was not so well received. Overnight Yves went from being a 'boy wonder' to a 'monster'. He lowered the hemline four inches at a time when ever shorter hemlines were front-page news. A year later, in the autumn of 1959, he went the other way, and shortened the hem to knee level. The knives came out. 'I think it is ridiculous for a youth of twenty-three to try and dictate to sensible women,' said a woman Member of Parliament in London. The debate raged, and newspapers, radio and television began quizzing people at length about their attitude towards knees. In the spring/summer Beatnik collection of 1960, Saint Laurent went all out for a youthful look. Motorcycle jackets were made of alligator, mink coats with ribbed sweater sleeves, turtle-necks worn under finely-cut suits. He had misjudged the staid clientele of Maison Dior.

It was at this point, after winning three deferments, that Saint Laurent found he could no longer avoid call-up for Algeria. Another assistant designer, Marc Bohan, took over at Maison Dior. Unfortunately, Saint Laurent's temperament was not suited to army life. Prone to headaches even in the genteel setting of Paris couture, he collapsed in the barracks. The trouble started when the trembly couturier was forbidden to take a bath for two weeks. The outcome was a complete physical and nervous breakdown. The tabloids had a field day and soon photographs of a prostrate Saint Laurent en route to a psychiatric clinic outside Paris were splashed across the papers. He was discharged from the army after two months as being 'unadaptable on military grounds', and went off to recuperate in Majorca. He never made it to Algeria.

•   •   •   •

'You know, publicity is the only thing that matters to Pierre,' said Roland de Vassal. 'Pierre is a man of the media. He was one of the first willing to have his dresses, his shoes, his apartment and even his dog photographed.'

Christian Dior, the inventor of the modern couture house, often said that it was better to be slammed on the front page than applauded in two lines on page eight. For fashion fortunes were built on publicity. Cardin learned that lesson well. Discarding his shyness in those pivotal years of 1957 and 1958, he called on his talents as an actor and began a charm offensive. His audience were the note-jotting journalists. 'He had wonderful ideas, extraordinary vision,' said Mont-Servan, 'and he was begging to talk about them.'

Cardin was a very modern designer in that he was one of the first to recognize fully the importance of the press, and he set about using it to his fullest advantage. He grabbed headlines with his modern, boundary-pushing clothes and by a barrage of immensely quotable one-liners liberally sprinkled throughout a rambling, poetic vision. 'A chic woman is never sexy,' he announced. 'Fashion acts as a stimulant on a woman's character,' he said, waving his hands. 'In our well-heated cities we have no need of a style that calls for long and befurred sleeves and thick materials, such as that of the Middle Ages.' He launched into monologues about himself that went on and on. All the fashion hacks scribbled down his sayings. 'It is the press that has made me,' he once said during a rare moment of humility.

But in 1958 Cardin also began giving the media romanticized versions of his life – something he continued to do throughout his career. There was the silly issue of his age. In 1958 papers reported he was 32; he was 36. And in 1960 he was still 32 years young. The story the press was given about his background was also incorrect. On 7 August 1958, the *New York Times* wrote: 'The son of a rich wine merchant, he was born in Venice – his parents were vacationing there at the time – which might account for his great love of travel.' No suggestion of abject poverty, or that he was Italian by birth, no mention even of little Sant' Andrea di Barbarana. Nothing at all about the years of degradation. Cardin's office released this somewhat sanitized version of his upbringing for decades.

No employee, other perhaps than André Oliver, ever heard Cardin discuss his family. What they learned about his background came from the papers. (And that was mostly inaccurate. Years later he told the press, 'I have neither a dog nor a family,' yet he still had half a dozen siblings alive. Few people close to him in fact knew he even had brothers living in France, or that he was the youngest of eleven children.) Cardin is self-made and his greatest creation ultimately became his public account of himself. When an annoying fact or two got in the way of his myth, he simply cut and sewed a version more in line with the image he wanted. It worked for thirty years. 'M. Cardin is an intellectual, cultivated and opinionated,' announced the *New York Times* in 1958. Undoubtedly he was embarrassed by his crude education and immigrant roots, for amongst the sandalwood fragrances he smelt of apples and garlic.

Dior's death gave Cardin an opportunity to shine publicly. The International Wool Secretariat, the association of the world's wool producers, was still running the design contests through which they had discovered Karl Lagerfeld and Yves Saint Laurent. Another of these contests was scheduled in late 1957 and Dior had been slated as one of the panelists. Thelma Sweetinburgh, who had left *Vogue* to organize the competitions, asked Pierre Cardin to step in and fill Dior's spot. It was very last-minute. And although the publicity had already gone out with Dior's name, Cardin jumped at the opportunity. The reticent tailor was shy no longer. He shone. 'He talked very well. He was very quick,' said Sweetinburgh. 'Like all shy people once he got started he was very good.'

The contest was held at the Théâtre des Ambassadeurs, an elegant theatre of chandeliers and red velvet chairs. As Cardin talked and thrilled people, his farmer's hands sawed through the air. His fingers were extremely long and flat with large diamond-hard nails. His thumb spread out like a spatula and, as he was essentially a labourer, flecks of dirt were permanently under his nails. His palms were meaty, the skin hardened with callouses. 'Pierre uses his hands a lot,' said Roland de Vassal. 'They are very flat, the hands of a real, good craftsman.'

'His whole story is in his hands. It's all there,' said Odile Moltzer, an employee in the 1960s.

•　　　　　•　　　　　•　　　　　•

Cardin began acting out his passion for travel. In 1957 he was invited to Japan by NDK, the federation of Japanese designers. He was sent three tickets, for himself and two mannequins. The purpose was to show the Japanese how to make clothes right on the mannequin without a paper pattern to follow. The curious Japanese had never heard of Pierre Cardin and they wondered if someone had garbled the name of Pierre Balmain. No, they were informed, he was a new designer who was trained at Dior.

NDK called in the portfolios of some sixty Japanese mannequins. The mannequin finally chosen to work with Cardin was a famous local model called Hiroko, a breathtakingly beautiful woman with a tiny waist. Hiroko was told to pick Cardin up at the airport in a kimono. Hiroko's mother took charge. She hired a car and chauffeur to keep a spot at the airport drop-off ramp, which she then lined with tatami-like mats. Hiroko changed there after having just rushed in from an earlier job. She made it by thirty minutes.

In 1957 it usually took two days to fly to Tokyo from Paris. Cardin got off the plane with a tall mannequin called Helen and a Japanese photographer, Yoshi Takata. Hiroko, in the traditional white make-up, bowed. 'I had never seen that kind of man before. He was such a smart man. He was very Italian-looking,' she recalled. Cardin was wearing a tartan suit and Hiroko's eyes kept falling to his cuffs which were so very, very white. The shirt had a high collar. 'He was so elegant. He was so beautiful and very sweet.' The two smiled at each other. They couldn't communicate.

Cardin spent a month and a half travelling with his entourage between Tokyo, Osaka and Kyoto. Still digging out from under the war's destruction, Tokyo's low slate-coloured buildings seemed to stretch endlessly. During the New Year fertility and good luck tokens of wheat, rice and bamboo were hung from doorways. Women in wooden clogs, their hair studded with flowers, tassels and tinsel ornaments, took little kimono steps through the muddy lanes, while a modern couple in fake-leather biker's jackets sped away on a motorbike. Penniless men in clogs appeared natty in ancient but immaculately kept suits. Cardin watched them as they slurped horrendously over a bowl of steaming noodles and fish cakes. 'It was like going to the moon,' he recalled. Certainly the stores were barren. There were few products on the shelves; no kid gloves, no lizard pocket-books, few stockings. Cardin, wide-eyed and curious, absorbed it all.

The high point of the trip was a fashion show at Tokyo's fashion school, Bunka. It was the first time a French couturier had come to Japan with a collection. Cardin created a sensation. Although Hiroko was already famous in Japan, the French couture clothes completely transformed her. The Parisian mannequin, Helen, was huge and the Japanese audience just gawked. In the audience was a young Japanese student who had never before seen a haute couture fashion show. His name was Kenzo. 'Before Cardin came all the French clothes I saw were very rigid,' he said. 'What was the most exciting thing to see was the fluid side of couture, the way it was draped. Everything was very soft.'

Cardin taught a course in making couture clothes. He showed the Japanese how to cut and actually make the dress on the model, how to structure the clothes. 'It was completely magical to see him cut the piece of cloth and put it right on the model. It was something they had never seen before.'

It was an important lesson. Kenzo had just started at the school and his teachers immediately realized that to become a designer it was very, very important to know how to cut. For these lessons — for the early trips and the

71

flattering attention – Cardin became the first French couturier to earn Japanese loyalty and awareness. His timing was perfect. His gnome-like Japanese photographer, Yoshi Takata, became his co-ordinator for the Japanese market and spent the next thirty years wringing it for all it was worth.

During that trip Cardin heard that his devoted assistant, André Oliver, had been called up by the French army to fight in Algeria. He was devastated and wanted to return to Paris immediately. He had his obligations, however, and left only after his tour was completed. But it was torture, an excruciating pain to sit through the endless shows. 'I spent forty-two days there,' he said. 'It was so difficult I crossed off each day as though I was doing military service.' (André Oliver was hardier than Saint Laurent and he did go to Algeria. But he did not receive the same treatment as, say, a Lyon mechanic. The president of the Chambre Syndicale, said reporters of the time, intervened with the Defence Ministry on Cardin's behalf. During his tour of duty Oliver was allowed twice a year to fly back to Paris to help Cardin bring out the collections. And during the preparations, claimed a Cardin mannequin, designs were flown to Oliver's barracks, where, at weekends, he worked on the garments and then returned them to Paris. Some said André Oliver was the only soldier in the whole army with a hand-made uniform.)

The next year Cardin took a ship to America. He did an eight-city tour, from New York to Los Angeles. Down Fifth Avenue swept secretaries in inexpensive, well-made Macy's dresses in bull reds and Caribbean turquoise. Finned Cadillacs in baby blue or cranberry and chrome sailed regally down canyons of cement. A jumble of ethnic-coloured faces passed by him. The colours of America thrilled Cardin, stimulated him.

'Shy Cardin backs trend to Chemise,' screeched Agnes Ash of *The New York Times*, announcing his arrival. 'Pierre Cardin, who looks like Louis Jourdan and acts like Jimmy Stewart, was saddened to hear that American men had denounced the chemise.' By comparing him to such stars, Ash was making sure the public understood that couturiers were no longer simple rag merchants but twentieth-century celebrities. Cardin played his role as the fey couturier to perfection. 'I think this tour will help me get better acquainted with the American woman,' he said. 'She is an inspiring creature.'

On that trip Cardin met a man who was later to become his American agent. Cardin had created six patterns for *McCall*'s magazine. A woman at the magazine was in charge of his entertainment, but of course she could not possibly take him to night-clubs or jazz bars at night. It wouldn't have been seemly. Instead, she turned to a man who was in charge of textiles in the trade department at the French consulate. His name was Max Bellest. He had originally come to the US to buy cotton for his family's import business in France. He eventually wound up in the French consulate and spent the war years playing golf in Pennsylvania with all the other Vichy French officials under house arrest. In 1958, however, Bellest was pleased to take Cardin into the bowels of Greenwich Village and show him the best dives the city had to offer. Together they went to smoky cellars where sweaty-faced musicians blew on saxophones and bearded poets picked fights. Bellest and Cardin parted friends. 'I liked him,' said Bellest. 'He was nicer in those days. You see, he was trying to climb the ladder, so he was nicer.'

•   •   •   •

Since his first trip to Japan in 1957, Cardin had continually asked the Japanese model Hiroko to come to Paris and model for him. She declined until 1960 when he sent her a ticket and she felt pressured to accept. But she immediately suffered a minor nervous collapse and went to bed for a month trembling at the thought. Her mother at length convinced her to look at it as a light-hearted shopping jaunt to Paris. That revived her.

In early July 1960 her Air France flight touched down in Paris eight hours late. She came out into the arrivals hall wearing the traditional kimono. No-one was there. Practically weeping she found a Japanese ground steward and asked for the next flight back to Tokyo. There was none for three days so, without speaking a word of French, she boarded the bus to the city of sin. As she got off at the bus terminal she was met by a throng of photographers and journalists. (The plane had been delayed so long that people had been told to wait at the Paris bus terminal.) It was a brilliant publicity stunt. Hiroko became Cardin's star mannequin and the first pure Asian model to hit the Paris catwalks. Cardin made plenty of capital out of it.

André Oliver, meanwhile, was not only important to Cardin as a companion but rapidly becoming vital as an assistant designer. He gave orders when Pierre was not there, his black eyebrows rising with unquestionable authority. Oliver had a natural, elegant taste very different from Cardin's bizarrely avant-garde bent. They complemented each other perfectly.

The drama was constant. Cardin had low blood sugar and carried two lumps of sugar in his pocket. Once, while working day and night on a collection, he passed out and toppled through glass doors on to the veranda. There were shrieks of alarm, but he was unhurt. He revived himself by nibbling the sugar and immediately went back to work. He was driven by a sense that only he could do everything correctly. 'Can you finish this?' he demanded of a tailor. 'No. I'll finish it myself or it won't be done properly.' He grabbed the 10-inch scalloping shears and began furiously snipping cloth into a dramatic sweep.

Cardin was terribly nervous, particularly during the shows. When he wasn't shoving mannequins on to the catwalk he was peeking through a hole at the audience, watching every reaction of Carmel Snow who was seated front row centre. If she dozed he went into a fit. Hiroko recalled that he once collapsed on the floor moaning that the collection was a failure. She and the other mannequins immediately surrounded him. 'The journalists were too busy taking notes to clap,' they said in an attempt to calm him and stop the moaning. He opened his eyes and saw half a dozen mannequins hovering over him. He suddenly shot back up. 'I need air, I need air,' he screamed. He ran to the windows, flung them open and took deep breaths while his mannequins looked on in alarm.

What went on behind the scenes belied the impact he was having in the fashion world. He was indisputably a leader. He started his cut-out phase in 1960, making cut-out diamond patterns at the breastbone of his models. Later came squares. Then circles. 'Pierre Cardin created the only excitement of the opening day of the Paris collections,' wrote the *New York Times* in the summer of 1960. 'Always a controversial figure and accused of making too advanced or severe designs, Pierre Cardin calmed down and showed softer, more feminine fashions than usual.' Slim wrapped coats made entirely of a liquorice-black mink or wavy broadtail were worn with matching fur cloches. They produced a thunderous applause.

In 1961 he led the pack again. 'Last season he was ahead of himself as usual when he showed loose-cut coat dresses with wedges of bias fabric set into the skirts to make them flare at the hemline. At that time they looked pretty odd to most people; in this collection they look just right,' wrote the respected journalist Carrie Donovan in January. And in July he had a financial winner. 'Although it was a mad scramble up the long curling stairway to Cardin's salon, an almost hair-tearing battle to hold on to one's seat and an exhausting wait for the collection finally to begin, it was worth it,' wrote Patricia Peterson. 'Store buyers jammed their notebooks with numbers of clothes to be bought for copying in New York.'

And in 1963 journalist Jeanne Molli placed her finger on Cardin's formidable influence on Paris. 'Cardin sizzles and pops with ideas. Just as the designs seem to follow a pattern, a new image emerges.' To a large extent he was Paris's ideas generator. Just one of his collections produced enough novel images to feed an army of second-rate designers for years.

•   •   •   •

In 1961 the French actress Jeanne Moreau was looking for the right costume. Joseph Losey was directing her in *Eva*, a film based on a James Hadley Chase novel. 'Joseph Losey was one of those directors who couldn't tell how Eva had to be dressed, but through what he said I knew exactly what was needed,' said Jeanne Moreau. She went to see Madame Chanel, who usually dressed her. Chanel was snippy. 'No, we're closing.'

Moreau was obsessed with costume details. It was the key to her film characters. 'It's like a trip when you make a film,' she explained. 'You prepare your costume as if you're packing. The intensity comes bit by bit, like a puzzle.' Her close friend Florence Malraux had worked on several films with the actress and knew how important the costumes were to Moreau's characters. Malraux made a suggestion. 'Florence spoke of a new couturier called Pierre Cardin,' said Moreau.

She went to 118 Faubourg Saint-Honoré. In Cardin's salon, panelled with a green silk-like cloth, she took her seat. It was a small collection but the clothes were beautiful. She had to see him right away. She went backstage. Cardin, very charming, draped her in his beautiful designs, listened to her talk about the costume needs of *Eva*. She returned again, and again, snapping up garments for herself. His long hands worked the material around her body, his intense energy and commitment to his work pouring from his gestures. 'I saw him. It was instantaneous,' she said. One of France's greatest actresses, Jeanne Moreau, was head over heels in love with Cardin. 'I knew his reputation as a homosexual. I didn't give a damn.'

Jeanne Moreau was the star of the Nouvelle Vague. Between 1958 and 1962 – when de Gaulle dragged France into a modern political constitution and ended the Algerian war – all the arts in France, not just fashion, began to twist and contort themselves in new directions. Film could not remain unchanged in a world so full of turmoil. A group of young film critics working for a periodical called *Cahiers du Cinéma* began turning their hands to film-making. They included François Truffaut, Jean-Luc Godard, Claude Chabrol and Eric Rohmer. It was the birth of the French New Wave and its best films between 1958 and 1962 – such as Godard's *A Bout de Souffle* (*Breathless*, 1960) – were steeped in a critic's knowledge of the classics, but unconventional and rough as the times dictated. The directors did away with the fluff of French farces. They went for grit.

A new style of film, of course, required new stars, and it was to Jeanne Moreau that one young director, Louis Malle, turned for inspiration. Malle had previously co-directed an underwater film, *Le Monde du Silence*, with

PIERRE CARDIN

Jacques-Yves Cousteau. At the age of 29 Jeanne Moreau had made twenty-one mediocre films; but in 1957 the already experienced actress was storming Paris with her steamy stage portrayal of Maggie in Peter Brook's production of *Cat on a Hot Tin Roof*. Malle wanted to make a film with her. In *Lift to the Scaffold* (1957), their first film together, he did away with flattering lights and make-up, and instead allowed the camera to explore the seething inner life that flickered across her face. Her looks were not conventional: she had a pouting beauty, her mouth pointed down in an expression of slight desperation. Her eyes were at times calm and kind, then fired up with passion and destruction. The skin was pampered, creamed, soothed and healthy, and yet it could not hide the dark rings under the eyes that spoke of a restless soul. A brave, dangerous spirit. 'She suggested intimate pleasures to everyone,' said the film critic Molly Haskell.

Malle continued the same film style in *The Lovers* (1958), in which Moreau's bored provincial housewife abandoned her husband and child for her new lover – a feminist film before the feminist movement. The crucial scene, a torrid love-making that closely explored a woman's reaction during orgasm, scraped through the censors and became an international sensation. That year the film won an award at the Venice Film Festival, and La Moreau, the thinking man's femme fatale, was born.

'The New Wave was an expression of what was going on in that period, but I lived everything from a distance inside the cinema,' she said. 'At 30 I didn't give a damn about what was going on in the world. My only concern was me, the way I was going to work and meet these extraordinary people.' And meet them she did. Between 1958 and when she met Cardin, Jeanne Moreau chalked up a list of critically acclaimed performances. She was lurid in Roger Vadim's version of *Les Liaisons Dangereuses 1960* (1959); on the point of breakdown in Marguerite Duras' screenplay for *Moderato Cantabile* (1960); and alienated in Michelangelo Antonioni's *La Notte* (1960). Moreau submerged herself in her roles. In *Moderato Cantabile* she started drinking wine in the morning, duplicating the troubling habit of the suicidal character she played. 'She emerges from her films a convalescent, both physically and morally,' said her friend Marguerite Duras.

In 1961 Francois Truffaut's film *Jules et Jim* was released. In it Moreau played Catherine, a woman involved in a complicated menage à trois that ends tragically in her suicide and the murder of her lover. The critics hailed Catherine as her greatest performance. Moreau by this time was at the top of the heap, a great star. Everywhere she went people ran after her, pressing on her programmes and napkins and arms to autograph.

And that was when she met Cardin. 'I was aware of the reputation he had in Paris. I knew all about it and I didn't care,' Moreau said in an interview.

'Quite the contrary. All the obstacles I knew were there only made him more attractive.'

Cardin had moved to a Left Bank apartment on the Quai Anatole France, with a dramatic view of the Seine. Moreau lived in Versailles with her son from her first marriage to the actor Jean-Louis Richard. She sent him flowers. She courted him. 'Moreau was completely mad about him. She kept after him for quite a while,' said Odile Moltzer, Cardin's press attaché in the early 1960s. 'I knew he was capable of loving a woman,' said Moreau. 'I had to be patient and gentle, not frighten him with the dreadful phantoms a sadistic society flourishes with such pleasure. I had to make him understand that I could understand, could admit everything – and that he should too.'

Cardin fell. 'I can remember that very night,' said Roland de Vassal. 'Pierre and Jeanne danced all night and she stayed after I left. She came for a New Year's Eve and never left again.'

André Oliver was crushed. Raymond Méjat was a television journalist at the time. He was sitting in the office of Edith Pasquier, one of Cardin's press officers, working out details for a fashion piece. Oliver burst into the room. 'He was hysterical. In shock,' recalled Méjat. 'He was walking around the room like some animal locked inside a cage and throwing everything he could find on to the floor. Pasquier followed after him picking up the debris. He was uttering every possible insult you could think of. That day, André Oliver looked so miserable I thought he was going to commit suicide.' They finally heard the reason for this incredible grief. 'He said that Pierre Cardin had just told him he was going to leave him for Jeanne Moreau. Their affair was over and it seemed like Monsieur Oliver could not get over it. I had never seen a man react like that over another man.'

James Brady was the Paris bureau chief at *Women's Wear Daily* at the time and watched it all happen from the outside. He was less sympathetic to Oliver's suffering and wrote his version in his autobiography: 'André was mooning about Paris, separated for the first time from the older gentleman who had brought him into business and into his life. It was reported that André was threatening suicide and that Cardin, upset at the reports, bought him a fine flat. Then it was said that André while well housed, was still depressed and was still talking about death. So Cardin set up charge accounts at some decent restaurants. Now André was well housed, well fed but still morose. So Cardin got Bernard Buffet to offer André one of his pictures. Andre was shown through Buffet's studio and supposedly announced, "There are three I can't choose between," and got them all. Later Cardin heard that André was staying out all night, drinking and dancing with young women at New Jimmy's, and Cardin announced he was deeply shocked.

PIERRE CARDIN

How could André's parents permit a young man to carry on so in wicked Paris?'

The papers, of course, exploded with the Moreau–Cardin affair. The paparazzi went mad, dashing after the lovers with white flashes and cameras with long lenses. The paparazzi's interest was understandable. Here was a fashion designer, with fey mannerisms and a reputation as a homosexual. There was the famous sex kitten, a reputed man-eater, whose reputation as a sensualist was fanned by touchingly frank interviews. All over the world the voyeuristic public followed the stream of stories about her alleged affairs with men that ran from young actors to famous directors like Louis Malle.

And now she was with Cardin. The two were photographed dining at Maxim's with Cardin's oldest sister, his arm draped protectively over Moreau's shoulder. Cardin even began taking vacations, lounging on the beaches of Saint-Tropez in skimpy briefs with Moreau and their poodle. As they strolled down cobblestoned lanes on the Greek island of Paros a trail of paparazzi snapped away at Cardin's dark good looks under a bleached sun-hat, at Moreau's defiant pout, white jeans and candy-striped summer shirt. Almost always, Cardin's large hands protectively grasped the back of her neck.

'I wasn't really tortured because I didn't allow that,' Moreau said of the constant trail of paparazzi. 'I never used the trick of dark glasses, wigs and things. Suddenly I thought, "I'm the rabbit and they are the hunters. That's because I run. What if I stopped running and faced them." When paparazzi followed us, in Italy or Greece, wherever we went, I stopped them and said, "So, what do you want?" Then it wasn't a game for them. They wanted me to run.'

Moreau's openness to the press perhaps explained the cynicism with which most people greeted their relationship. When the two were at a banquet, opening, show, lunch they hardly talked to each other. Instead they batted eyelashes at the press. 'You know damn well he didn't have an affair with Jeanne Moreau,' said Robert L. Green, a fashion editor who later became a friend of Cardin. 'I was sure that he adored her because she was terribly bright and witty and amusing and was a powerfully important dramatic actress. But you also got the feeling that one of his eyes was watching who was going to photograph them.' That view was the consensus of most outsiders looking in, and particularly of Cardin's homosexual colleagues.

It was, however, an utterly authentic love affair. Perhaps it was unconventional, but they were not conventional people. 'I didn't think of our relationship only in terms of sex. It was two humans, two souls. It was love. He was very important in my life, and I know that I was very important in his,' said Moreau.

And Cardin's closest employees of the time all swear that it was very real. Some noticed that Moreau squirmed with jealousy over the other women working with Cardin. 'They were exactly the same,' said Moltzer, Cardin's press director, explaining their attraction in terms of narcissism. 'When one looked at the other they saw themselves.' A bond was the near-religious commitment they both had towards work. 'Pierre is a man who worked a lot,' said Moreau. 'We shared the same curiosity about things.'

Moreau more or less moved into his apartment on the Quai Anatole France. She kept her house in Versailles, where her son was, but she increasingly spent time at Cardin's. The apartment had a winter garden overlooking the Seine where huge rubber plants, which seemed three storeys high, had wound themselves around the room. The main salon had a black marble-flagged floor. The armchairs were in deep purple, ink-blue and green velvet stripes. Low coffee tables were cluttered with buffalo and mouflon horns set in silver. A rearing head of a cobra seemed ready to spit at visitors, while everywhere the apartment was filled with white, dainty flowers. The view from the apartment was cut from a New Wave film: houseboats and barges lined the Seine, and German shepherds lazily watched their masters hang linen out to dry. In front of the Louvre the leaves of the chestnut trees turned russet and amber, while for a few francs children rode donkeys around the Rodin and Maillol sculptures in the Tuileries.

Together Cardin and Moreau went to flea markets, bought knick-knacks by the cartload. 'We met him every Sunday for lunch,' said Roland de Vassal. 'We would spend the afternoon reading or listening to some music and he would cook dinner for us. André Oliver or Jeanne Moreau was there. I went to Pierre's for dinner several times when Jeanne was there. He looked sincere although I never really understood what was going on.'

It was also a period of relative light-heartedness for Cardin. Compulsive work habits were lightened with moments of humour. An employee recalled that one day, walking down the Faubourg Saint-Honoré, Cardin noticed a policeman with beaten-up old shoes. The Italian padrone in him was touched by this sight. He dashed across the street and told the policeman to come with him. When he emerged from Cardin's boutique half an hour later to pound his beat he did so in some fabulously expensive Cardin shoes. And this was the time, too, when Cardin behaved as if he were the star of some movie playing in his mind, an English movie. Hiroko recalled that he drove a convertible MG and liked to wear a red cap and khakis. His maid, meanwhile, delivered his lunch every day in a wicker basket. He and André retreated into his office to sup as if they were in the British countryside.

Thelma Sweetinburgh, who had left the Wool Association to become Paris editor at *Women's Wear Daily*, was one of the privileged few allowed to interview Moreau at the Quai Anatole France apartment. Her hair freshly washed, she met Sweetinburgh in the salon. Next to her was a hyper-active, blue fox-coloured poodle. Moreau introduced the dog as 'Voyou' – guttersnipe. 'Ever since I started making money I have ruined myself on clothes and shoes,' she confessed in a deep voice. 'Pierre Cardin's collection appeals to me because it's infinite fantasy. I love all the ostrich-feathered crêpe dresses, the little suits with high rolled collars, and the brimmed hats which add mystery to the eyes.'

No wonder, then, that there were sceptics in the crowd. Moreau and Cardin plugged each other's careers, and the notoriety of running with La Moreau of course propelled his fame into a new stratosphere. It was, observed *Women's Wear Daily*'s chairman John Fairchild, the first time in the history of dress-making that a star had openly declared her love for her dressmaker. The lowly nineteenth-century status of the dressmaker had been truly transformed during this century. John Fairchild (nicknamed 'Unfairchild') was quite fascinated by the Cardin–Moreau link. 'Pierre Cardin came out with Jeanne Moreau, hand in hand,' he recalled of one of Cardin's shows at the time. 'The photographers demanded: "Monsieur Cardin, please kiss Mademoiselle Moreau on the mouth . . . please, a kiss." Cardin kissed her neck lightly and squeezed her at the hips. Moreau looked like Alice in Wonderland, her to-the-shoulders long hair, her wide searching eyes, her tiny frame, her mouth sad, drooping; then a warm, melting smile.'

In 1962, a year after they met, Moreau was working on *La Baie des Anges*, in which she played a brassy gambler in a white suit designed for her by Pierre. 'We wanted to have a baby,' said Moreau. She could not become pregnant. After trying for a while, they both went to doctors to be tested. Moreau found out she had lumps. The doctors suspected uterine cancer and immediately operated on her. The operation was successful. Moreau, however, was incapable of having children after that.

Around this time Fairchild visited Cardin at the Quai Anatole France apartment. It was winter and the furnace had just blown up. Cardin wasn't a bit concerned. They snuggled into the striped library armchairs with space heaters and listened to scratchy Japanese music. Cardin stood, his hips swivelling like an African dancer, while he lambasted 'Les Americains'. Fairchild was a captive. 'They steal all my ideas and never buy a model. Why should I struggle to create "the new" when the other couturiers in Paris rehash over and over again?'

Perhaps this was the time when the idolatry of the fashion press, the constant movie star-like treatment by the paparazzi, began taking a toll of Cardin's sense of self. During the same period Cardin took over two buildings opposite the Élysée palace. 'I bought them so, on the front of the building, we can put up a neon sign with my name,' Cardin told his photographer, Roland de Vassal. He was quite serious. 'It will go on and off all the time and even de Gaulle will see it from his desk.'

WHAT'S IN A NAME? 6

'Monsieur Cardin has been assessed as a great talent, especially in the tailoring of suits and his choice of colours, and yet he has still to win many of the top professional buyers. Money, it is said, is still missing from his cash register in Paris,' wrote *The New York Times* in July 1961.

'It was very hard,' said Cardin. 'All of my money had been invested in the company. The bubble dress was very successful, but not enough to have lots of money for the haute couture shows. I had hundreds of people and myself to pay.'

Cardin had overexpanded and he couldn't sleep. It was all too much: the atelier at 118 Faubourg Saint-Honoré, the cost of putting together 120-piece collections; the high-profile life of a great couturier; the wild travelling. It was beyond his financial reach. There was no control and cash-flow was far short of covering the aggressive expansion. When Cardin's photographer asked for some money to get him and his equipment home, Cardin gave him enough for a métro token.

On top of that he was being robbed blind. 'In the early sixties he experienced business reverses that were in no way aided by his personal financial excesses or by the fact that one of his trusted aides absconded with thousands of francs, leaving the books in such a state of disarray that Cardin's lawyers advised against bringing any action,' noted James Brady in his official recollections. 'There was simply no way to prove there ever had been any money there in the first place. We so reported in *WWD* and Cardin, as might be expected, was furious. But then Cardin was generally furious at something or somebody.'

Several similar cases of theft came to light. Cardin often hired rather unsavoury, though handsome young men, mostly for manual labour. 'One day I was carrying out the garbage and there were ten costumes hidden in it,' said Odile Moltzer. 'I told Pierre that one of his boys was stealing from him. I was sure. He was furious with me that I told him. He must have known, but he didn't want to hear about it.' Throughout his career a procession of lower-level employees have taken advantage of Cardin. Some former members of his staff think he asked for trouble by surrounding himself with young men who were tough and streetwise. 'He adores being stolen from,' claimed one. 'Not on a very serious basis. Just a little petty thievery.' Others were more kind. 'He is very naive,' explained former employee Henry Berghauer. 'It is part of his charm.'

Cardin lacked a steady stream of income. His couture customers only saw the charming, elfin man. But his suppliers and employees knew there was trouble. The fabric manufacturers were not getting paid for their deliveries and they threatened to pull the toile from under him. The consequence would have been disaster. Without fabric he could not produce his couture line on time and his star would immediately plunge. But Cardin's publicity temporarily saved him. Daniel Gorin, the Chambre Syndicale's president, intervened behind the scenes. He called the suppliers together. 'Are you crazy?' he yelled. 'Don't you read the papers? He's considered one of the top Paris couturiers. Are you going to destroy one of the brightest hopes of the business?' Sheepishly they backed down.

Cardin, meanwhile, went to the banks. Across the street from 118 Faubourg Saint-Honoré was the London and South America bank. He asked for a loan. They granted it, but were nervous. Weren't designers prone to erratic behaviour? The loan officer called up a friend, Monique Davidson, the former publicity officer at Paquin who was working at Jacques Griffe.

'Do you have confidence he can pay back a loan?'

'Yes,' Davidson replied. She really didn't know Cardin or whether he was to be trusted to pay back a loan. But she did know he was talented.

In 1961 a queue of fashion groupies lined up after the show to congratulate Cardin. When Jean Manusardi, the able administrator working at the Chambre Syndicale shook his hand, Cardin asked him to stay for a talk. As the room cleared the two men sat down amongst the chaos of tipped-over gilt chairs and discarded programmes. 'I want to build up a business,' he said, 'by which only things made in the house, or on behalf of Cardin, are shown at Cardin. I don't want to be like the others. I don't want to borrow shoes from X, hats from another, handbags from a third. I want everything to be Cardin.'

Would Manusardi help him build the empire? 'The trouble is', and here Cardin smiled sweetly, 'you are certainly aware that I am broke. I have no money. So if I ask you to join the company you must be prepared to gamble on the future. We'll make a deal and you can share in the profits.'

Manusardi thought it over. 'It sounded a bit megalomaniacal, but all couturiers are megalomaniacs. They have to be,' he recalled. 'No, it really was very intelligent. The word "Environment", of course, wasn't even used at the time, and perhaps he didn't have the idea in his mind, but everything was included in his speech. He wanted everything to be Cardin.' Even so, Jean Manusardi turned Cardin down. With young children at home Manusardi felt he needed steady income. It was a decision he was going to regret for the rest of his life.

By this time the financial and creative pressures were taking a personal toll on Cardin. Employees began noticing erratic behaviour. The tiniest and most inconsequential matter – something wasn't where it was supposed to be – provoked a violent fury. It was dangerous to walk in front of 118 Faubourg Saint-Honoré. Quite beside himself with rage, he sometimes raced his battered car out of the courtyard without looking, missing unsuspecting pedestrians by inches. He could be intolerable. Like all designers he dressed his principal female employees. On occasions they arrived at work in the morning after a disagreement to find all their outfits up for sale.

There were other signs of stress. The 118 Faubourg Saint-Honoré had a huge basement that seemed to stretch for ever. Sometimes Cardin disappeared for hours until employees discovered him hiding in the dark cellar sweeping dust from one end of the basement to the other. 'That's when you knew it was serious,' recalled an employee who insisted on anonymity. 'We would stay out of his way then.'

Pushing a broom obviously helped Cardin relax. It did not, however, have the same effect on his staff who grew alarmed at his compulsive sweeping. He discovered a small device that mimicked the sound of the heartbeat. He bought a number of the machines and installed them in the basement. Soon, out of the basement floated a very loud and constant 'tick, tock' which resonated up into the floors above. When employees fearfully stuck their heads into the basement they saw him in swirls of dust, sweeping to the soothing sounds of the heartbeat.

But Cardin was a fighter. His assets were his name, his image, his press coverage, all of them intangible. Somehow he had to cash in on those assets. First he set out to boost his business staff, to help lay the foundation for his vision. Although he had failed to hire a seasoned professional like Jean Manusardi,

PIERRE CARDIN

Cardin had his pick of sincere, hard-working young men who were eager to work for couture's new avant-garde star. Henry Berghauer, who had once met Cardin at a Cocteau party, applied for work at the Faubourg Saint-Honoré salon. He waited politely in the house decorated in the style of Napoleon III. The furniture was black and gold, the walls lined with rich dark-green material. Berghauer knew several hopefuls were competing for the job opening at Maison Cardin.

After interviews with a string of other employees Berghauer finally met Cardin, who was preparing a collection. The young man was led into the studio where Cardin was working on a fairy-tale bridal gown. White, crisp cloth had rained down upon the room.

'Do you know anything about couture?'

'Not at all,' admitted Berghauer, although he could not take his eyes off the other-world bridal gown in front of him.

'Are you married?'

'No.'

'Will you marry one day?'

'I suppose.'

'Would you offer this dress to your wife?'

'I'm not sure,' said Berghauer, 'because if you wore such a dress, the wedding would have to be in a church.'

'You won't get married in the church?' asked a perplexed Cardin.

'It would be difficult. I'm not Catholic.'

'What are you?'

'I'm Jewish.'

'Oh,' said Cardin. Pause. 'Jews are sharp people. They know how to make money.' On that reasoning, Cardin hired the 22-year-old, inexperienced Henry as an assistant business manager. When Cardin fired a discredited business manager shortly afterwards, Berghauer was promoted into the managerial position.

•   •   •   •

'Cardin had big problems with his social position. It goes back to his humble background,' said G. Y. Dryansky, a former *Women's Wear Daily* Paris bureau chief. 'When he came to Paris couturiers largely were fournisseurs of the rich. Some of them were well off; some of them even revered as celebrities. But when Cardin came to make his way he needed powerful patronage, he needed more social prestige. Cardin very wisely hired himself people who could lift his social prestige, who could help him climb.'

Paris could be frigidly cold to the outsider. The stifling feeling of old money and education reverberated up the Rue de Grenelle in the curlicue-chiselled stones of the hôtels particuliers. And nowhere was this snobbism more apparent than in the world of couture. No man or woman timidly entering this world could bypass the haughty toe-to-head stare with which pinched women in fox stoles sized up background, education, content. They lingered most emphatically on the shoes, somehow correctly intuiting that the true value of people lay in their soles. And yet this was the world that the dirty-nailed labourer, Cardin, was trying to penetrate. Ultimately, he was earthy enough not to care truly about being accepted by snobs, but business-wise he knew he needed them. Particularly during those early years. To get his revenge he somehow had to enter their fold.

Cardin first latched on to Madame Juliette Achard, a Parisian socialite of the first order married to Marcel Achard, the bespectacled, rotund writer whose intellectual power delighted fashionable Paris. Juliette herself was coolly elegant, with short curly red hair, pearls and plain gold bangles worn with simple little black dresses. Only her eyes were thickly made up. Heavy black mascara and inky eyeliner leadened the lids over her eyes, which appeared half closed like a lizard's.

'Pierre and Juliette became very friendly,' recalled André Ostier, a close friend of Achard. 'She kept on saying, "Pierre Cardin c'est merveilleux, Pierre Cardin c'est merveilleux." ' Said another friend: 'She was his slave.'

Cardin returned her patronage. 'Cardin was probably giving her special prices,' said Ostier. 'He was always saying, "Ooh, yes, you must have this suit, this evening gown. If you go to this party you must have something beautiful." '
It worked. In 1958, as the decade of the costume ball drew to an end, Cardin was invited to the spectacular Hôtel de Coulanges ball. He went as a Venetian Doge, dressed in a tight-fitting, dark velvet costume. In eight short years he had gone from stitching the ball's costumes to attending the ball.

Like a butterfly collector Cardin pinned people to his cork board. His major social coup of the time came in 1961, soon after *The New York Times* published his financial difficulties. *Marie Claire*, a French magazine, decided to commission an article on people in the Arts who were expected to become very big over the next ten years. Cardin was one of the artists selected.

A freelance journalist was cobbling the article together. Today she is happily remarried as Odile Moltzer. Back then, however, she was Princess de Croy. She was beautiful, 30 years old, and au courant with everybody. After *Marie Claire*'s group photograph of the ten artists, Cardin broke away from the crowd and timidly approached her.

'I want you to be the directrice of my house,' Cardin blurted out awkwardly.

Moltzer looked up, her eyes widened. 'I thought he was completely mad,' she recalled. 'He didn't know me.'

'Come on Thursday at 3,' he said abruptly and left.

That Thursday she found herself at 118 Faubourg Saint-Honoré. She entered the green salons and a man came out. 'Pierre Cardin will receive you now.'

Moltzer followed him into the office. As soon as she was in the panelled room she recognized the man who had just ushered her in to see Cardin. It was Pierre Cardin himself. To her utter amazement she realized that he talked about himself in the third person. 'He was talking like royalty,' she said. ' "Pierre Cardin intended to do that and that." '

Moltzer grew accustomed to Cardin's peculiar way of talking. And then she learned why he was interested in her. 'I want you to turn my house into a snob establishment,' he said. At the time Cardin's directrice was the Baroness Geneviève Davillier, a charming black-frocked woman of 75. She had at one time owned a mansion off the Champs-Elysées complete with a large garden. The baroness brought in a very smart set, but they had reached their prime around the First World War. It was a rather wrinkled clientele. To reverse his fortunes Cardin knew he had to attract a younger crowd that would actually buy his avant-garde cuts. He needed patronage, prestige.

'When he saw Odile he understood through her he could have a younger and more fashionable clientele,' said Kim Moltzer, her future husband. 'This is where he is very clever. He feels how people can be useful to him, without appearing cynical and calculating. It's based on intuition. He is not a man of reflection or thought, but his intuition is usually right.' Odile Moltzer explained it more succinctly: 'I was Princess de Croy. It was surely the reason he asked me. Let's not have any illusions. It was like cream for him.'

But the job would be unique and fun, so she took it. She started working at Maison Cardin in 1962 but received another jolt on her first day on the job. As soon as she arrived she found out not only that the baroness was still there as directrice with a complete staff, but that Cardin had not even told the elderly woman that a new directrice had been hired. It was awkward. Horrified, and really a little timid of having to direct a large staff, Moltzer told the baroness to stay. She herself would concentrate on public relations. (Within a year, as it happened, the baroness was dead.)

The upgrading was swift. Moltzer was well known by le beau monde and, while Cardin's first benefactress, Juliette Achard, had made some valuable introductions for him, it was Moltzer's connections that really plugged him into Paris's mighty. Her first major publicity event was a very elegant party which included many of his future clients: Rothschild, Agnelli, Onassis, and Niarchos.

It terrified her. She had to introduce Cardin to some 100 guests. Afraid she would make a blunder she even wrote some of the names on her hand. But Cardin, the abrupt and awkward peasant, never appeared. In his stead was the actor: humble and urbane. 'He was very shy and nice because he didn't know anyone,' said Moltzer. 'He was simply fantastic.'

•   •   •   •

The economics of couture had changed since Dior opened in 1947. Escalating labour and material costs were making it exceedingly difficult to earn returns. As costs climbed the market shrank. By the early 1960s only some 3,000 ultra-wealthy women worldwide could afford the trips to Paris, and the number of women paying their bills on a timely basis was a fraction of that. Poor cash-flow was instant death in a seasonal business where hundreds of thousands of francs were tied up in bloated inventories of fabric. Yet most clients tended to be very cavalier about paying bills. Some compulsive fashion addicts were understandably afraid to show their husbands the incredible sums owed. Others, however, simply could not have cared less that for every silver-threaded evening gown they wore, for every sleeve embroidered with ruby-red beads, and every chinchilla collar on satin dinner coats, couturiers were thousands of francs out of pocket. And social etiquette forbade couturiers from shaking down delinquent clients. But they were equally to blame for the sad state of affairs. They were the first to bat eyelids at the press and majestically claim that the mundane realities of finance had no part in their creations. They, after all, were creating fantasies in cloth. They were providing life's esprit. Maybe, but esprit was not paying the Faubourg Saint-Honoré overheads.

Yet all these difficulties could have been coped with had there not been a more serious, more structural problem just below the surface. Parisian designers were ignoring a twentieth-century truism: for all practical purposes couturiers had become obsolete, undone by 100 years of developments in clothing manufacturing.

The perfection of the sewing-machine by the Massachusetts farmer Elias Howe in 1846, and the exploitation of the invention by Isaac Merrit Singer, ushered in the era of mass-produced clothes. The demand for uniforms during the American Civil War so improved the method of production for ready-made garments that by the 1890s it was estimated that 90 per cent of the men and boys in the USA were wearing them. For the first time it became possible for men of all social classes to wear clothes of identical design and cut from the same factory. Even language had to catch up to the Clothing Revolution. The Americanism 'hand-me-down' and the Briticism 'reach-me-down' referring to the shoddy clothes that were handed down from a rack – were replaced by the more genteel 'ready-to-wear' in the early twentieth century.

From then on the industry never rested, and by the 1960s new flexible manufacturing techniques and electronic machinery had greatly reduced the visual differences between haute-couture gowns and ready-to-wear garments. The bridge between the two worlds of couture and ready-to-wear was the copyist, the professional buyer who purchased Parisian gowns and remade them cheaply as ready-to-wear. These were the real villains eroding the Parisian couturier's business. In the early 1960s the American copyists were going full throttle, their knock-off techniques so perfected that they were inflicting serious economic damage.

To enter the couturier's salon, the copyist was required to pay a non-returnable deposit ranging from $280 to $1,400. The deposit was credited against the purchase of a model that cost anywhere between $700 and $2,800. Once bought, the model was then picked apart and copied. Alternatively, at a more favourable price the copyist could buy a toile made of cotton, which was unlined but had the dress's details sketched in. The least expensive means of learning the technical mysteries of a haute-couture gown was to buy a paper pattern.

The designers were in a bind. As fewer and fewer traditional couture clients checked themselves and their blue-haired poodles into the Ritz hotel during collection week, they were increasingly forced to rely upon these professional buyers for orders. Couturiers competed among themselves for the attention of the buyers – the wealthiest of whom were invariably from American stores like Bonwit Teller and Lord & Taylor – and aggressively sent out sales staff to pamper these clients like film stars. Cigar-sucking New Yorkers from the garment district were seduced with chauffeur-driven cars, boxes at the opera, suites filled with peach-coloured orchids and lizard clasp-purses for their wives. The fawning was necessary, for the department store was king. In the late 1950s and early 1960s, some manufacturers' hard goods became brand names, such as 'Cadillac' by General Motors. Most apparel, however, was graced simply with the manufacturer's label. In the US, for example, Arrow or Hathaway or Van Heusen were shirtmakers. With a sea of manufacturers' labels an individual brand left only a snowflake impression.

It was the department store label, however, that carried the fashion clout among the masses. 'Department stores virtually in themselves guaranteed the fashion, styles, and colours which they carried. They were fashion's dictators,' explained Kurt Barnard, publisher of the Retail Marketing Report. 'If Lord & Taylor or Macy's edited, selected and consequently carried it, it was something

I, the customer, could wear. The name of the store guaranteed the quality and fashion timeliness.'

So the large department store purchases offered short-term financial relief to the couturier, but they also carried within them the seeds of destruction. In April 1962, some 3,000 women crowded around Macy's whitewashed catwalk. These were sophisticated New York clients under the Waterford crystal chandelier; women who tended to wear gold Omega watches and coral-pink Elizabeth Arden lipstick. When the show started two mannequins strutted towards the audience wearing identical outfits – Givenchy black-and-white, fitted check coats worn with white marshmallow hats, cotton gloves and sleek umbrellas. To the untrained eye the two coats appeared identical. And yet the original Givenchy coat cost $1,000, the knock-off only $70. A $1,200 Lanvin-Castillo white party dress – 240 petal-shaped panels fanned into a skirt and lashed with a black bow – cost only one-eighth of the original as a Macy's copy. The show was a knockout. The women stampeded over to the racks, elbows and umbrellas flying.

High fashion was accessible to all budgets. Even Saks, with pricier imported copies, managed to cut the price of a Nina Ricci full-skirted suit in hot-pink wool with brass-buckled belt from $800 to $325. But no case better illustrated the power of copying than Yves Saint Laurent's pea jacket.

After his departure from Christian Dior, Saint Laurent teamed up with Pierre Bergé, a savvy bulldog of a businessman, and opened his own couture house at 30 bis Rue Spontini in January 1962. The spacy, awkward 26-year-old immediately began producing fun, irreverent looks that undermined a history of formal suits and frocks. One of his first lines included a sailor look. Saint Laurent elevated the lowly pea coat by using fine wool and carved silver buttons. It cost his clients a princely $800.

The sailor look was seized upon. Immediately at Ohrbach's cash-and-carry counter the pea jacket in melton cloth and YSL's identical silver buttons cost only $56. The sportswear firm, Reid & Reid, came out with a $12 copy in sailcloth. And the savviest shoppers could feel perfectly chic by simply picking up an original pea jacket of navy wool and anchor-studded buttons for just $10 at any Army & Navy surplus store. With quality so improved, prices so competitive, who was going to buy the prohibitively expensive couture clothes in Paris?

That was the true malaise underlying Cardin's financial problems, and he knew it. The 1961 *New York Times* article that announced he was experiencing financial difficulties also printed his rebuttal. 'But I am copied,' he said. 'My coats are copied on your Seventh Ave. and they sell.' Somehow he had to cash in on the demand for his clothes which existed, not so much in the élite circles of Paris but amongst the comfortable middle classes of the world.

Cardin's answer lay in the details of a little-known business deal that had taken place at 30 Avenue Montaigne just a decade earlier. After Christian Dior's first show in February 1947, an executive of an American stocking manufacturer, Prestige, asked for an appointment with Dior and Rouët. He offered to provide Dior with some $10,000 worth of stockings, a small fortune in those days, in exchange for a credit on the Dior programme and the right to advertise the connection in *Vogue*, *Harper's Bazaar* and *Town & Country*. Dior inspected the stockings – they were sheer nylon in interesting patterns and spicy colours – and agreed.

At Dior's next three collections the mannequins wore Prestige stockings. But after the July 1948 collection Dior spoke to Jacques Rouët. 'I don't see why we should have our mannequins wear American-made stockings,' groused Dior. 'Why don't we make Christian Dior stockings that someone would manufacture for us; that we could sell in our boutique and possibly in some quality stores? Why don't you think about it?'

Rouët did. It made sense, he figured, if the manufacturer maintained the exclusive Dior image by selling in only the best stores. Rouët went to work and found a partner in the American stocking manufacturer Kayser Roth. In late 1948 Christian Dior signed the first licensing deal in fashion history. Chanel had previously licensed her name for the first modern flacon of perfume, Chanel No. 5, but Dior was inaugurating the first fashion licence. It was simple, really. The company manufactured and distributed the Dior stockings, but on all sales the Dior house was paid a royalty. In 1949 Kayser Roth distributed the stockings to Saks Fifth Avenue, Bergdorf Goodman's and Bonwit Tellers. Women, now well aware of the Paris couturier after the resulting media hype, bought the stockings by the dozen.

At the same time another American visited Rouët. Benjamin Theise made silk ties in the US. 'Jacques, why don't you make Dior ties in the States?' Theise asked Rouët. 'Look, women buy 80 per cent of men's ties. Dior means so much to women. When they see your ties in the men's stores, they'll buy them immediately.' In the late 1940s there was no such thing as a designer tie, and Bronzini and Countess Mara were the two names that dominated the US tie market. So this time Rouët spoke to Dior. 'Why not?' Dior replied, 'but only do it in the US because they have the only retail stores that are good enough.' Theise introduced Rouët to the right manufacturer and the second Dior licence was signed.

'We were criticized by some peers,' recalled Rouët. 'At the time they could not understand how a couturier that made evening dresses – sumptuous, very expensive dresses designed for queens and international stars – could print his name on stockings or ties. It was beyond their understanding.'

Some ten years later Cardin returned to this novel if controversial business arrangement for quick money. The attractions were considerable. With a stroke of the pen he immediately received a cash infusion. It was doubly attractive since none of his own money was at risk; the manufacturer paid for the expense of producing, marketing and distributing. Yet if the product sold well, Cardin was guaranteed royalties above and beyond his initial cash packet. On a risk-reward basis it was an exceptional deal. However, the true benefit was disguised: by licensing his name Cardin could earn a return whereas before he was cut out by the copyists. He was moving down-market. 'Everybody was copying my clothes, so why shouldn't I do the ready-to-wear myself?'

In 1959 Cardin signed a licensing deal with a French manufacturer of women's ready-to-wear, Vaskene SA. Licensing deals were utterly simple and basically covered three essential points: product and market, minimum deposit, royalty rate. Cardin supplied Vaskene with some designs and technical assistance; the company modified the designs to suit mass production, substituting cheaper materials, until the factory could produce affordable watered-down versions of a Cardin couture coat or dress. But the process differed from the traditional copying in a very important way. Attached to the dress was the all-important label, 'Pierre Cardin – Paris'. It was the first time in fashion history that a couturier had put his name on lowly, off-the-rack clothes.

Cardin had launched the designer label era. He was 37.

The managing director of the Printemps department store, Robert Schoettl, had just been touring American stores like Bloomingdales and Macy's. He came back full of ideas. 'We needed to upgrade,' he said. In 1960 the ground floor of Printemps was littered with rows of free-standing boxes out of which jumbles of household wares were peddled: bolts of cloth, thread and needles. Printemps was selling as it had done for nearly 100 years. Fabrics, needle and thread were low-margin business and not nearly racy enough to pull people off the street. Borrowing on ideas he had picked up in the US, Schoettl decided Printemps should sell products with added value – why sell the raw material for making dresses, as department stores had done since the nineteenth century, when you could earn more by just selling the dresses?

The presentation of wares at Printemps also left much to be desired. Again he turned to the American department stores. 'The idea was to re-create street boutiques on half a floor,' explained Jacques Gourbaud, head of the women's wear division at Printemps. 'The space between the boutiques mimicked the streets of Paris.' Gourbaud signed a deal with Daniel Pérou to open a Pierre Cardin boutique at Printemps. (Cardin's version of how the deal was put together involved a complicated series of introductions through a friend of his working at the department store.) By early 1962 the Paris newspaper *Le Monde* reported that Printemps' Pierre Cardin women's line was reinvigorating the department store. Readers learned that a month after the spring collections shoppers at Printemps could buy a flouncy Pierre Cardin orange blouse for FF 59 and a complete suit of a red or beige fitted wool coat and bell skirt for FF 75.

The publicity never translated into sales. The line was discontinued after only a few seasons. It had to be revamped. 'The prices were fairly high,' recalled Gourbaud. 'It was rather disappointing.' Henry Berghauer had another explanation: 'It was before its time.'

But the publicity was considerable. Cardin once again had created a first. No élite Parisian designer had ever put his name on ready-to-wear. Even more shocking was for him then to peddle the wares in a large department store. 'There was a great outcry,' said Cardin. 'Rouët, Bergé, Gorin [Chambre Syndicale president] told me it wasn't possible. How could they accuse me of vulgarizing fashion? I said: "My decision is made. Your concept of fashion is not mine. I know fashion, since I'm a professional." I told Bergé, "I'm more professional than you . . ." Incidentally, he didn't like that.'

'Pierre Cardin created such a shock among designers who would follow him ten years later that his reputation as a revolutionary was made,' observed G.Y. Dryansky in *Vogue* many years later.

The Printemps experience did not deter Pierre Cardin and he began signing department store boutique deals with as many stores as possible. In Japan's Takashimaya department store, 'salaryma' – the Japanese corporate employees – were greeted by bowing saleswomen and the latest Pierre Cardin look from Paris. Cardin also signed up the German giant Hertie, and Britain's Selfridges. One such deal was with La Rinascente in Italy. To promote the agreement Cardin wanted to give a fashion show in Rome. The French embassy was in a beautiful palace and Moltzer suggested taking it over for the occasion. It was not easy. Embassy officials were concerned it would appear as if an impartial government was endorsing one couturier at the expense of others – a terrible precedent. And this was sordid private enterprise, after all, not suitable for the hallowed halls of diplomacy. But Moltzer's considerable charm melted the objections and she soon received the approval. It was a major coup. 'Tout le monde' was coming.

The day before the show Moltzer received a phone call. It was Pierre Cardin. 'I won't come.'

She froze. 'If you don't come I'll kill you.'

They argued back and forth. Finally Cardin boarded a plane. He arrived in Rome unshaven, unwashed and in a rage.

'You look awful. You can't stay like that,' Moltzer snapped. 'Go and take a bath. Do that for me.'

When the party started he was just charming.

•   •   •   •

Fresh from signing his women's ready-to-wear deal Cardin went to London to have a suit made. 'It had always been my assumption that English men were the best dressed in the world,' he told an interviewer. 'When the tailor brought it over to Paris for the fitting it was the most awful suit I ever saw. The seam between the legs drooped to the knees, the waist came up to the chest, and the jacket was narrow. The suit simply did not do. I am an athletic man, with broad shoulders and narrow hips – built like the ancient Egyptians – and here was a suit contrary to my physique. I said to myself, "This is impossible. I am going to design men's clothing that I would wear myself." '

Cardin had dabbled in men's clothes ever since he opened his 'Adam' boutique in the 1950s. Now he tackled it head on and turned to his new business tool, the licensing agreement, for a new fashion breakthrough. His first menswear licensee was a small factory in Lyon, but he quickly grew dissatisfied with the results and instead sought out one of the largest and most respected menswear manufacturers in France. Daniel Pérou first approached S.A.M. Bril & Co. in 1960. He asked for a 10 per cent royalty and one million new French francs up-front, in return for the rights to manufacture Pierre Cardin's menswear worldwide. The company's owner, Georges Bril, and its managing director, Jean Manigot, counterproposed. They finally settled on an 8 per cent royalty limited to Northern Africa and Europe only. 'Pierre had a head this big. A thorough understanding of our problems. And ideas, ideas like lightning flashes in a storm,' recalled Manigot.

In those early days, Cardin was obsessed by quality: only expensive fabrics, cloth mounted not glued, sleeves attached by hand. He had the right to approve every line, and he did. He had control over the entire catalogue. Bril presented its first ready-to-wear Pierre Cardin collection on 7 July 1961. 'It was an immediate success,' he said. 'The professional male model didn't exist then. We hired university students.'

A year earlier Cardin had presented the first men's haute-couture show in history. On 26 February 1960, the international press crammed into the Hôtel de Crillon salons at 5 p.m. Cardin was presenting a bold new silhouette, modelled by men, and the excitement was palpable. Realizing that his suits would primarily appeal to a younger, irreverent man, Cardin had in preparation written to the dean of the Sorbonne inviting 200 students to his fashion show.

PIERRE CARDIN

The students were at the Crillon at the appointed time, strategically placed among the sceptical fashion press.

The lights dimmed, the music began. The first outfit came out. The second. The third. The only reaction was a stony silence. Cardin became visibly pale. 'What have I done?' he mumbled to himself.

The fourth model came out. The young men were modelling lapel-less and collarless corduroy suits – buttoned all the way up – over starched white shirts and narrow ties. Some had sun glasses on, their hair neatly slicked back with gel. Finally, the students came alive with rude hoots and hysterical cheers. 'Bravo! C'est formidable!' Cardin started shaking.

Cardin had come up with a New Look for men. His men's collection, reported *Le Figaro*, was 'certainly going to produce a great deal of controversy'. Besides 'clergyman' haircuts, the show was packed with a 'quantity of other new details'.

The silhouette of men's clothes changed rarely, but when it did the designer who first caught it could ride on its crest for a decade. In the 1950s good men's clothes meant Savile Row. Period. In teak-panelled fitting rooms English tailors dressed gentlemen in hushed tweeds and wools and flannels in a muted atmosphere of reverence. Men's ready-to-wear was even less imaginative. Boxy suits were limited to a few shades of grey and dark blue. An army of identically-dressed men read the financial papers on the 7.37 into the city. Only the cities differed.

'At the time, when a woman walked down the street with her husband she looked like she had just inherited a million dollars. The husband, on the other hand, looked like the lawyer who read the will,' said Nicholas DeMarco, an executive at Pierre Cardin. But a spicy counter-movement was bubbling below these rigid 1950s fashions. This was not being imposed by Paris's Faubourg Saint-Honoré, but percolating up from the streets of London.

It began shortly after the war when a small group of wealthy men from Belgravia and Mayfair revolted against the patriotic shabbiness of the days of rationing. Pining after the fast-vanishing privileges of their class, they labelled themselves the Neo-Edwardians and dressed richly in narrow trousers with raised seams, step-collared or brocaded waistcoats, and skirted jackets with a single or double vent in the back. Young men fastidiously positioned the pearl pin in their cravat and then grasped the mustard, calfskin gloves in one hand while hooking the bamboo-handle umbrella over the other forearm. The most colourful of such dandies were often dressed by Bunny Rogers, who went in for a 'saucy-cut toggery' of gold and crimson vests, cravats of pink and purple, and a plethora of accessories ranging from monocles to gold watch-chains. The Edwardian cult was restricted to a small group, but they were influential.

Britain's economy picked up in the mid-1950s. Clothes rationing ended at last. Brand-new council flats rose majestically in the bombed-out neighbourhoods surrounding London's railway stations; seagulls screamed as Dockland crane operators worked overtime unloading crates of modern tooling machinery from Brooklyn. In the streets of the East End, in the 'caffs' smoky with prattling bacon and the queues for jellied eels, semi-skilled boys enjoying full employment began strutting their own version of the Edwardian look. These were the 'neo-Neo-Edwardian' or Teddy Boys of the East End. They sank their pay-packets into padded-shouldered jackets that fell to the knee; skin-tight drainpipe jeans were meant to show off the bulge of their crotch; white shirts were jazzed up with the black, slim-jim ties popularized in Westerns. On the Teddy Boy's feet were two-inch-thick crêpe-soled brothel-creepers. Influenced by Elvis the Pelvis, this was a grittier, more erotic version of the Belgravian Edwardian dandy, brought alive by a duck's-arse haircut, brass rings and flick-knife.

By 1956 the drainpipe trousers and brothel-creepers were out for the truly fashionable Ted. In their stead came trousers with turn-ups 18 inches round, the polished toe-caps of the aggressively pointed winkle-pickers, and a short crew-cut borrowed from Marlon Brando but spiced up with a stiff quiff quivering from the forehead. America, James Dean, greasers and motorbikes influenced their adaptation of the Edwardian Look. So did the new music, Rock and Roll. The 1954 Bill Haley and the Comets hit, 'Rock around the Clock', created screams of approval at the Teddy Boy dance centre of north London's Tottenham Royal. A Teddy Boy in an outfit costing as much as £100 would coolly comb his greased hair in front of the girl of his choice while staring at her with his eyelids drooped half shut. With a flick of his head he invited her on to the dance floor. The Teddy girl – in flatties, Hound-dog Orange lipstick and pony-tail – first put a price on everything he was wearing before agreeing to dance. Britain's working classes wore their outfits as badges of arrival.

In 1957, meanwhile, John Stephen opened a tiny boutique in London's Carnaby Street and started a 'crusade to brighten men's clothes'. It was the dawning of mod clothes. Bearded beatniks, marching in sandals at Ban-the-Bomb rallies, hid their academic bodies under black sweaters, flannel shirts and duffle-coats. But Stephen's anti-establishment fashions went in another direction. As the 1960s rolled in, he was earning a reputation for his Herculean struggles against men's inhibitions. He jazzed up the traditional shirt, suit and tie with pink and red pants, frilly shirts and boldly-striped jackets. Once he noticed how men often pushed their waistbands down. So he invented the hipster, a tight-fitting trouser that sat low on the hip. Rockers like Chuck Berry blared over the shop speakers, while the new kaleidoscopic lighting practically induced epileptic fits. Britain, the frumpy, forgotten aunt at the fashion table, was shaking awake.

Cardin was thrilled by anything youthful. 'In life you must always start with the young, because they can wear anything. Fashion must be tomorrow, not yesterday, so I aim my designs at youth,' he said. He immediately set about bridging the needs of businessmen with the vibrant, youthful fashions of Teddy Boys and Carnaby Street. Out went the grey, skinny-lapelled sack suit. In came Cardin's version of the 'Edwardian' silhouette: long jackets, deeply-slashed vents, narrow trousers, squared-off waistcoats. (He preferred to call it the 'cigarette silhouette'. As the 1960s progressed and the ties became louder and wider, he was said to have spearheaded the 'Peacock Revolution'.)

Bril's salesmen were sent to all corners of France. Pierre Cardin suits were distributed through the 'chemiserie', the local haberdashery usually sandwiched between a Société Générale bank branch and the local, tight-lipped electrician. Military-stiff dummies wore wide ties and tight-fitting, green tweed jackets with peacock-fanned lapels. Socks were folded seductively in the window like Swiss rolls; wide-collared and tautly folded synthetic shirts were piled high in a crisp pile of abundance. The maître peered invitingly over his bifocals at the customer entering the shop, ready to jump with his yellow tape-measure and pin-cushion. Pierre Cardin's ready-to-wear suits retailed for between $100 and $150. A long-line Edwardian overcoat cost up to $170.

A men's boutique opened at Printemps. 'The opening of the Pierre Cardin boutique was fabulous,' said Michel Bouret, now manager of the purchasing department at Printemps. 'For us, it meant a visit by all the top designers and distribution people. They all came because it was so unusual that someone like Pierre Cardin would agree to sell in a department store.' The Cardin boutique radically shook up how clothes were presented in France. 'At the time stores were dull, each department selling one item and nothing but that one item. If it was suits, there was nothing else,' said Bouret. But at Cardin's boutique, shirts, and later ties and accessories, were nattily draped against the suits. It was the launch of the 'Total Look' boutique and top designers came from all over to see this marketing innovation.

Cardin also custom-made suits. After he saw the men's line was going to be a success he moved his tiny 'Adam' boutique out of the 118 Faubourg Saint-Honoré building and over to a new shop across the street. At the corner of Place Beauvau, adjacent to the Palais de l'Élysée where de Gaulle reigned supreme, Cardin's shop-windows swelled with the high armpits of the Peacock Revolution.

In front of the Élysée palace, the tricolour snapped in the wind on white flagpoles. Guardsmen in navy-blue uniforms and white gloves twirled wooden carbines. From their left shoulders red cords drooped; red-tufted nineteenth-century kepis perched over chiselled jaws and razor-shaved heads. Caped gendarmes with batons and white patent-leather pistol holsters strolled backwards and forwards, tension creasing their brow. They were all on maximum alert against fanatic Algerian colons attempting to assassinate President de Gaulle. A dozen motorcycle policemen sat on fat BMWs, ready to roll out the escort.

A dozen yards away, however, Cardin's 'sissy' revolt raged. Men stared into the full-length windows that were stuffed with waistcoated dummies. The ground floor of the building was wrapped in black Italian marble. Inside the boutique the handsome Robert Bruno, an employee, stood crisply to attention in a brown tweed three-piece Pierre Cardin suit. It cost $360. Men entered; passed to and fro. Despite the price tag the store was humming with 'Cardinists', loyal customers clothed entirely in his designs. Scarlet carnations were worn on extremely long and wide lapels instead of a handkerchief. Scaled-down top hats with curly brims cost $40 and were worn over green, wide-collared shirts. But the key was the fit. 'If you can drive a car with the jacket buttoned, it is too loose,' salesmen told the Cardinists. Besides fashionable young men, Cardin boasted clients ranging from Rex Harrison to the Beatles.

The old boys in Savile Row were not pleased by Cardin's breakthrough. They reached for their pin-cushions. At the Master Tailor's Benevolent Association annual dinner in London, Teddy Watson, tailor to the Duke of Edinburgh, attacked 'the weird and gimmicky garments which have emerged from these people trained and raised in women's dressmaking, applying their often absurd ideas to men's tailoring'.

Additional problems were closer to home. Across the street from 118 Faubourg Saint-Honoré was an élite men's tailor. Gilbert Feruch was a very respected technician of men's clothes, a sort of tailor's tailor, dressing clients who included Yul Brynner, Nelson Rockefeller, Aly Khan, Cary Grant and the Shah of Iran. Today Gilbert Feruch alleges Pierre Cardin stole the designs of the Peacock Look from him. According to Feruch, in the early 1960s he designed a new type of suit. It had big vents, high armpits and was very fitted. In short, the Parisian interpretation of the Edwardian Look. One day Cardin came to buy himself a suit and he was enamoured of the Feruch creations. 'We must make your suit,' Cardin told him. 'Everybody must know about it. Even doormen.' Feruch laughed, not really taking him seriously.

In 1963 Pierre Cardin and André Oliver entered the tailor's atelier and ordered about fifteen suits, claimed Feruch. Several months later he was walking down the Faubourg Saint-Honoré when he saw several models returning from a Cardin show. They were wearing exact copies of his suit. It was made by Bril and 'designed' by Cardin. Feruch went crazy. André Oliver saw him, said Feruch, and quickly ushered him to Cardin's office. He stomped up the stairs and confronted a very embarrassed Cardin. Cardin proposed they work together. How? Feruch could design for the Pierre Cardin label, said Pierre. Any clothes he designed had to have his name on them as well, retorted Feruch. No, Cardin would not allow that. Feruch left in a rage.

It did not end there. According to Feruch, Cardin felt guilty and suddenly grew concerned that Feruch would go public with the story. Cardin came to his atelier 'with hat in hand', he said, and 'begged' him not to sue. 'He said that he was just starting out in the business and that a lawsuit would ruin him,' said Feruch, who had no intention of suing but warned Cardin that he himself would make his own ready-to-wear men's line.

The truth? 'I vaguely recall Cardin had a dispute with Feruch,' said Bril, 'but it must have been inconsequential.' (Although an argument seems to have taken place, the story needs to be seen in context. Stealing ideas in toto would be completely out of character for Cardin. Like all couturiers he occasionally borrowed design ideas, but they were always transformed by his ego and imagination into his own very distinctive currency. Furthermore, the fashion industry has always been rife with claims and counterclaims as to who started what and when. Designers known for establishing a look have often not been the first to create it, Dior's New Look being the most famous case in point. The general rule is that the designer with the muscle and timing to make the look a trend earns the credit. In that case, Pierre Cardin should rightfully be credited with the 'Peacock Revolution'.)

By 1965, just four years after signing the initial agreement, Bril had sublicensed Cardin's men's line in Britain, Germany, Spain, Greece, Portugal and Holland. He was distributing in Luxembourg and Belgium. In France alone some 250 retail outfits were pushing Pierre Cardin suits, and the full line included men's ties, shirts, dressing-gowns, sweaters, shoes, hats, socks, overcoats, and bathing suits. 'Cardin is the couturier who broke through the French indifference four years ago with ideas that have become an $8 million business in men's clothes,' reported The New York Times.

•   •   •   •

'Cardin, who in those days could never say no, would smilingly sell [model] number 227 to Macy's exclusively and then turn around and sell it to Lord & Taylor, also exclusively,' recalled James Brady. Cardin's antipathy towards the American copyists flared up in 1963. That year some hundred American buyers were jostling for their seats at the Cardin show. Cardin threw them out. 'He just told them to get out,' said Odile Moltzer. 'It was one of his hysterical rages. They were shocked.'

The collections of 1963 sent the press into rhapsodies. 'The dress collection was a gentle spring rain that released fashion thunder,' wrote Jeanne Molli about the January show. As always, Cardin's genius did not lie in establishing a cohesive look but was concealed in minute details. He made pie-crust ruffles for collars; leather was pleated into a horse's feedbag and used as a handbag; a solid cummerbund dramatically grounded a floating draped chiffon dress with cape back. That summer he received the same rave reviews: candy-coloured scarves fluttered with knee-high kid boots; turtle necks were soft or transformed by stiff cadet collars; a dress in tangerine orange showed through the cut-out holes of a perforated grey tunic.

But without the big American buyers the collections did not sell. Patience was required to build his licensing markets; in the meantime, Cardin had to struggle through the precarious finances. While she was in Paris Hiroko recalled that sometimes employees were asked not to cash their pay checks before a certain date. 'We didn't have a bean,' said Henry Berghauer. 'It was tough.'

America, of course, was home to the widest and most lucrative market, and Cardin knew he had somehow to reverse his damaged reputation among US buyers. He asked Moltzer for some ideas. Fresh from the success at the embassy in Rome, she suggested they try the same kind of fête at the French embassy in Washington. Cardin agreed.

In Washington the 45-year-old John F. Kennedy had been president for two years. His tenure was heavy with the Bay of Pigs, Nikita Khrushchev, Vietnam, the Berlin Wall. He galvanized the nation's energy and imagination with his space programme. But there was a much lighter side, too. It was the Kennedy style, the immense good looks and charm of the first family. There was the president – matinée handsome, drank milk and Scotch, stole his dad's socks when he could. He devoured James Bond novels and obscure nineteenth-century biographies. Around him was a platoon of attractive secretaries. He had a natural flare for turning a phrase, for speech-writing; and he sat on an estimated $10 million share of the Kennedy fortune. He was always unpredictable: the night after he was inaugurated he went to the all-stag Alfalfa

PIERRE CARDIN

Club Dinner. Jackie and her young children, Caroline and John, captured the nation. As soon as she was installed, Jacqueline began redecorating the White House, establishing it as both an informal family home and a vibrant repository of the nation's heritage and culture. Children romped at official parties; fires crackled in fireplaces previously boarded up; bowls of blossoms decorated niches and table-tops. Martini hour gripped the nation as the Kennedys instituted the first open, honest-to-goodness White House bar (previous presidential slurping was conducted on the sly). Their terrier, Charlie, sniffed ambassadors' trouser-legs.

As soon as the Kennedys arrived at the White House, Washington's society columnists began to gasp. After the president appointed his cabinet he invited them over for a Sunday night reception. Betty Beale, columnist at the capital's evening paper, the *Star*, listed eight social precedents shattered during that evening. President Kennedy ruled with his wit. 'The reason for this reception', he told his guests, 'is the desire to see some of the names I have been reading about in the newspapers.'

Jackie ruled American fashion. Within 24 hours of becoming first lady she unwittingly created a sensation. The press corps spotted her walking through the White House halls in riding breeches. And then her style came in a rush: the white pill-box hat, Chanel-like beads, peach three-quarter-length sleeve jacket, and the trademark long gloves. Oleg Cassini became her official designer, and her high-necked silk ottoman evening gown, and fawn-coloured, semi-fitted wool coat with removable circular collar of Russian sable, were widely copied. In suburban homes in New Jersey girls dressed Jackie Kennedy cut-out dolls in shocking pink and red suits.

Such style appealed to the French, particularly to Nicole Alphand, wife of France's ambassador to Washington, Hervé Alphand. The intimacy between the Kennedys and the Alphands started almost immediately. At the Kennedys' first White House reception, daughter Caroline enthralled the press corps in her fancy party dress and requests to the Marine Band for a rendition of 'Old MacDonald had a Farm'. Outside on the White House lawn gardeners had sculpted a snowman with button eyes and carrot nose. Jackie had just repainted Caroline's room in pale-pink with white woodwork. In the White House receiving rooms, African and Scandinavian ambassadors milled, awaiting their chance to greet the US president and cable the details of their 'conference' back to respective capitals. The president approached Nicole Alphand. 'Comment allez-vous?' he asked, and then laughed at his own accent. 'My wife speaks good French. I understand only one out of every five words . . . but always de Gaulle.' *Quelle charme*. The French adored it. It was the beginning of a close friendship between the Alphands and the Kennedys.

Nicole Alphand's influence in Washington grew rapidly after that. She stormed Washington society with her perfect power parties. Her sway over the capital's social life was such that she made the cover of *Time* magazine in November 1963. 'Short of a summons to dinner at the White House, few invitations are treasured as highly as those to 2221 Kalorama Road, site of the grey stone Tudor-style French embassy and home of Nicole Alphand,' wrote *Time*. A whip-smart 46-year-old, with bronzed skin from Bar Harbor summers and Palm Beach winters, Alphand wore her trademark honey-rinsed blonde mane as if it were a regal crown. Her blue-green eyes flashed with passion and she was admired up and down Pennsylvania Avenue. She had a talent for flirting without inspiring Washington wives to grab steak knives; a talent for effortlessly combining fun with the power play. Style that held its own with Jackie Kennedy's. When Kennedy met de Gaulle in Paris, Nicole Alphand's dress created a stir even with the Scotch-swilling, cigar-chomping press secretary, Pierre Salinger: her gown was a pale orange sherbet, the exact colour of the dessert served at lunch. One 'high-ranking Administration official', noted *Time*, was so entranced by Nicole during a dinner, 'he almost fell into her soup'.

In 1963, Odile Moltzer asked Nicole Alphand to help her promote Cardin. They were old friends and the ambassador's wife agreed to help Paris fashion. She dipped into her $80,000 a year entertainment budget and sent her famous chef, Maurice Bell, clanging through his copper pots.

The party was a smash. Cardin was there; Moltzer danced with John Kennedy. Bobby and Rose and Ethel made the rounds, the whole Camelot clan. Nicole Alphand wore Cardin, smelled of Dior, and circulated among the crystal goblets. The fashion show sent jolts of electricity through the bureaucrats. Over the sound of the twist one could hear snippets of conversation: 'No, darlings these models don't have anything on underneath. They don't have anything to hide.' Ambassador Alphand disappeared at 1.30 a.m. up the elevator to his room. His wife said goodbye to her last guest at 3.30 a.m. Cardin must have been awed. 'You know, before coming to these embassies I had already been to many consulates,' he told Moltzer defensively.

Behind the scenes not all had gone well. Nicole Alphand did not like André Oliver. 'This is all very nice but I won't have them in my home,' she told Moltzer. 'You can stay.'

'You can't do that,' gasped Moltzer.

'Why not? It's a nice little hotel.'

There was a compromise: Cardin could stay, but Oliver was packed off to the hotel. The two women friends gossiped a lot during that Washington trip, and in their chit-chat Alphand casually mentioned that if her husband was sent back to Paris she wanted to get a job.

PIERRE CARDIN

On 22 November 1963 – in an instant when the sun shone and a reporter tracking the president casually mentioned she would rather be shopping in Neiman Marcus – three shots rang out and John F. Kennedy was dead. Ambassador Alphand, so deeply associated with the Kennedy administration, was brought back to Paris to become the Secretary General of the Ministry of Foreign Affairs.

Odile Moltzer, in the meantime, had had enough. She was in love, wanted to remarry, wanted to stop working. Fishing for a graceful exit, she recalled Nicole Alphand's desire to get a job if she returned to Paris. 'If you want the Americans you have to take Nicole Alphand into your house,' Moltzer told Pierre. 'She can take my place.'

Moltzer called her old friend. She accepted the job in late November 1965. Brouhaha. It was terribly unseemly for the wife of an important diplomat to work. A press conference to explain her new job was cancelled without explanation after the French papers exploded with the pros and cons of her risqué move. But, ever feisty, Nicole Alphand sneaked out a comment: 'It was time that someone does something for the French woman. She must have the possibility of having clothes with the label of a grand couturier, even though she has only a small amount of money to spend.'

'The day after she started,' recalled Moltzer, 'she had all the American buyers back.' Alphand had tremendous stature. She had a Margaret Thatcher-like sense for the practical and, at 5 feet 8 inches, she was the only one at the house who could smack Cardin around a bit. Where Cardin was unpredictable, disorganized and inarticulate, Alphand brought solidity and organization. She was vital to his early development. She packed the house to the rafters with precisely the right kind of customers.

Cardin's America push continued. Back in 1962 André Oliver and Cardin checked into the St Regis hotel in an effort to interest New York buyers in his men's wear. One visitor recalled: in a tiny suite with a 9 foot by 12 foot living-room André and Pierre themselves put on a fashion show. In the bedroom Cardin put on a suit from the huge steamer trunk, while Oliver strutted in the living-room, showing off the deep vents. Then they switched.

John Kornblith, president of a menswear company called Fashion Park Inc., was dragged down to the St Regis by his advertising executive, Don Robbie. By that time Cardin had returned to Paris and Oliver alone made the presentation. 'It had a body that I had never seen in the United States, except in riding clothing,' said Kornblith. 'It was in a lot of fabrics which were not conventional men's fabrics. It was really one of a kind.' He tried to sell the idea to his board of directors. It was met with a complete lack of interest. 'At the time there were some designer toilet waters for men, and there were some ties. I think it was even before the first Polo ties,' recalled Kornblith. 'But Fashion Park was much more staid. It was kind of caught up in the Kennedy craze, which was destined to turn America from the three-button to two-button clothing which has lasted ever since. Americans didn't know anything about Cardin. He was doing some men's clothing in Europe, but none of it had reached these shores.'

No-one took the bait. On another trip Cardin went to every specialty shop in New York trying to place his wares, but again the cut was so different from the traditional American men's clothes that nobody was interested. In a fit of desperation Cardin called Eleanor Lambert, a leading fashion publicist in New York, who told him that if Saks turned him down it would then probably interest Mildred Custin, president of Bonwit Teller. Lambert made the introduction.

The men's department at Bonwits at the time was a shabby hodge-podge of pyjamas, cuff-links and gift items. After meeting Cardin, Mildred Custin sent her new executive, Danny Zarem, over to Paris. The report he relayed was glowing and Custin took the lure. 'We had at that time a very drab and dull men's haberdashery department on the 57th Street side that I had wanted to do something exciting with. So I thought to myself, this might just be the right time for men's fashion to explode in the United States. It was time for the Peacock Revolution to start here.'

Mildred Custin ordered the Pierre Cardin suits from Georges Bril. The Bonwit's boutique was modelled after Cardin's 118 Faubourg Saint-Honoré decor of luxurious dark-green fabric covering walls and furniture. The suits were priced at $495 a pop. The year, 1966. For the opening party, in the stores 57th Street window Custin installed a mime frozen like a mannequin into position. As the guest came in the model dropped his paper or looked up, making the guests practically jump out of their jewels. The party was held on the third floor and as the guests ascended they saw photographs of themselves flashed up on the walls. New York's narcissistic glitterati fluttered delightedly at the touch.

Oliver and Alphand were there; Cardin was nowhere to be seen. It was a replay of Moltzer's experience with him in Rome, but with worse results. 'He was afraid it wasn't going to go over,' said Custin. 'The *Daily News Record* wrote an open letter to Pierre Cardin. It said: "Pierre, it was your great night and you missed it." '

The first boutique collection was drawn from clothes previewed earlier in the year in Paris. Cardin's menswear was still considered incredibly novel, shocking. That season people burst out laughing when a male model walked out wearing a velour hat shaped like a cut-off stovepipe. The wide-lapelled jackets were so tight that the models could barely breathe. The wide ties were bunched thickly around the throat with Windsor knots. Leather boots came from Brazil where Cardin had just been. Shiny shirts were in purple, orange and mauve. His show was heavily laced with a smouldering, homo-erotic virility. 'Some of the models came out, smoking, with a hunted look in their eyes,' wrote Gloria Emerson in *The New York Times*. 'They all had lots of courage and good legs. Everyone knew about their legs because they also wore silk bathrobes and very abbreviated bathing trunks.'

But under Georges Bril's hands the suits were toned down, the results fabulous. 'Everyone thought we had taken leave of our senses because American men weren't going to wear slightly nipped waists, tennis-rise trousers and vents in the back,' said Custin. They were wrong. Rapidly the small boutique built up a $2 million turnover, an unheard of amount. 'It was a small shop,' said Custin, 'but if you went in on a Saturday you found celebrities from every walk of life there – theatre, literary, they were all there. It was a passing show every Saturday.' (Custin quickly followed up with a Cardin woman's boutique which sold dresses from $110.95 up. At the launch a huge sketch of Cardin took over Bonwit's Fifth Avenue window, while inside models hung from swings.)

'Cardin made it totally acceptable to upper middle-class and above people to feel they could wear designer men's clothes, without having to apologize or be identified as fops,' explained Robert L. Green, the men's fashion director at *Playboy* and perhaps the most influential voice in US men's fashion at the time. 'It was accomplished by Mildred Custin understanding that the times were a-changing. There was a hunger on the part of men to change their attitudes to women, work and holidays. It was the product of the 1960s. Men were accepting that clothes were not something they just embarrassedly put on to cover themselves. They had their own interests in feeling free, to be able to use colour to enhance their attractiveness, or line of silhouette to make them look taller or slenderer. This was a new kind of freedom.'

With the American market cracked, Cardin needed an executive to develop it further. Through a series of coincidences he wound up offering the job to his old Greenwich village guide of the 1950s, Max Bellest.

'On one condition, Pierre,' said Bellest. 'Only one. No salary and I pay my own expenses. I only want a percentage of your royalties. But I want that till I die. I have no fortune, but I eventually want to be able to leave something.'

Cardin looked hard at Max, his head calculating the pros and cons. 'Ooh,' said Cardin excitedly. 'But this is very good, Max. If we don't do anything I don't owe you anything.' Then he added, 'But if we make money I'll be glad to share it with you.'

Cardin's general manager, Daniel Pérou, drew up a contract. 'They gave me a contract that I didn't dispute. I accepted it right away. I received a 10 per cent royalty of his royalties.'

Cardin generally paid his people poorly unless they worked on a commission basis. After signing up Bellest, he generously gave away additional shares of the yet untapped American market. Nicole Alphand, whose job was to develop the US in terms of publicity and contacts, was given a 9 per cent share of his North American income. André Oliver, assigned to create an ill-fated American-based women's ready-to-wear operation, also received a 9 per cent royalty.

It was a move Cardin was going to regret.

•   •   •   •

'When Cardin was in financial difficulties, he fell in with the lovely Jeanne Moreau,' mused James Brady in his autobiography. 'Moreau was at the top of her career, and she was a careful businesswoman who invested her money shrewdly. She moved in with Cardin and André Oliver moved out. Moreau had the reputation of being a tigress and Cardin had the reputation of being, well, a fashion designer. No one really knows the truth of what their relationship was, but it was rumoured that Moreau put a great deal of money into the Cardin business, got him to organize his work habits, inspired him to branch out into the menswear business and generally straightened out his affairs.'

With the success of his menswear Cardin's reputation as a poor businessman began to change. In May 1967, he was the subject of a leading article in *Women's Wear Daily*. 'Je suis un industriel,' he boasted to Thelma Sweetinburgh. 'In the beginning we always thought he'd be a couturier,' said André Ostier. 'We were really surprised.'

Was Moreau the cause? It is unlikely that Jeanne Moreau had quite the influence on Cardin's business that Brady suggested. Her tenure, however, did coincide with the dawning of Cardin the businessman. 'Whether he hired someone or she took command or there was a sea-change within Cardin himself – whatever it was he suddenly started making money,' noted Brady. That was true. But the relationship ended in 1965. Or rather it eased, faded. Because of Moreau's operation she could not have children, and Cardin once said that was what made them grow apart. 'Things just end sometimes,' she told an interviewer. 'He has a very strong personality, and mine is not exactly a weak one either.'

Jeanne Moreau had just filmed Louis Malle's *Viva Maria* (1964) with Brigitte Bardot. She flew Air France into Mexico city for the shoot. Bardot's arrival produced riot police, tear-gas pistols, a fight, grown men fainting. In comparison, Moreau arrived very matter of fact. Just a warm smile. The only hint of her stardom: her luggage was 260 lbs overweight. Cardin flew to Mexico to be with her and, giving George Hamilton a temporary brush off, she flew off with him to spend ten days lounging in Acapulco.

Soon after that film Moreau fell into a deep depression. She could not tolerate light, suffered intolerable insomnia. 'Yes, I had broken up with Pierre, but that wasn't the reason,' she recalled. 'In 1965 I found the pressure of "you must do this for me", "you must get that amount of money", "you mustn't do this one" unbearable. I couldn't stand it. I was too aware of the system. In fact, it was a very healthy reaction because I cut the star system and began to lead a different life.' Moreau began an intensive self-analysis. 'Some people are addicts. If they don't act then they don't exist. I had to check to see if I was an addict. Well, I know now that if something happened I could make a decision to do something totally different. I can live without acting.'

For the next few years, however, Moreau and Cardin remained friends. Marguerite Duras, one of Moreau's closest friends, wrote in August 1966: 'Until last year Jeanne had been living for four whole years with Pierre Cardin. Says a friend: "She will always go back to Cardin. She needs him for continuity – which has nothing to do with sex." At any rate she probably still thinks of him as dearly as she does her ex-husband, whom she allowed to direct her in *Mata Hari*.' Cardin designed her costumes for a few more films. 'He was very important in my life,' said Moreau, 'and I know I was very important in his.'

André Oliver had changed, too. He remained fiercely loyal to Cardin but he had grown. He was no longer living in Cardin's shadow, but a sophisticate respected in his own right for his couture gowns. He had an active private life that swirled contentedly independent of Cardin. 'André was very beautiful. Young and gorgeous and chic,' said Don Robbie.

Oliver's social life changed dramatically. While Odile Moltzer was at Maison Cardin, she said, she often brought him along to meet her friends, such as the Rothschilds. She introduced him to Georges Pompidou, the future president, and his wife, whom she had known for years before he was elected into office. 'In two years André knew everybody,' recalled Moltzer. 'He was delirious with pleasure.' Soon he was dining regularly at the Élysée palace, advising Claude Pompidou what to wear for her husband's functions. André became famous for his urbane parties, his flower arrangements. 'His life is caviar and flowers,' said a friend.

Cardin filled the hole in his own life with work, and Nicole Alphand lined up a series of events for him to whirl through. The day after the 29 January 1966 collection – a white crêpe sleeveless dress blasted with a huge yellow, orange and black bull's-eye; a pin of porcupined black-painted iron nails around large

Harry Winston diamonds – Alphand and Cardin hosted a party at his Quai Anatole France apartment.

It was 'un cocktail'. Some 600 invitations were sent; 1,100 people showed up. Les Viscounts clanged and thumped their drums and guitars in the music room where, on the other side of the window, Paris and the Seine sparkled in the winter night. In the din and the roar total strangers ravaged platters of Westphalian ham, smoked salmon en brochette, chunks of garlicky roast pig. Amongst the canapés were tiny pastry-wrapped Russian meatballs. Mildred Custin in a salmon-pink chemise chatted with a Lord & Taylor buyer. Nicole Alphand kept an eye on the staff, while Mireille Mathieu, the very young Edith Piaf-style chanteuse, belted out love ballads. Mathieu wore a coal-black page-boy haircut and nervously licked her protruding teeth. (Cardin had taken to her – she had a similarly humble, big-family background – and he was now pushing her.) Meanwhile Gore Vidal assisted the auburn-haired Lady St Just up the stairs – she had just broken her leg while skiing in Villars, Switzerland. In all this activity Cardin was frail and shy and poetic, quite charming.

Not so behind the scenes, said his employees. 'Socially he is badly behaved,' claimed one employee too afraid to talk on the record. 'He really doesn't know how to speak. He has no manners. He puts his legs under the table, slumps, sticks his hands into his trousers, leans over his food. It's like that. It's a bit ridiculous when you know what he is really like. It's embarrassing.' If that was the true side of Cardin, few people learned of it. Publicly, as he was at this party, he was irreproachably elegant.

But his cruder side did bubble to the surface occasionally. Like all couturiers Cardin launched his own perfumes. The packaging and bottle of his women's perfume, 'Singulier', unfolded like flower petals. 'Much like a woman's sex organ,' he told his employees. He wanted 'Bleu Marine', his men's perfume, to smell faintly like semen, an 'olfactory suggestion of sperm', he said. The packaging was novel. The fluid floated in a glass phallus, the shaft exploding into a silver tip. (The planning, pricing and launch were botched. The costly packaging was never recouped in the retail price and Cardin lost money on what should have been a bonanza. Disgusted at the outcome, believing that ready-to-wear and licensing were the true cash generators of the future, he sold the worldwide perfume rights to his name.

'When he was in an interview with journalists,' said Barbara Ligeti, a press officer who worked for him, 'he sprayed the cologne all over himself. Real dramatic. "Ah, it smells like sex," he'd say.'

As a former member of his staff said, with much eye-rolling, 'Thank God sex didn't smell that bad.'

PC IN SPACE

7

'Frenchmen, Frenchwomen,' appealed Prime Minister Georges Pompidou on television on 16 May 1968. 'It is up to you to show, by your coolness but also by your resolution – whatever your political preferences may be, whatever your social demands may be – that you reject anarchy. The government will do its duty. It asks you to help.'

Spring usually arrived gently at the Jardin du Luxembourg. Mediterranean winds brought out daffodils and geraniums. Students sat on bottle-green benches, near the uncurling of peach roses, and read Rousseau. In 1968, however, spring brought riots. Students seized the Sorbonne, protesting over-crowding, terrible conditions, an antiquated university system. The hard-core radicals agitating at the centre of the group – Trotskyites, anarchists, Castroites – sang the Internationale and opposed France's bourgeois and capitalist establishment. To make their point, 3,000 students seized the Théâtre de l'Odéon and rejected 'consumer culture'.

On 10 and 11 May fierce fighting broke out between riot police and students at the Jardin du Luxembourg. Helmeted, shielded and booted police advanced steadily upon student barricades made from torn-up paving stones, signposts and red flags. Gas grenades were lobbed at the students, wool scarves wrapped tightly around their faces, while the night sky lit up as cars were torched and then exploded. Hundreds of billy-clubbed students and pavement-pelted police were sent to hospitals. By morning Rue Gay-Lussac was littered and blackened with forty burned-out cars.

The unions joined the student protests, and on 19 May 2 million workers walked out. President Charles de Gaulle pledged economic and educational reforms while street battles continued to rage all over Paris. Students armed with axe-handles, wooden clubs and iron bars attacked the 'Temple of Gold', setting fire to the Bourse. Throughout May battle raged. Students erected barricades from sawn-off trees, heaps of garbage, overturned cars; police clubbed and tear-gassed their way through the debris.

By the middle of June parliament had been dissolved, a new cabinet appointed, promises made, a referendum held, the tension diffused. The night before the new cabinet was formed, Gaullists staged a massive demonstration. Some half a million Frenchmen marched from the Place de la Concorde to the Arc de Triomphe, carrying the Tricolour and singing the Marseillaise. They attacked the socialist leaders capitalizing on the unrest, chanting 'Mitterrand to the firing squad' and 'Communism shall not pass'.

'Nicole Alphand took Cardin by the hand and started dragging him, saying "You're coming, you're coming," ' recalled the former Cardin employee Daniel Fallot. 'He left the house with a trench coat pulled over his face. But there were so many people, and it was very moving, the force of all those people. By the time he got to the Arc de Triomphe he was standing erect, wanting to be counted.'

'He definitely became a Gaullist when Pompidou became president, because André Oliver was eating at the Elysée palace three times a week,' said Manusardi. 'Cardin accepted the fact and officially became a Gaullist. But until then he absolutely wanted to be neutral.' He apparently did not have a political bone in his body. 'Pierre Cardin was allegedly impressed by the slippery, long black coats worn by the riot squads during the Paris street fighting,' reported *The New York Times* in 1968.

•　　　•　　　•　　　•

On 27 January 1968, cognoscenti were crammed into the salon of the new darling, André Courrèges. Suddenly, a man in the audience jumped out of his white plastic cube seat and began removing all his clothes. Women gasped as he stripped down to a pair of white jersey boxer shorts. He gyrated his hips to the tattoo of drums; fluttery fashion editors ogled the black, rippling muscles in his back and buns. And then Courrèges's freckle-faced mannequins hit the runway. The show was on.

André Courrèges was the leader of a group of couturiers called the Space Age designers, all of whom were obsessed with the future. The dictatorial powers of the traditional French couturier had been steadily eroding. The crochet-bikini hedonists of Saint-Tropez or the Beatles and their Mao-jacketed followers in Liverpool's Cavern were the engines; street fashions were the inspiration. But in 1964 and 1965 Courrèges created a sensation with his bra-less, bronzed models with bare midriffs and backsides. His women were bizarre, tall things with short hair, flat-heeled boots, blinking through giant white spectacles in his laboratory-white showroom.

Along with Mary Quant in London, Courrèges established the age of the mini-skirt. (Cardin, of course, has also claimed he invented the mini-skirt.) He presented skirts that ended several inches above the knee and matched them, not with shoes, but with boots of soft white kid. (In Britain during the early 1960s, one major manufacturer had an average skirt length of 25 inches; by 1966 the same mass producer had cut 9 inches off its average length, to just 18 inches.) Courrèges also put grandmothers in gaberdine trouser-suits, another outfit that stormed the beehived streets. His pants had a long elegant line that flared slightly over the top of the feet. Hats were helmet-shaped.

Hot on his heels was Emanuel Ungaro. In 1965 Ungaro struck out on his own while the Swinging Sixties were just coming into full stride. He went on a silver binge: silver wigs; silver-soled boots; silver buttons, collars and mesh stockings. In 1967, the year he opened a glamorous new house, he was heralded as the New Star (the Paris fashion world has the same sense of proportion as Hollywood). Ungaro's wild prints and well-tailored clothes were always sprinkled with Space Age lunacy. Aluminium necklaces doubling up as bras were juxtaposed with see-through flower-appliquéd trousers.

Cardin, too, was considered a Space Age designer. His trademark pale wool and lovely scalloped skirt suits of 1960 were soon replaced by his 'crazy furs', starting in 1962. That year's crazy fur was a white fox hat and coat hand-painted with big, ugly black polka-dots. In the mid 1960s he began his shocking stocking look: candy-striped body suits plastered with cut-out vinyl necklaces and skirts of white vinyl strips. The look was difficult to wear — logistical problems in the lavatory — yet it was photographed endlessly by the press. (In the midst of his body-sock craze, however, were infinitely wearable dresses, such as a multi-layered, utterly romantic evening gown which made the mannequin look as if she was cushioned in orchids. Most likely these were the creations of André Oliver.) What lasted from Cardin's stocking look, however, was the idea of solid-coloured tights, which he effectively teamed with the mini-skirt.

Cardin anchored strapless tube dresses to dog collars. In 1968 he came out with moulded dresses: synthetic fibres moulded to pop out in the impression of an egg carton. In 1968 a simple stewardess-like dress was fitted with two large white breasts; a brassière-like top looked like the headlamps of a Volkswagen. And above all was his love of vinyl, which striped, fluted and plastered everything. 'Creation is an evolution; if one follows fashion, it is not creation,' he was fond of saying. 'Creativity causes provocation. If one shocks it changes the spirit of things. Provocation eventually causes acceptance.'

His Space Age tag crystallized with his 'Cosmonaut' collection of 1966 (the 'Astronaut' look when it was being marketed in the US). In the throes of the Soviet–American race to the moon, Cardin's Space Age vision was a sort of ski outfit for the cartoon family, the Jetsons. A blouse was tucked into nylon-like ski pants that were again tucked into heavy black boots. The look was topped off with a Newfoundlander's cap. The press coverage was measured in tons. When, in 1969, Neil Armstrong walked on the moon, Cardin gasped, 'You see, I was right.'

The thread that bound his 1960s designs together was a preoccupation with youth. He fought to remain with it. He was obsessed with remaining young, with being close to the fresh-faced men and women who threw Molotov cocktails. Unlike, say, Givenchy, Cardin seemed to detest the wealthy, elderly women who were the traditional mainstay of the haute-couture world. 'Ageing women with their stupid desire to please make the work of pioneering creative fashion designers extremely difficult,' Cardin told *Penthouse* magazine in a scathing, rather misogynistic attack on his own couture clients. 'Whenever we produce something a little daring or unusual, public opinion starts to scream. "This is ugly! This is obscene!" Of course it is, if seen on the body of some old hag . . . In the nineteenth century Balzac gave women thirty years as the limit of their emotional and sexual life. Let us not be over-generous today and double this figure in order to feed the female vanity . . . I'm not concerned with youth pills, rejuvenation clinics, face-lifts, and silicone injections. If there is one thing I hate it is vulgarity – and there is nothing more vulgar than a middle-aged woman disguised as a hippy or, as we say in French, a "ye-ye" girl.'

Outside Cardin's little world the pictures were changing fast. And it all seemed to be happening faster, more furiously, in America. In 1968 a set of assassin's shots, just two months apart, closed the dreaming eyes of Martin Luther King and of presidential hopeful Senator Robert Kennedy. Violence seemed to scorch everything. President Nixon's administration carpet-bombed Vietnam while award-winning pictures graphically brought the bad war home. In New York's Washington Square park hippies believing in flower power strummed cracked guitars; around them zonked Vietnam vets danced hysterically. Everything was in a jumble, turned on its head. *Archie* comic books lost ground to underground characters engaged in cartoon oral sex. Even Wall Street was doing drugs, overheating in the 1960s 'go-go' market. Bernie Cornfeld and his IOS mutual fund empire was rocketing away with gullible money. 'Do you seriously want to be rich?' he asked. The Beatles went to India, wore beads; Mick Jagger squeezed into skin-tight satin jeans and jumped around the stage screaming he couldn't get any satisfaction. Torrid images – Soviet tanks rolling over Prague and US soldiers razing an Asian village – seemed to rush past in a confusing blur of 20-second TV spots.

The confusion of the news was mirrored in fashion. The decade ended in the maxi, the longest day-length hemline since the army coats of the First World War. Battle raged between communists and capitalists, and between maxi and midi and mini. In that battle Cardin took a stand. He boldly killed the midi and instead had his models wear the mini under a maxi-coat.

The young styles of the 1960s, unlike some of the earlier important fashion trends of the century, could not be tagged to a specific year or a particular designer. The world had simply changed too much for a handful of élitist couturiers to dictate styles. Anything went. Ready-to-wear designers who could pick up on the casual fashions of the street became more influential than the powdered, turn-of-the-century Faubourg Saint-Honoré salons.

One designer who successfully bridged the fashions of the street with couture was Yves Saint Laurent, easily the favourite of *Women's Wear Daily* and most of the fashion press during the 1960s and 1970s. In 1962 he held his first haute-couture collection in his own name, under the auspices of his business partner, Pierre Bergé. He combined utter simplicity in line with some very tongue-in-cheek details. His 1960s creations were neither reconstructed gilt chairs disguised as day-wear, nor aluminium-foil wraps passed off as evening-wear. In the first year, 1962, he made his famous pea-jacket collection. In 1965 he made the 'Mondrian' dresses, very simple wool jersey shifts that borrowed the primary colours and patterns of Mondrian's palette. They were copied everywhere. In 1966 and 1967 he shocked with his 'Pop Art' collection of cartoon strips, nude torsos, pink lips. Gone for ever was the journalists' diet of understated elegance. For evening, those same years, he began creating women's trouser-suit ensembles based on men's formal wear – a tuxedo look that became the signature of Liza Minelli. And throughout such achievements Saint Laurent continued to make very controlled, elegant clothes in the tradition of Chanel.

As the 1960s closed Saint Laurent produced his 'happy hooker' or 'rich hippie'. 'Following the May 1968 student riots in Paris, Saint Laurent confessed that he found himself depressed by politics and the world situation generally.

PIERRE CARDIN

Out of this depression came what were, for their time, some of the ugliest clothes in years,' recalled James Brady. 'For several seasons Saint Laurent persisted with a look he called the "happy whore". It had broad shoulders, short skirts, ankle-strap shoes, vivid streetwalker make-up, frizzy hair. France's internal difficulties, the American urban riots, Vietnam, made it impossible for a sensitive designer to turn out "pretty" clothes. Saint Laurent was reacting violently to the world he thought he saw around him. Those of us who criticized Saint Laurent were proven wrong within a year when young women began to pick up the "ugly" look . . .'

In her own time-warp, ever fashionable, was Coco Chanel. As always, she had an opinion on everything. The mini-skirt? 'C'est une exhibition de viande,' she sniffed ('It's a show of meat'). Surely she liked Courrèges' clothes? 'The most ridiculous thing in Paris.' What about Saint Laurent? 'Monsieur Saint Laurent has very good taste. And the more he copies me, the better taste he displays.'

Nor did Coco spare Cardin. In fact, she seemed to detest him. Their mutual antagonism came to a head when Chanel, who was not a member of the Chambre Syndicale, started maliciously scheduling her shows at the precise time Cardin scheduled his. This went on throughout the 1960s. Buyers and press were forced to make agonizing choices as Chanel had her press attaché warn everyone that the doors closed promptly as scheduled, foiling any reporter trying to catch the first half of Cardin and the end of Chanel. The origin of their feud was never known. Perhaps it was because he pooh-poohed her achievements. 'I have no admiration for Chanel as a creator,' he told anyone who would listen. 'Imagine doing the same suit all your life.'

In the late 1960s a rumour swept Paris that the octogenarian designer had died. At 118 Faubourg Saint-Honoré there was great excitement. Nicole Alphand was assigned the task of telephoning the House of Chanel for details. She rang and Chanel picked up the phone. Alphand, a diplomat when need be, stammered out some greeting and asked if she could come over one day to be fitted for some evening dresses. 'Although I must be Madame Cardin by day,' Alphand said, 'I would like to be Madame Chanel by night in my private life.' 'You can be Madame Cardin twenty-four hours a day,' Chanel snapped and hung up.

Soon after Coco had dinner with Jim Brady and told him about the rumours of her death and the call from Maison Cardin. 'No,' Chanel told him, 'when I die I'll simply lie here on the couch for six months or so, only close friends are to be notified, and there'll be none of this filth in the papers or chez Monsieur Cardin and that lot.'

•   •   •   •

'Maison Cardin was less organized than any other house, but this is how you could really see the genius of Pierre Cardin at work,' recalled the embroiderer Jean-Guy Vermont. 'I saw him do things I never saw another couturier do. He took a toile, he put it on the mannequin, took the scissors, cut here and there, then tied something here. In five minutes it was done. Or else there was a toile he didn't like. Three cuts of the scissors and all of a sudden you saw a gown very well architectured and interesting.'

Cardin created out of chaos. A few months before collection day, couture suppliers arrived with their various wares at 118 Faubourg Saint-Honoré. The task of picking fabrics usually fell to André Oliver. 'I go through about 10,000 fabrics to choose the final 2,000 lengths that we use as the basis of a collection,' he claimed. From Zurich, a salesman from Abrahams AG arrived. Abrahams was a silk processor, and its salesmen came with samples of the newest fabrics that had been concocted in its Zurichberg labs. From Paris's Right Bank came Jean-Guy Vermont, the force behind the capital's second-largest embroidery house. André Lemarié descended from his atelier near the Rue Saint-Denis porno district to show artificial flowers and feathers. At Marescot-Riechers the latest black grand lace, perhaps hand-embroidered with little green flowers, went on display. A house like LeMarchand, meanwhile, peddled the latest bull-horn or teak buttons. In these tiny ateliers, up creaking staircases, behind bolts and dummies, the artisans of Paris worked their trade in century-old family businesses. This was the backbone of the couture industry.

These suppliers were amazed at the Cardin house. All fashion shows came together at the last moment but Cardin was in a category of his own. He was always breathlessly behind schedule. One well-known fabric manufacturer, Nattier, once discovered that by mid-June Cardin had still not unpacked the rolls of cloth needed for a mid-July show. Getting paid was another matter. 'He didn't have trouble paying bills any longer, but he was the only one allowed to sign the cheques. When he wasn't there, there were no cheques,' said François Lesage. 'It was a monkey-ass business.'

One year Jean-Guy Vermont dropped off his embroidery samples. He usually made some twenty-five or thirty models for Cardin every season, or about 10 per cent of the Cardin show. On this particular occasion, as he had not heard from Maison Cardin, Vermont called the house a week before the collection. One of Cardin's assistants told Vermont that Cardin had decided he was not going to use embroideries that season. On the Friday evening of that week, five days before collection day, Renée Tixier, Cardin's assistant, called Vermont.

'Monsieur Vermont, you must come and see him tomorrow. He has decided to use some embroideries.'

'I don't think I am going to do it, Renée,' said Vermont in shock. 'Tell Monsieur Cardin I don't want to waste his time. I won't be able to complete the embroideries on such a short notice.'

Vermont hung up. But Renée called back again two minutes later. 'Don't worry,' she said. 'Monsieur Cardin is not going to order very difficult embroideries.'

Early Saturday morning Vermont was at 118 Faubourg Saint-Honoré. They worked out an agreement. Cardin ordered about ten neck-band-like pieces that were embroidered to look like large jewels. Cardin would make the dresses and then the bejewelled dickies could be rapidly stitched on the dresses at the last moment. It was agreed that no changes could be made. Vermont's suppliers were closed over the weekend and he could only use what was in stock.

Vermont and his staff started work immediately. They had, of course, orders from other couturiers. The pace was gruelling. They worked all day Saturday, through the night, all day Sunday. On Sunday evening Vermont started the staggered delivery of the embroideries to Maison Cardin. The completed pieces were whisked over to 118 Faubourg Saint-Honoré right up to the fashion show. But Vermont had done it. Exhausted he went to see how Cardin used the embroideries. He sat through nearly 300 skipping models. Not one of his embroideries appeared. For whatever reason Cardin had yet again reversed his decision. (Embroiderers make their money from the reorders that come when clients buy a gown, so this was a financial blow. 'He still has them. A few years ago I saw the pieces in a drawer,' said Vermont.)

Cardin's mannequins, too, had their crosses to carry. He didn't work like other couturiers. They were designers and not, like him, trained tailors. Rather than endless sketches, Cardin preferred to make the dresses right on the mannequins. No plan, just a wild deluge of ideas, some that worked brilliantly, others that failed miserably.

Cardin waited until the last possible moment before entering the studio. But then, in a fierce work binge that resembled a debauchery, he worked days on end without sleep, without bathing, in the same clothes. Terrified assistants ran back and forth, carrying swatches and scissors and tapes and pins and half-eaten baguettes. And in the background, like mimes, mannequins stood stock-still for hours, days, months while he cut the toile right on them. Cardin's favourite was Hiroko, the exquisite mannequin who did fourteen of his collections. With Japanese grit Hiroko endured better than the others, which allowed a self-absorbed Cardin to make forty to fifty outfits of a collection right on her.

'It was very hard work,' said Hiroko. 'I would stay with him from 9 a.m. till 7 p.m. in the studio, sometimes for a month-and-a-half. Many girls fell down, collapsed with hunger. But I didn't have problems because I was excited to see him work. He was making unique clothes right on me.'

Nor were his shows conventional. In the mid-1960s Eugenia Sheppard of the *Herald Tribune* tagged along with Cardin on collection day and was allowed to see him work backstage. Cardin was fussing around Hiroko. 'The neckline of this coat is all wrong. The show will be a fiasco,' he cried, ripping the suede garment apart. With just a few hours left before the show, Cardin's assistants could not hide their despair and fatigue. Hiroko, accustomed to his tirades or perhaps not understanding what he was saying, stood emotionless. Elsewhere 60s-skinny nude mannequins tried on glittering evening gowns or tweed suits. Dresses hanging from hangers had scooped-out fronts with big bow-covered bras, or giant lapels that stayed primly closed and then could be sensationally opened out like petals on a flower. Laid out on a table were the dresses' accessories, including flowered stockings, buckled shoes, fur hoods, sombrero hats, and evening head-dresses of ostrich feather or curled organdie shavings that hung like ringlets of hair.

Outside, the salon filled. Cardin's shows were always embarrassingly late. The speakers pounded with 'Eleanor Rigby'. People waved invitations, pushed and jostled. Militant clients sometimes, like English soccer hooligans in high-heeled Valentino shoes, waged elbow wars with fashion journalists shaking with caffeine. Paparazzi, meanwhile, toted two-foot-long lenses and whacked unsuspecting bystanders with steel-edged camera cases.

The seating at such shows rarely varied and was a fascinating study of contemporary anthropology. In the centre of the front row the ever-feared critic John Fairchild sat like Toad of Toad Hall. Only royalty could usurp his position. Close to his sides were the 'front row ladies' – Jeanne Moreau, Shirley MacLaine, Charlotte Rampling, Claude Pompidou. Fanning out from the centre were other fashion journalists seated in a pecking order based on their publications' power. Beyond that suppliers and licensees were shunted. Together the crush of bodies produced a heat and smell reminiscent of a Nairobi market.

Finally, Cardin emerged to make a curtain speech before the collection. 'Head cocked to one side, speaking without the slightest regard for the microphone, Cardin goes on interminably expounding his fashion philosophy while restive Italian editors shout, "basta, basta",' wrote James Brady. 'Nothing perturbs Cardin. He goes on talking through the roar of the crowd and when he is good and ready, the first model steps onto the runway.' *The New York Times*'s Emerson noted in a 1969 column that 'Pierre Cardin feels he must make a speech, which 80 per cent of his audience cannot follow.'

PIERRE CARDIN

For many journalists that was just the beginning of the torture. Cardin believed in the deluge approach. Whereas other couturiers would show some 100 models, clearly focused and well edited to get their message across quickly to fashion journalists, Cardin blasted away for hours with some 300 models that ran from aluminium helmets and hula-hoop skirts to immensely wearable, deceptively simple black evening gowns. His collection showed every possible length, silhouette and fabric. 'His shows have always been shotgun treatment. If you shoot a shotgun with enough shot in the cartridge, it will eventually hit something,' explained fashion editor Robert L. Green. 'Whatever became the thing that was that year's fashion statement, Cardin could say, "I did it." '

During collection week fashion journalists dashed, notebook in hand, from the Left to the Right Bank, from 9 a.m. to 7 p.m., watching some half-dozen shows in a day. In that context Cardin's shows grated on the journalists' nerves. 'Why does he do it? Is it a sort of megalomania? We long to know, for everyone's story (even a couturier's) is better by being kept brief,' snapped fashion writer Serena Sinclair.

His shows were wildly entertaining, driven by hysteria. The models never appeared in the order of the programme so clients, buyers and journalists were left frantically trying to identify numbers that had caught their interest. 'Cardin was not systematic,' said Hiroko in a classic understatement. 'In other houses the order had all been set up the night before. Cardin hated to set things up. We were very free and I would arrange my order so the changes were easiest.' The result was chaos. 'It was a circus, with Cardin pushing people on stage,' said Green. 'It wasn't like an ordinary fashion show which is chaos alone,' recalled Arnold Linsman, the US licensees' press officer. 'His was chaos in spades, because one model didn't know from one show to the next if he was wearing the same outfit. Cardin would say, "No, you put that on." And the guy's waiting to go on stage. I couldn't stand it. It drove me crazy.'

Mannequins emerged stumbling from a shove, heels caught in bizarre loops of material. When several were on stage, they sometimes backed into each other and ricocheted out of the sight lines. And the models were often not finished. Pins stuck out of hems, buttons were occasionally missing, threads hung from sleeves. The perfection of other couturiers was never reached at Maison Cardin. 'The last model usually emerges with André still pinning on the sleeve,' recalled Brady. Cardin, nervously peeking through the curtains at the audience's reaction throughout the show, finally appeared unshaven and rumpled to take his bow.

Everyone had an opinion as to why he needed to produce 300 models. 'The secret lies in Cardin's immense wealth of creativity,' wrote Sinclair. 'He acts as an ideas factory for all Paris, but in his own work he cannot be ruthlessly disciplined, and is reluctant to edit any of his innovations.' His business associates, meanwhile, claimed there were practical reasons for his endless ballads in cloth. As his licensing empire started to grow in different parts of the world in the 1960s, Cardin began designing more for his licensees. His shows became stuffed with American, Oriental and South American executives who were manufacturing the PC merchandise in separate corners of the globe. They came, of course, in search of the next season's style that they could adapt to local fabrics and market tastes. Cardin had to satisfy them. 'The shows were enormous. It was a trick Cardin had,' said Mario Sala, Cardin's Italian manager for nine years. 'The Italian licensee could find something that suited his market, the Indian licensee something for his market. It was very international.'

But perhaps the most important reason was related to the media and Cardin's brilliant sense of public relations. The numerous models allowed Cardin to satisfy his hunger for the press while balancing the practical needs of his licensees. Ever mindful of the needs of the fashion editor, Cardin was careful to lace his show heavily with unwearable get-ups that grabbed headlines. 'Cardin was the first designer to sense that the general press could be more interested in a sensational picture of what was New-In-Fashion than in a lengthy report on what women were likely to wear,' wrote the journalist G.Y. Dryansky. 'He helped the big dailies all over the world sell newspapers, and they helped sell Cardin. And the masses got their money's worth: they could ease their envy of the rich by believing that rich people's dress was wacky, and they could, with no evident contradiction, partake of a certain communion with luxury by buying, at a price they could occasionally afford, some simple item labelled "Pierre Cardin".'

Editor Patricia Corbett agreed: 'Cardin is also the author of notorious commercial flops that were nevertheless worth their weight in publicity,' she wrote. 'His electronic dresses, twinkling like Christmas trees, and 3D shifts, whose brief skirts were held out by a series of hoops, caught the public eye and are perennials in graduate design students' collections the world over.'

His shows became his trademark: brilliant and not so brilliant ideas blasted like buckshot at the public, executed in a slap-dash way. 'Observers are divided into two distinct camps — fans and scoffers,' observed one journalist. 'There's virtually no neutral zone. And business booms.'

Sant'Andrea di Barbarana, Italy.   (AUTHOR)

La Tour-du-Pin, France, *circa* 1930.   (GILLES MOREL)

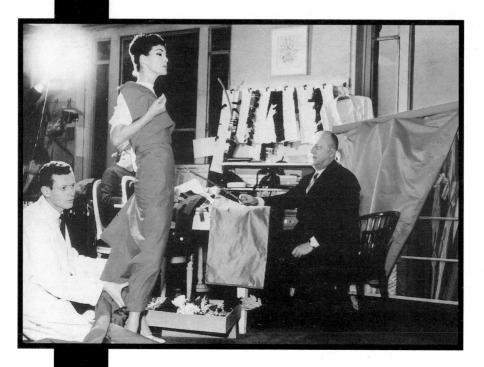

Christian Dior at work in his studio. (ARCHIVES CHRISTIAN DIOR)

Pierre Cardin (*left*) was one of Dior's top tailors
during the 1947 launch of the New Look.

(ARCHIVES CHRISTIAN DIOR)

Jean Marais as
the Beast and
as Prince
Charming in
Jean Cocteau's
1945 success
*La Belle et La
Bête*.

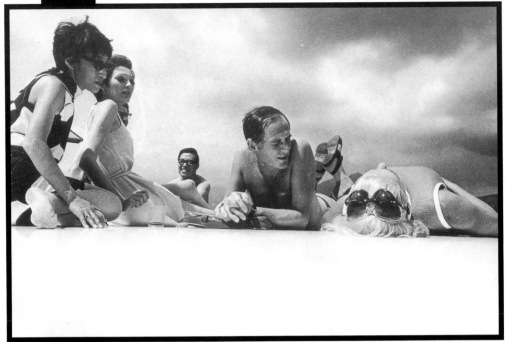

Pierre Cardin and Jeanne Moreau at play, and at the theatre.

A party with the Princesse de Croy, now
Odile Moltzer, in the background.

A party in Cardin's apartment
overlooking the Seine (Françoise Sagan,
Anne and Charlotte Ford against the
window).

Nicole Alphand sitting
next to Pierre Cardin at a
1970s show.

André Oliver, Pierre Cardin and models.

(REX FEATURES)

Pierre Cardin with his industrial designer Alain Carré in front of Espace Pierre Cardin.

(ALAIN CARRÉ)

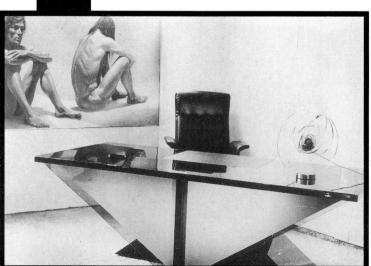

Cardin-'designed' desk and chair in his Espace office.

(REX FEATURES)

The press listening to one of Cardin's famous monologues.

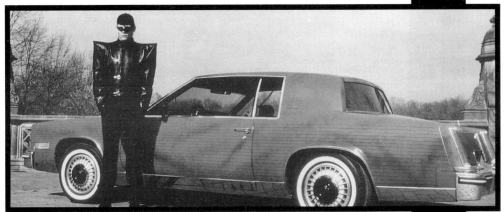

Cardin model poses beside Cardin-styled car.

Cardin discovering his US line of furniture during the 1977 launch party.

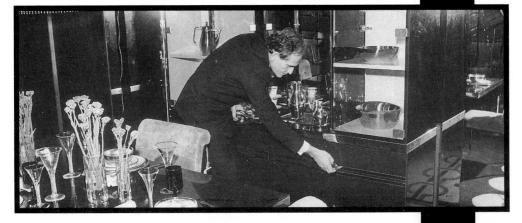

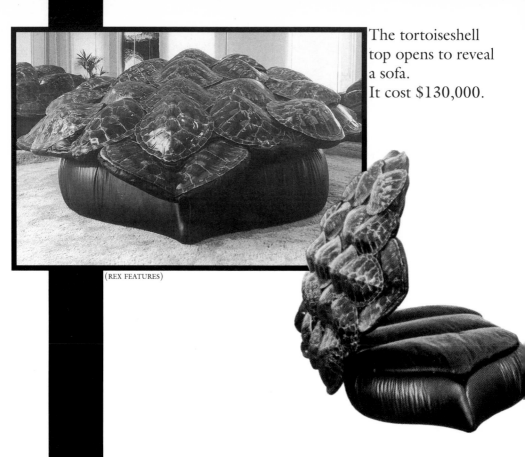

The tortoiseshell top opens to reveal a sofa.
It cost $130,000.

The Pierre Cardin Westwind I by Atlantic Aviation.

(GAMMA / FRANK SPOONER)

In 1981 Cardin bought the famous restaurant, Maxim's.

Long before anyone else
Cardin was breaking
down the last great frontier:
Communist China.

(GAMMA / FRANK SPOONER)

It was the Soviets, however,
who took the first leap.
Cardin designed a Soviet
line of 'Pierre Cardin'.

(GAMMA / FRANK SPOONER)

(REX FEATURES)

(REX FEATURES)

(REX FEATURES)

(REX FEATURES)

1960s

.300

$10

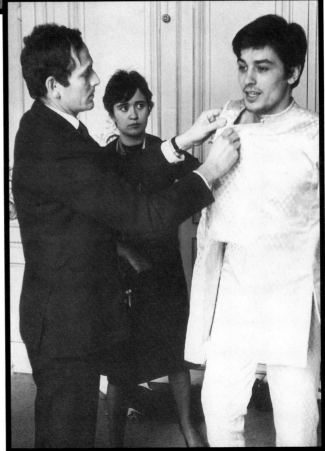

1960s

1960s

1960s

(REX FEATURES)

1970s

(GAMMA / FRANK SPOONER PICTURES)

(GAMMA / FRANK SPOONER PICTURES)

1980s

1990s

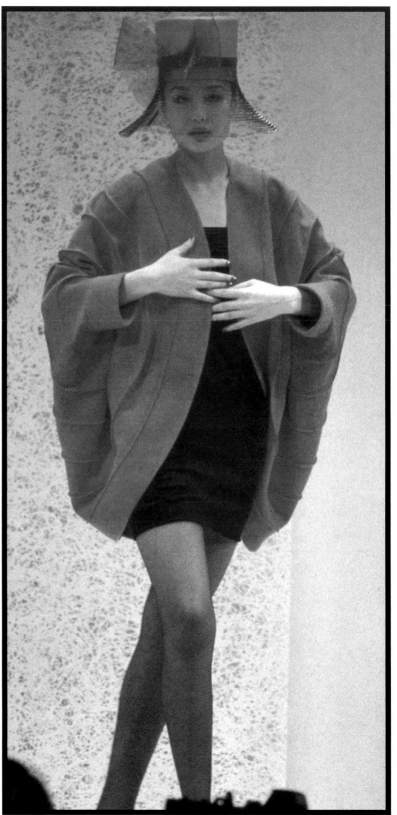

RETURN TO VICHY   8

By 1967 ten years had gone by since Pierre Cardin burst on to the scene with his
first full collection. That year Gloria Emerson hit hard in her 29 July article in
The New York Times. 'Pierre Cardin doesn't have to be a rebel any more because
he is too famous and too influential,' she wrote. 'It is almost a pity. His new
fall–winter collection today is evolving. The Cardin revolution is over. The
déjà-vu sensation hit some people because Cardin has been imitated so often.
It is boring when he repeats himself because so many others already have.'

Fashion's law of gravity was starting to pull Cardin's star to earth. 'A
designer's influence rarely lasts more than a decade,' explained Suzy Menkes,
the *International Herald Tribune*'s fashion editor. 'It's a young man's game.'

The powerful John Fairchild seemed to cool towards Cardin overnight. No-
one really knew why. Perhaps he had decided Cardin was too gimmicky – clever
but in bad taste. Perhaps it was personal – some thought Fairchild simply did
not like Cardin. In any event, a chance to repair fences came when the irreverent
James Brady was replaced by G.Y. Dryansky as the *WWD* Paris bureau chief.
Dryansky was very bright, but utterly green in the ways of Paris couturiers.

On collection day in 1966 Cardin swivelled up to the new *WWD* star
and said, 'Let me undress you.' Dryansky raised an eyebrow. He took the

comment metaphorically and allowed himself to be shoved into a room. Seasoned journalists knew never to give a couturier an honest opinion, even if he asked for it. What the couturier really wanted was flattery. Only back in front of the word-processor did the experienced journalist undress. Dryansky, however, took Cardin's request at face value.

'The evening wear is beautiful but the day wear is a bit, well, dingue,' he said.

Dingue was French for odd. The evening wear, of course, was the work of André Oliver, while the day wear was generally designed by Cardin. Not only had Dryansky told Cardin his assistant had done a better job than he had, but Dryansky had also called Cardin's creations weird. Cardin's face stiffened with incredulity. And then he went berserk. He shut himself away in a room. André Oliver flew out of the room to berate the shell-shocked Dryansky.

'You have very bad manners,' he scolded. 'The best thing you can do is leave.' Dryansky did.

What exactly happened thereafter remains cloudy. There are several versions, but according to James Brady a *WWD* photographer who had arrived to take Cardin's photograph found the designer sobbing on the carpet. The photographer's arrival was just too much for Cardin to take. He jumped to his feet and hysterically ordered a member of his staff to call the police (some say the fire department, although why he should want the fire department is utterly unclear). The next evening Brady had to attend a formal dinner for Cardin, given by Nicole and Hervé Alphand. 'Cardin by then was under icy control, but it was not the most pleasant dinner party I'd ever sat through,' he recalled. The fence-mending with *WWD* was not proceeding as planned.

Cardin remained a great talent, a technical wizard, but instead of new ideas with every garment, as had been the case for so many years, journalists found they were being served yesterday's lasagne. In January 1968 – a year after Emerson's cutting column – Prudence Glynn at *The Times* in London drew more blood. 'One of the most depressing experiences is to watch a collection by a designer, who you believe to be extremely talented, which does not do him justice,' she wrote. 'Looking at Cardin's clothes today it was hard to imagine that this same man has in the past been considered one of the most original and exciting designers in Paris. His collection was not gimmicky, it was not fancy dress; it was just dull with occasional bright patches.' *The New York Times* agreed: 'Pierre Cardin . . . seems tired and in need of rest.'

Cardin still had plenty more days in the limelight. His flame flared up periodically and dramatically, particularly when he went back to the classic coats he created in the 1950s. But there was a definite shift after 1967. Cardin had begun his slow, downward spiral. At first the fashion editors took time out to berate him, which was a compliment in itself. He could still command a full article. But then they followed up with something much, much more deadly. Indifference. In February 1974, Bernadine Morris of the *New York Times* buried Cardin in 120 words. Worse yet, the brief reference was at the end of a long article, in paragraph fifteen. 'There are some pretty things, but they're overshadowed by the hobble-skirt dresses, the batwing outfits, the split-level skirts edged in feathers, the tufted-and-tasselled sofa effects and the coloured baubles the size of a baby's head that border the cape-back of a black dress,' she wrote. 'Possibly they were meant to be amusing.'

Cardin moved on. Creating clothes was becoming boring, anyway. He had grander ambitions.

•   •   •   •

'As I have long predicted, the haute couture will become a laboratory for ideas. Haute couture alone can never make a financial success. Today I have as clients the ten most-talked-about women in Paris. The Baronne Guy de Rothschild orders thirty models a season . . . But what is that? Perfume? That too is a myth. I agree it provides very good salaries for a number of people, but when all is done there is not much profit left for the house itself,' Cardin told *Women's Wear Daily* in 1967.

'The only way to make money is with Ready-to-Wear. You have no idea how I was criticized by my couture colleagues when I started a department at the Printemps store. But what are they all doing now? Look at Saint Laurent selling jersey dresses for $60 . . .'

The long-simmering conflict between haute couture and ready-to-wear surfaced in 1966, when Pierre Cardin had a fight with the Chambre Syndicale de la Couture Parisienne. The Chambre Syndicale had always been biased towards the glossy magazines like *Vogue* and *Elle*, and the syndicate had instituted a rule whereby photographs of the models were forbidden for about thirty days after collection day. Ostensibly the rule was meant to prevent copying, but it also effectively wiped out any advantage newspapers or television might have over a magazine. The fast-moving Cardin, meanwhile, was dead against it. His licensees in Argentina or Japan needed instant publicity. They needed photographs of Cardin and his creations splayed across the dailies.

So in July 1966 he resigned from the Chambre Syndicale. He couldn't work under the constraints of the association, he said in his brief resignation letter. (Later, in a fit of exaggeration, he claimed he was thrown out of the Chambre Syndicale for launching designer ready-to-wear.)

In 1967 the Cardin licensing empire encompassed some thirty-five licences and sub-licences. That year he came out with ready-to-wear for two- to eight-year olds. Little boys could wear miniature cosmonaut outfits, complete with capes and big ring zippers over everything. Deals were coming together in such faraway countries as Australia and Mexico. In Paris he worked fourteen-hour days. Otherwise he was flying to Lebanon, Germany, America, Israel, Brazil, Italy, Argentina, and Japan visiting his new licensees. In 1969 *Time* magazine reported that he was earning royalties on a $27 million turnover.

Business was growing so fast that he needed more executives. Jean Manusardi, who had turned Cardin down in the early 1960s, finally joined the house at the insistence of Alphand. Manusardi – big like a bear, erudite, honest – was paid a fixed salary, given a desk, had no specified duty or title. 'You heard the gun on the left, you went with the cavalry to the left. You heard the musketry on the right, you went there with footmen. You never knew. You just had to act,' was how Jean Manusardi described his initiation into the Cardin business empire.

The first musket fire came from Italy. Daniel Pérou had signed a licensing deal with an Italian fabric manufacturer, Filla. It was going to produce fabrics under the Cardin name – a huge mistake that came from helter-skelter growth and careless planning. Clothing manufacturers could buy Filla's PC fabric, make clothes with the signature all over them, and then advertise the Cardin connection. It could have been the end of the house, cannibalizing the business of finished-garment licensees like the menswear manufacturer, Bril.

'My first assignment was to kill that deal in Italy. I managed to do that without breaking too much glass,' said Manusardi. 'My first achievement was negative. It was a bad omen.'

A few months after Manusardi was hired, Cardin discovered a salesman called Daniel Fallot. He was very handsome in a British–German mould: grey flannel, club tie, married with children, played tennis. He had a strong image and was well versed in the clothing industry. 'Cardin was seduced by the aspect and look of Daniel Fallot,' said Manusardi. 'André Oliver was not very happy because Cardin obviously thought Fallot was a good-looking fellow.'

But Fallot, too, was in for a shock. As had happened a few years earlier when Odile Moltzer arrived at the house, Fallot discovered that no-one knew he had been hired to co-ordinate the French licensees. 'Cardin didn't say anything to anybody,' said Fallot. 'I was the one who had to say, "Mr Cardin told me that I was in charge of this and that . . ." '

So a few months after Manusardi had been hired, he found he was on the way out. He had not made any egregious errors. 'From one day to another, which is also proof of Cardin's disorganization because these things should build up slowly, Fallot was a great man and I was down in the cellar,' recalled Manusardi. 'All of a sudden everybody was forbidden to tell me anything. I was there from 9 till lunchtime, from 2.30 to 6.30, and nothing. Barely anything. I answered a few phone calls but no letters. The licensees were supposed to talk to Fallot and not me.'

But the two men, Fallot and Manusardi, became friends. They explained their friendship as partly due to the fact that they were both heterosexuals. It was a bond through which they subliminally protected themselves against a cliquish homosexual club where sexual orientation was often rewarded above ability. (A female employee in the early 1970s estimated that during her time 80 per cent of the male staff was gay.) Their bond was strengthened, too, because the two men's stars regularly rose and fell in opposition. Rather than become enemies, they joined forces to beat Cardin's capricious system. The one who at that moment Cardin had turned into a star often acted as the front man for deals worked out by the executive in disgrace.

'Unbelievable as it sounds we became friends,' said Manusardi. 'We should have hated each other; 90 per cent of the people encouraged me to hate him, and him to hate me.' But the truth was they needed each other's expertise. While Fallot was in favour he had to negotiate contracts, and for that he urgently needed Manusardi's guidance. When Cardin dropped Fallot and reinstated Manusardi, Manusardi turned to his friend when he needed assistance with the French licensees. 'We had secret meetings at our homes. Never in the office,' said Manusardi. 'People were forbidden to talk to me.'

In the US Max Bellest was moving things along nicely. Bellest was a character in his own right. He pinched pennies: he ate fast food for lunch; took the bus instead of a cab; always called the licensees collect. 'He wore nylon-tricho shirts he could wash and hang up in his shower to dry,' said a friend of his. And eating with Bellest at a restaurant was one big scene, with food and wine repeatedly being sent back. ('There's only two things you do in life three times a day from the day you're born to the day you die,' Bellest once told shirt licensee S. Miller Harris. 'One is make pee-pee and the other is eat. So when you eat it might as well be good.') Bellest was really extremely charming, his eccentricities harmless. But he was also tough as nails when required and fiercely protected Cardin's interests. In just a year or two Bellest had signed up half a dozen important licensees, a roster of products which included jewellery, ties, menswear, womenswear, and belts.

The most important licence, menswear, went to John Kornblith, the man who had seen André Oliver's St Regis fashion show. Besides running Fashion Park Inc., Kornblith was also one of the early licensees of the McDonald's Corporation, a business he built into a huge organization. He was, like Cardin, a visionary. He saw huge potential in US-made Cardin suits.

In the spring of 1967 Kornblith resigned from Fashion Park with the idea of cutting the deal with Cardin. He joined forces with Marvin Kirsten, a menswear

PIERRE CARDIN

manufacturer with a factory on Astor Place in lower Manhattan, and the two men founded Intercontinental Apparel Inc. with some $100,000 capital, later to rise to some $300,000. It took almost a year to negotiate the deal with Daniel Pérou, Nicole Alphand and Max Bellest. But finally it was all done, approved by Cardin. Kirsten and Kornblith flew to Paris to sign the contract.

'Cardin would not descend from his ivory tower to sign the contract. We waited in Paris for three or four days for the man to appear. He didn't,' said Kornblith. 'Nicole was mortified, Pérou was embarrassed, Max was furious. And we were waiting.' Finally Kirsten and Kornblith just walked away and decided to enjoy themselves on Lake Como, Italy.

But then Kornblith had a brainwave. The two men dashed back to Paris and Kornblith immediately told Fairchild's Paris bureau chief that he was signing a deal with Cardin to make suits in the US. 'We met over a drink, and I asked if he would be interested in being at the signing with a photographer. That's exactly how it happened. It was forced to the head by Fairchild, because Cardin liked publicity. Under the gaze of Fairchild, Cardin appeared and we signed the agreement.'

Not appearing at scheduled meetings was a permanent fixture in Cardin's business dealings. 'He's famous for standing people up, but usually not the press. He always had great sensitivity to the press,' recalled Kornblith. 'But my people would go to Paris and get stood up by Cardin often. He's just strange.'

Intercontinental Men's Apparel Inc. began its business in November 1967. It started shipping merchandise in the following August, and that year sold $816,655 worth of suits. A year later the figure had nearly quadrupled to over $3 million. 'It was pretty easy, a lot easier than I thought it would be,' said Kornblith. 'But Mildred Custin had pioneered it, to some extent. A lot of merchants had gone through Bonwit Teller, although none of them understood it. These merchants were used to selling in great volume and simply did not understand what a boutique was. But they saw Bonwits getting one hell of a lot of publicity, and, if nothing else, they saw it as a way to attract attention.'

More important, customers cottoned to the New Look for men. Throughout exclusive department stores in America, fashionable men stood in front of mirrors, not believing their own reflection. 'Pierre and André had very small upper arms. Those clothes put on a muscular American or German made the guys who put the clothes on think they were Tarzan. They were putting the clothes on to fuck, to be sexual objects,' said Don Robbie, John Kornblith's designer who interpreted Cardin's suits for the American market. 'Pierre and André were putting the clothes on to be effeminate and tasty and chic. But the suits all went on people with big upper arms, muscular thighs, fat asses. The guy

126

turned around, looked at himself in the mirror, and it wasn't him. He couldn't take a breath, but he was transformed. That's why the clothes were a success.'

Max Bellest's third American licensee was Eagle Shirtmakers Inc. S. Miller Harris, the president of the company, cut a straightforward deal: A 5 per cent royalty, with a minimum guarantee of $15,000. That meant that to break even Eagle Shirtmakers, which was owned by the Hat Corporation of America at the time, had to sell $300,000 worth of shirts. In 1968 it sounded like a lot. It turned out to be a conservative target. But Harris, like Kornblith, was in for a shock. 'Cardin did not conduct himself in business the way I was used to dealing with people,' he said.

In the 1960s shirts were traditional, with plain button-down collars, and retailing for around $8 or $9. Harris wanted something new and designed a fitted shirt that mirrored the silhouette of Cardin's suits. 'We made it a fly-front – so the buttons were hidden. And we had architectural seaming, which meant you could make the shirt fit tighter. The long straight-point collar had construction inside so there was no way someone could press a wrinkle in the collar. Up until that time, every shirt had had either a back or side pleat, or was shirred to give some extra fullness. Our shirt had a perfect straight back – there was no excess material. And instead of having shirt-tails, it was straight across the back. From a manufacturing point of view, it was like making a boat in an airplane factory. It was completely different.' The price, too, was different. Men spent $300 on a suit, but only a few dollars on a shirt. Harris retailed his PC shirts from $18 to $25 and the price mould was forever broken.

The shirts, completely novel, flew off the shelf and surpassed all expectations. The first year in business Harris sold five times his break-even target – $1.5 million worth of shirts. (Some 10 years later Eagle Shirtmaker's PC sales peaked at around $35 million, claimed Harris.) Early on it became obvious the company had to build another factory to meet demand. Harris thought that since the company was investing so much money in the Cardin label, it should pay a sliding-scale commission – as Cardin sales went above $5 million, say, the royalty should drop to 4 per cent and then down to 3 per cent, and so on. Higher volume, lower commission.

'Nicole Alphand and Pierre Cardin and Max Bellest all said they couldn't because all the licensees would want the same deal,' said Harris. But when Intercontinental Men's Apparel went public in November 1970, Harris discovered that the men's suit licensee had long enjoyed a sliding-scale commission. Fuming, he confronted Nicole Alphand. 'She said, "So, we lied. It was a little lie",' he recalled.

Harris flew to Paris to negotiate the new contract with Alphand and Manusardi. Bellest, of course, was in on all the US negotiations. They negotiated hard for two days. Finally they emerged with a two-page agreement, in French and English, that covered seven succinct, crucial points. 'They called Cardin in and they went over all the points with him. He agreed to them and signed it,' said Harris. 'When I returned to the US and he had sent the agreements to write them into the contracts, every single point had been changed in his favour. They had changed the royalty rate. The time frame. Every single term we had agreed to they had changed.' Harris was disgusted. Yet he did what most of Cardin's licensees did. He swallowed his anger and accepted Cardin's method of working. He did so for fourteen years. Why? 'The name was just too important,' he said.

Cardin had not just revolutionized menswear in France but throughout the world. 'I don't think that Pierre Cardin has ever really gotten the amount of credit that he should have as far as what he did for the men's fashion industry in this country,' said Wilkes Bashford, the respected American retailer who was fashion director for the Associated Merchandising Corporation at the time. 'Many names have become big since but the truth of the matter is that Cardin was the pioneer. He was a good five to seven years before anybody else.'

•   •   •   •

Cardin always wanted to be unique, the first to experiment with new ideas. And for years he had expressed a vision: 'If I dress the man why shouldn't I dress everything around the man, his surroundings.' In May 1968 the French Minister of Industry, Olivier Guichard, asked Cardin to join the Council of Industrial Aesthetics. The Council's job was to try and inject interesting design into utilitarian industry. 'Ugliness sells badly,' reasoned Guichard. 'The useful object is not necessarily ugly,' said Cardin. 'Cookers are looking more and more lovely . . .'

The wheels were turning and he began discussing the concept of a total Cardin 'environment' with Fallot. Manusardi was out of favour at the time, but as they were wont to do Fallot and Manusardi discussed the environment concept in their clandestine meetings away from the office. Manusardi knew just the company, and he took Fallot to see an exhibition that included ultra-modern ceramics – not just ceramic vases and flatware but futuristic ceramic office toys with rolling steel balls and clacking magnets – made by an Italian firm called Ceramica Franco Pozzi.

'That's the guy,' said Fallot. 'That's exactly what we want.'

'OK, Daniel, but you discovered it,' said Manusardi. 'If Pierre knows it's me there will be an instant abortion.'

An appointment was set up with Cardin. The Pozzis, two brothers, also brought their attorney along with them. Mario Sala was a smart, straight, thorough lawyer. He already knew Manusardi, who was at the meeting strictly as a powerless interpreter, and now he met Daniel Fallot. 'We talked about Italy, Italy's capabilities, Cardin's concept of the environment, and what he wanted to do,' recalled Sala. Opposite Cardin's office was a store he had just rented. 'He asked if Pozzi could send some things right away to inaugurate the shop. In fifteen days Pozzi changed some colours, made some modifications to the ceramics, and got them to Paris for the store opening.'

'Pierre Cardin by Pozzi' was launched. For the first time a designer had broken out of the narrow milieu of fashion. It was 1968. Of course Cardin hadn't 'designed' the products, he was simply lending his name for a royalty. But the public as a whole didn't know that. Cardin had pushed through the licensing barrier with his ready-to-wear deals some eight years earlier. Now he was opening a new frontier.

The next year he was pushing his new product-line in Milan. 'Designing for the home is fun for me,' he told the *Washington Post*, though he had no more designed the Pozzi ceramics than the Eiffel Tower. 'These are the hors d'oeuvres . . . there are more to come. I will do furniture, lighting and interior design . . . everything that makes up the total environment.' As many journalists discovered, when shy Cardin started talking he was overcome with poetic visions. 'My goal is to offer the absolute best in design at low prices. To do this, I rely on science – new materials, plastics, electronics, mass production. Through my environment idea, I want to make it possible for everyone to live in the future.'

But as often happened when Cardin threw together his ideas, there were blunders that grew from poor planning and organization. Back in Paris, the new 'environment' store opposite 118 Faubourg Saint-Honoré was decorated by exclusive decorators and at its grand opening the press stood elbow-to-elbow. But a few weeks after it had opened the landlord sent Cardin an injunction forbidding him to sell the Pozzi merchandise from the store. Daniel Pérou had not read the lease carefully enough; it stipulated that only textiles could be sold. Understandably Cardin was furious and started screaming at Pérou. 'So now we had to transport all the chinaware back into our cellar,' said Manusardi. Out of the cellar Cardin's sales people peddled flatware stacked away in crates.

Another outcome of the Pozzi meeting was a deal with the Italian attorney, Mario Sala. Manusardi and Sala were having coffee in a bistro across the street from the office; the first Pozzi-Cardin meeting had just broken up. As they were chatting they noticed Daniel Fallot running across the square towards them. 'Maître, maître,' bellowed Fallot, 'Monsieur Cardin wants you for Italy.'

Sala, like Bellest in New York, became Italy's super-agent. No salary, just a 10 per cent commission on all of Pierre Cardin's Italian royalties. When he took charge Italy boasted only a few sub-licensees, mostly from Bril. By the time he left the organization some nine years later he had signed up nearly forty licensees in Italy alone. They included tiles, glassware, womenswear, costume jewellery, bags, shoes, ties, scarves, and sheets.

Around the same time Fallot was sent to Italy to find a store. The licensees that Sala signed up could gather around Cardin's Italian boutique, using it for the promotion of their products. Fallot found and negotiated a beautiful space in the heart of Milan's leather-heavy shopping district. Again Cardin poured a small fortune into the decoration, and the store's inauguration took on the proportions of the Second Coming. The street was closed to traffic. There was a fashion show under the portico of the Galleria. 'There were so many people they couldn't get in, they couldn't get out,' recalled Sala. 'Even the mayor of Milan was blocked. Literally all of Milan's high society was there.'

One person, however, was not. Daniel Fallot, the man who had done all the work, was forbidden to go to the opening. After being a star, with Manusardi the outcast, roles had abruptly switched again. Fallot had done something very small to bring about his fall from grace. He discovered a manufacturer, Sylvain Benillouche, whom he thought should produce Pierre Cardin's womenswear. Benillouche, however, was having cash problems and needed an infusion to take on the licence. But he made such a strong impression that Fallot figured it was well worth Cardin's investment. Cardin signed the deal and loaned Benillouche some tens of thousands of francs. But then Pierre started thinking about what had just happened.

'For the first time in Pierre's life, when he signed a contract he had to pay. He was paying someone to use his name. This was blasphemy. Cardin is a man who wants a royalty on the air you sniff in his office. It was Fallot's undoing,' recalled Manusardi. 'Fallot didn't know he was walking into a minefield and, of course, it exploded.'

Cardin became terribly suspicious of Fallot and immediately turned to the only other person in the office, the once disgraced Manusardi. 'Keep an eye on Fallot,' Cardin whispered to Manusardi. 'You know he is a friend of Benillouche. Be careful.'

Shortly thereafter Fallot was pushed out of the Cardin house. Summoned to Cardin's office, he was told he was no longer working for the house but for the licensees as a Pierre Cardin liaison. From then on Fallot was the French licensees' employee.

Time proved that Fallot's instincts about Benillouche were absolutely correct. A few years later Cardin himself admitted that Benillouche was one of his most loyal, productive and honest licensees. But by then the damage to Fallot was done.

•   •   •   •

On a typical Monday morning an employee carrying a brioche and café crème entered the 118 Faubourg Saint-Honoré entrance and mounted the stairs to his office. It had vanished. Over the weekend Cardin had come in with workmen and without a word to anyone totally rearranged the house. A photographer recalled the particular method Cardin used to move his employees: everything on and in the employees' desks was swept into giant grey rubbish bags and unceremoniously dumped at the new desks.

This didn't happen just once a year but often, repeatedly, without warning. As a result the offices took on a temporary and sterile look. Employees stopped personalizing their offices with photographs of their families, posters of Jean-Paul Belmondo movies, postcards from Marrakech. It was futile.

'I was particularly stable. I only had to change offices seven times in ten years, which was nothing compared to the others,' recalled Manusardi. 'My reluctance towards this sort of thing was one of the reasons why he never accepted me one hundred per cent. I saw him pulling things and transporting things from one floor to another. I just looked at him with my hands in my pockets. I have problems with my back, so I never helped. He was a bit disgusted by this. Everyone else in the office helped.'

Broom-sweeping in the basement was gradually replaced by compulsive furniture moving or office swapping. One person to pitch in with the hauling of furniture was a teenage designer called Jean-Paul Gaultier, later to become the irreverent Enfant Terrible of Paris fashion. Although only at Cardin's briefly, Gaultier has said that Cardin's wacky insistence on regularly moving the furniture was actually a great plus. It was impossible to take anything too seriously.

For the more conventionally minded it made work at 118 Faubourg Saint-Honoré very difficult. In a typical scene, licensing directors waited nervously for Cardin to show up at an appointment with a manufacturer. The agreed time passed – by half an hour, an hour. The chit-chatting with the manufacturer, who had come all the way from Canada or Australia, became strained. Excusing himself, the licensing director started searching for Cardin. On one such occasion an employee found him cleaning out a sock drawer. When reminded of the appointment, Cardin flatly refused to come to the meeting. He would not budge from his task at hand, which was the restacking of socks.

In the late 1960s Cardin went on a boutique binge, opening up shops at a frenetic rate. Cardin stores opened on the Left Bank, on Rue Jacob, and all around the Élysée Palace. The boutique manager had his crosses to bear. Cardin would come in on a Sunday when the shop was shuttered and start rearranging all the clothes by colour. Or if they were already done by colour, then he would switch to rearranging the clothes by size or fabric. Sometimes he didn't complete the job and the poor manager returned to work on Monday to find the shop partly organized by colour, partly by size, partly in a ferocious jumble. 'Monsieur Cardin has whims, fancies – he suddenly gets very enthusiastic over something, but then never finishes it,' said Jean-Paul Demichel, a former boutique employee.

Arnold Linsman was in Paris for one such whirlwind decorating attack. 'I arrived in Paris on a Friday,' recalled Linsman. 'I walked into the boutique on my way upstairs and everything was normal until about 6 o'clock. Then suddenly this whole crew descended on the place. They completely redecorated the boutique. You know this had to cost Pierre a young fortune, but that didn't seem to bother him.'

Cardin's need to rearrange the furniture often struck at the most inopportune moments. S. Miller Harris and his wife, Marie-Louise, were included in an eight-person black-tie dinner one evening. Two cars pulled up at the salon to pick up Cardin. They let him know they were waiting downstairs and then started chatting. They waited. And waited. Finally one of the group went up to see what was taking Cardin so long.

'There he was in his tuxedo and he had decided to move a refrigerator from one end of a hall to another. He didn't say, "Get me five people to move this refrigerator." He just started pulling at it,' said Harris. 'It was compulsive. "I want to move this refrigerator and they'll wait." There were times that I would make an appointment with him in Paris and reconfirm it, and reconfirm it, and reconfirm it, and get there to discover he was moving . . . Sometimes he wasn't even in Paris.'

        •   •   •   •

In 1968, at the age of 46, Cardin went back to Vichy – back to the parc ancien, the casinos and gallerias and sulphur waters; back to the old boutique, Manby, where he had once worked; back in time. But the store had seen better days. The eggshell-white hotels, once so elegant, were now faded and pathetic. The beautiful town of Vichy had never fully recovered from the war, its name for ever linked in infamy with the Pétain government. No renaming of the town streets after American presidents was going to erase the scars of war.

Cardin took over the lease of the trapezoid-shaped building on the parc ancien where he had launched his career nearly thirty years earlier. He asked Blanche Popinat, the ancient Manby directrice who had helped and protected him during the war, to become the directrice of Vichy's first Pierre Cardin boutique. He brought in decorators from Paris and together they refurbished the old store from top to bottom. It was done in 1960s space chic. The walls of the 200-square metre store were covered in green jersey, the track lighting covered in cloth so that an orange light soaked the room. And at the back of the first floor Cardin built a small apartment so that he could sleep, when he wanted to, in the store in which he had been so happy many years before. For the opening, models came down from Paris for a show at the grand casino; close by his side were his women, Blanche Popinat, Juliette Achard and Nicole Alphand, and his Japanese licensing director, Yoshi Takata.

The Vichy staff thought him odd: 'We always saw him wearing black or dark clothes and sometimes with a two- or three-day beard,' recalled Jean-Paul Demichel, a salesman at the boutique. 'Monsieur Cardin flares up very easily,' said Marie-Reine Véron. 'I remember once, someone didn't give him the welcome he was expecting and he left right away. He's very touchy. But when he likes people, he does whatever they want him to do.'

The Vichy boutique did not make economic sense; it made emotional sense. Rightfully and deservedly he was pampering himself with a sentimental gift. And although he never ever talked about it, neither did he forget his days in Saint-Etienne, how his family was made to feel like second-class citizens.

Cardin as a boy swore revenge. As a man he got it. His mother had owned a stud farm in Italy. In the 1960s, his brother said, Cardin secretly bought a stud farm in Alençon, Normandy. It, too, was not an economically motivated purchase. In fact, once purchased he rarely even visited the farm. 'He bought it to be able to say, "I have avenged my mother",' said César Cardin. Cardin had restored the family fortunes tenfold. But revenge is often bitter. 'One day he visited the farm with my three sisters and found the people who were looking after the place sleeping in his own bed,' said César. It was the end of the dream. In a rage, Cardin immediately sold the farm.

THE IMPRESSARIO 9

In 1969 the city of Paris was looking for a tenant for the Théâtre des Ambassadeurs, an elegant pavilion in a little park off the Champs-Élysées, just a five-minute walk from Cardin's offices. The theatre's stone porch and façade looked out on chestnut trees and gravel walks and a tiny little kiosk selling hard citron candies and *Le Figaro*. This was where Marcel Proust once bought madeleines. Through the park elderly women walked schnauzers and poodles, occasionally dressed in tartan suits and matching booties. In the other direction, crew-cut Marines snapped to attention in front of the US embassy, where chauffeured diplomats came and went.

The theatre was linked to Cardin's past. It was here, after Dior's death in 1957, that he had burst on to the scene with his colourful speech at the International Wool Secretariat competition. Fresh from signing his first environment licence with Pozzi in 1969, Cardin ran in a new direction. Daniel Pérou quietly went into negotiation for the Théâtre des Ambassadeurs.

'Cardin called me one morning and told me he had bought me a theatre on the Champs-Élysées for my Christmas present,' Jeanne Moreau told the press. 'But we're not in love any more. That's life.'

Cardin did not want just any theatre. This was the man who imagined moon residents dashing around in velour and vinyl jump suits. He dreamed about city residents strolling nude on moving pavements heated by infra-red units. 'We will all be stark naked,' he said. 'The streets will be climatized, and if they are not, we'll wear something, a belt or a necklace which will climatize our body heat individually.' His theatre had to have that sort of a feel. Its shell, a historical monument, was sacrosanct. But he wanted the interior ripped out for his vision, and he renamed Les Ambassadeurs, Espace Pierre Cardin.

For some inexplicable reason he hired a Belgian company to remodel the theatre. As was his wont, he spewed forth a grab-bag of decorating ideas and then dashed off somewhere else. Trying to make sense of his confusing vision, the contractors went to work. Cardin was working as he did in haute couture: do it, and if it doesn't work rip it out and do it again. And that is what, essentially, happened. One day Cardin came by and told the contractors that what they had done was all wrong, and gave them completely new and unexpected instructions. An architectural volte-face, in effect. The Belgians had had enough of Cardin's method of working. They slammed shut their toolkits, walked out, and demanded payment. Cardin refused to pay them a centime, claiming that they had never followed his instructions. The dispute went to court. Cardin had to pay up.

The theatre was now a mess. A jumble of sheet rock, bricks and cement. Cardin had to hire a new contractor to complete the work, but now the job was running into millions and the 20-year lease for the theatre was devouring cash. Again he had depleted his resources, overexpanded. He decided he had no choice but to borrow from the loathsome banks. He sent Jean Manusardi and his accountant, Huguette Brillouet, to the London & South America and Société Générale. His licensing contracts guaranteed minimum payments over a specified period of time and Manusardi offered these minimum guarantees as collateral. The banks agreed to discount the contracts, but at a price. They wanted their pound of flesh and a curb on Cardin's free-wheeling style.

Never. Cardin would not give in. At this point, however, he began receiving flak. First Georges Bril started sewing panic with the other licensees. 'I don't understand Monsieur Cardin . . . what the devil is he up to? He doesn't realize how much it costs,' he said. And then the French press unsheathed its talons, sniping that this Italian émigré was not quite the person Paris wanted owning the Théâtre des Ambassadeurs. Even Cardin's lawyer started blanching. 'He doesn't know when to stop,' he clucked to Manusardi. 'A theatre! That's another kind of business, you know.'

Once again, Cardin was alone and walking his high-wire act. It always brought out the best in him. The tougher the opposition, the more determined he grew. 'I do not drink, I do not smoke, I do not gamble and I don't take drugs,' he snapped at anyone asking him why he was risking his fortune on a theatre. 'I have no interest in cars, yachts or Riviera properties. I therefore have to find some way to spend my money. I can afford to lose money. All I want is satisfaction.'

It made good press and gave the illusion that he was richer than he actually was. In the meantime, however, Manusardi had concocted with Sylvain Benillouche, the women's licensee who was unwittingly the cause of Fallot's downfall, a way to drum up the cash. It was time for heavy arm-twisting among the licensees. (Manusardi, of course, kept Cardin abreast of his manoeuvring. If it works, fabulous, he told Manusardi. If it fails, I've never heard of you.)

Manusardi ordered all the licensees to Paris. They took their seats in the conference room, cigarettes and gold pens on the table. In a measured tone of voice Manusardi informed the licensees that the theatre was bankrupting the house. To save the house every single licensee had immediately to pay up six months to a year's worth of the minimum guarantees stipulated in their contracts. If they refused, Cardin and the licensees were all going to go down in flames. There were a few moments of silence. And then mayhem. The licensees began yelling across the table, protesting, haranguing. Manusardi began to defend Espace Pierre Cardin. 'Thanks to Espace, our and hence your reputation is going to skyrocket,' he pounded back. 'You can consider yourselves very fortunate in dealing with a man who is not just a fashion creator.'

And then Benillouche, in on Manusardi's ploy from the beginning, moved in. 'Everybody knows about my cash-flow problems . . .' he started coyly. However, he thought the Espace principle sound and he was willing to back Cardin. The other licensees looked daggers at Benillouche but the damage was done. There was no united front, and two hours ten minutes later they had agreed to cough up 3 million francs (about £240,000) in the next two weeks.

Cardin now had the money to complete Espace. He went shopping. In 1969, a young designer was showing his line of furniture at the 'Salon des Artistes Décorateurs' at the Grand Palais. Alain Carré, a thin, sandy-haired young man, practically died with delirium when Cardin stopped at his stall and began buying his futuristic furniture by the cartload. Cardin asked Carré if he could make additional items. Carré went to his drawing-boards and furiously started designing for the great man. 'Of course, when Pierre Cardin bought something, the name Alain Carré was dropped for Pierre Cardin,' said Carré. As with Pozzi, Cardin presented Carré's work as his own. But Carré did not mind. Cardin was so famous, he rationalized, it would undoubtedly aid his career.

Cardin ran up a bill in excess of 50,000 francs, claimed Carré, but never paid. After not hearing a word from him for six months, Carré sent a letter. 'I didn't mention the designs I had done for him without being paid, I just told him I was still at his service,' he recalled. Cardin called him at home. When Carré went by with his portfolio he asked Cardin for a salaried position. Cardin agreed. 'He asked me how much I was making,' said Carré. 'Cardin has never paid his employees well, particularly not the artists. So, I tripled what I was earning and [gave him that figure].' Carré immediately started as Cardin's manager of design.

The theatre was taking shape. At the time, Cardin seemed to have become enamoured of a brilliant young society boy. 'I never met an adolescent with such a deep intelligence of life and people,' he said of François-Marie Banier, an irreverent teenager with curly blond hair, elongated blue eyes, and a face described as that of 'a fallen angel'. (Banier would not talk about Cardin, but he did make it clear they were not lovers. 'People said that [we were lovers] – because Pierre was what he was and I was what I was – but it wasn't that way at all,' he said. He also claimed that he thought up the name for the theatre, Espace Pierre Cardin.)

Women's Wear Daily, writing about Banier, reported that the young man had left his wealthy bourgeois family home for a maid's room at the age of 17, and lived off his drawings. (Banier scoffed at this account.) Before he reached 20 he had published a widely acclaimed novel, *Les Résidences Secondaires*. But more than that he was a brilliant talker – a fresh, witty sparring partner who constantly shocked in the tradition of Jean Cocteau. Talent and good looks often inspire jealousy and Banier received his share. He talked back to everybody in a way that awed Cardin. He had absolutely no reverence for age and position but somehow he managed not to offend. He just made people gulp a few times. In 1970 Banier was working on a novel, *Sunday Afternoon*, which he said was about incest and imposture. 'I write for love and to be loved,' he told *Women's Wear Daily*. 'I met myself at seventeen. This made me really happy. You know . . . I am a narcissist.'

Cardin hired the 20-year-old in 1967 as a press attaché. When Espace opened he sent Banier over to the theatre. 'Pierre gave me confidence,' explained Banier at the time. 'He believed in me and took the risk of protecting me when everybody hated me. I will never forget.' (Banier however, did not stay and left shortly after the appointment.)

Espace finally opened on 1 December 1970, eleven months after Cardin was assigned the lease. The renovation reportedly cost $2 million. He had built an 1,800-square metre cultural emporium. It housed a 550-seat theatre, a bar and a 400-seat restaurant. (Cardin's fashion shows, from then on, took place at Espace.) In the basement was a small cinema with ninety-six of the latest uncomfortable purple seats. The art gallery was awash with plexiglass luminescent sculptures, or hanging UFO-shaped discs known as the 'Hydro-space City of Kosice'. In the spherical conference room with black walls visitors sat in bright orange foam armchairs that looked like polyethylene breasts. Cardin's office and small conference room was furnished with an electric console desk that lit up, a huge spherical speaker system, wavy foam armchairs. The 'multi-functional' room could be, at short notice, turned from the scene of an avant-garde production to an art auction, to a telecommunications conference. From the Pierre Cardin boutique consumers learned about his latest products: adhesive wall surfaces, blankets, watches, inflatable boats, lighters, stereo units. In the hallway of Espace visitors threaded their way through lumpy rubber furniture, foam 'pebbles', plastic bubbles. And, of course, Espace also housed a hideaway for Cardin.

The Espace insignia, the symbol for this new emporium, was tacked onto the side of the building: a vaguely abstract plastic penis penetrating a vaguely abstract plastic vagina. 'Espace Pierre Cardin echoes the contrasts of modern living and anticipates men's hopes for their future,' declared the promotional literature.

Espace became Cardin's obsession. Jean de Rigault, one of the Espace co-ordinators, showed a journalist around the theatre. In one of the interminable foyers some workers were setting up for a publicity shoot. They were unwinding a long, snake-like, stuffed seat-sculpture and rearranging some mauve and orange slabs of foam rubber in a conversation pit. De Rigault stiffened. 'Please! Please don't move those things. Monsieur Cardin has personally arranged them exactly the way he wants them. He won't like it if they are all scattered about.' The publicity team promised to put everything back. Later, lively children were found bouncing foam stones around. De Rigault put an end to that, too. 'You see,' he explained to the journalist, 'this really is like Cardin's home. Everything here has been personally selected by him. It is arranged just the way he likes it.'

Utterly obsessed, Cardin did not simply insist on overseeing the decorating of the theatre, he also wanted to hang every exhibition personally, position every lamp, and, if he could, choreograph every dance and sit in every seat. It was terribly difficult for him to delegate even the smallest decision.

In 1972 the *Los Angeles Times* did the must-do pilgrimage to Espace Cardin. The newspaper's journalist, Cynthia Gremier, was chatting with Madame Janine Alexandre-Debray, the woman Cardin had appointed to run Espace, when he slid into the room. 'Bonjour Janine,' he said softly, waving to her not to interrupt the conversation for him, and then moved over to the windows against which were propped several framed Fernand Léger drawings. All of a sudden the conversation stopped. Cardin had fallen to his knees and was holding up a Léger frame, moaning in distress.

PIERRE CARDIN

'Oh Janine! I'm sorry, but . . . oh no, no. No,' he wailed softly. 'No. No. These bolts! These terrible big brass bolts in the corners. Oh no. That'll make 600 bolts on the wall for this exhibition. No one will see the Légers for the bolts. It's got to be changed. Made very simple. Just plain glass. Janine, tell him,' Cardin pleaded, still on his knees. Before he had finished Janine was on the phone firmly telling someone the bolts had to go.

Cardin became an impresario, a modern-day Diaghilev, a patron of the Arts. Jeanne Moreau, naturally, performed at Espace, electrifying and terrifying the audience in a low-cut sequin dress in Peter Handke's *The Ride Across Lake Constance*. Parisians loved Blues singers. Shirley Bassey belted out boozy love songs, her voice brassy, her fingers outstretched and fluttering. Ella Fitzgerald and Dionne Warwick raised their arms in thanks to the thunderous applause, clutched white roses. A relatively unknown blond actor, Gérard Depardieu, beefy with a face like a construction worker, lumbered across the stage in a production that required him to carry a mummy.

Cardin seemed to have a large appetite for avant-garde productions loaded with nudity. A giant, bald, stark naked Othello flitted across the stage. Bare-chested men with eyes heavily made up crouched in a production of *120 Days of Sodom*. The floor was seething with half-naked couples clutching each other's foreheads when New York's Liquid Theater came to town. Stringy, tanned bodies and poky penises stared from the canvases of Bruno Schmelz. But as soon as Cardin was pigeonholed, he slipped away: the great cellist Mstislav Rostropovich, the operatic soprano Renata Tebaldi and a group of Japanese Buddhist monks with their Sho-Myo ceremony also performed at Espace. 'Somewhere the businessman Cardin figured out that association with Art was the next big rub-off,' said Dryansky. 'But at the same time, I think he sincerely thought this was a good thing for humanity, for the city. It was both.'

Cardin spent a small fortune sponsoring young unknown talents, a fair share of whom went on to become famous. He thrilled at discovering the New. One of his discoveries was Robert Wilson, the acclaimed avant-garde director. In 1971 Wilson was an unknown writer/director of an eight-hour-long play with a cast of 80. Cardin brought Wilson and cast to the Espace, picking up the tab for everything. The 'Prologue', as the first three-hour segment of Wilson's epic was called, started every day at two in the afternoon. The audience was let in, in tiny groups of two or three, to a semi-darkened auditorium and seated atop sponge-rubber cushions. Around the central space four men and one woman lay stark-naked, motionless throughout the three-hour performance. The whole performance was acted/danced in slow motion. People appeared – some naked, some not – lay down on the floor, passed a baton. A girl skipped across the stage; a live caged rabbit made an appearance. The actors passed a plate of raisins and almonds to the audience. Towards the end, the audience was led through a hall, through a labyrinth of naked bodies lying on staircases.

Richard Roud of the *Guardian* didn't particularly like 'Prologue' and noticed that no-one gave the naked bodies any raisins or nuts. 'A joint might help,' was his advice to anyone wanting to see the production. But Roud was in the minority. Most Parisians raved; felt it was a near-religious experience. 'I have never seen anything more beautiful in my life,' wrote Louis Aragon.

Robert Wilson was discovered and went on to be one of the hottest directors of epic avant-garde. 'That established my career. Afterwards I received a lot of offers to work in the theatre,' he recalled. 'If Pierre hadn't done that I wouldn't be doing what I am today.'

Cardin's early love of gymnastics and naked bodies led to his discovery of Pilobolus, muscular Dartmouth-educated American gymnasts bounding across the stage like dancing acrobats. After a successful début at Espace in 1975, Cardin financed Pilobolus with a monthly payment in exchange for Espace-performed new choreographies. 'He was very much like a father figure,' recalled Moses Pendleton of Pilobolus. On one occasion Martha Clarke burst into tears because she had to take her three-year-old child on tour. Cardin quietly delivered flowers to her. 'She'd break down and cry again, and, you know, just dance her heart out. He just seemed to know,' said Pendleton.

Another group that Cardin introduced to the West was the Japanese Ondeko-Za Drummers, a religiously precise group of muscular, monk-like drummers, naked except for tiny loin cloths and headbands. Their bodies were honed from hours of rapid drum beating. On stage they dripped sweat and rained down upon the heads of the audience a tattoo of ferocious drumming. It was breathtaking. Insiders claimed the Ondeko-Za were Cardin's favourite, because he could house them cheaply upstairs in his Espace apartment. Unflappable and ascetic, the group slept on the floor. But it was easy to be snide. The truth was that Cardin was truly generous to these young performers and launched the careers of many of them.

Alain Carré remembered Marlene Dietrich's performance at Espace. Carré was put in charge of making Dietrich comfortable. She was a great star, even at her ripe age. 'She demanded a red curtain, and a dressing-room covered with roses,' he said. 'She acted very much the grande dame, and Cardin was very timid, always bowing to her wishes.'

Andrew Wargo, Max Bellest's associate in New York, remembered Cardin telling him another version of Dietrich's time at Espace. 'When she first met him she was very cold. Sort of, "You are Pierre Cardin, who are you? I was Marlene Dietrich before you were born." He just smiled, turned and said to the manager, "Whatever she wants, do it. Don't bother me. Just do it." It was really expensive changes she was asking for – like red carpets and curtains. And even though she was still cold to him, every night at intermission he had roses handed out to each person in the lobby, so at the end of each performance they could throw roses at her feet. And then they were all gathered and put in her room at the Hôtel de Crillon so after three days you couldn't get into her room.

'He never showed up. He would just go to the top of the theatre's balcony and watch the performance with a few friends. She tried to call and he never took her phone call. She then went to Hermès and sent him a little leather notepad. He never wrote to her. He finished his story by saying, "I may know who Marlene Dietrich is, but now she knows who Pierre Cardin is." ' (If this story is true, it is a tale of sweet revenge.)

But the point was that the licensees were wrong about Espace. Cardin was right. The prestige of being associated with such avant-garde productions, such legendary stars, earned him enviable press. Not all the press was good. 'Cardin can only have a theatre in his image,' charged the French critic Philippe Bouvard. 'That is to say snobbish and anguished.' The food was considered 'devoid of taste'. And, in fact, most of his risky productions failed miserably. But no matter. His name was at the centre of the brouhaha.

It was also expensive. Espace lost money. Some said $200,000 a year, but, like haute couture, it enhanced the cachet of his name. And that was a saleable if intangible commodity that he could parlay into even more licensing deals. 'I finance l'Espace myself, and it should be obvious that operations are on the deficit side,' he told Glenn Loney of *After Dark*. 'The expenses are enormous but I am compensated by the publicity . . . It contributes to the reputation of the label Cardin. What I'm losing on the productions, I'm gaining in publicity.'

To capitalize on Espace, Cardin moved Alain Carré's design office into the theatre. With the futuristic world of Espace as a springboard, Carré and ten designers galvanized the growing family of environment products with their technical and marketing know-how. Their job was to translate some twelve approved designs into usable technical blueprints for modern manufacturers. Cardin rarely had any input into the products that carried his name, although he had final approval. His vague ideas, said Carré, were usually too bizarre to be of use. 'Pierre Cardin couldn't understand a thing that I was doing,' he claimed. It appeared that Cardin could not read a blueprint.

But that didn't stop Cardin from being on the cover of *Time* magazine in 1974. 'Those Designing Europeans' featured the 52-year-old Cardin naked but for a PC towel wrapped around his midriff and some PC socks sagging at his ankles. He is standing in front of a mirror, holding up a PC electric shaver. 'The most successful practitioner of this design proliferation, as well as one of the Continent's most talented designers, is France's Pierre Cardin, that shrewd fantasist who has tacked his name onto just about anything that can be nailed, glued, baked, moulded, bolted, braced, bottled, opened, shut, pushed and pulled.'

With the Espace as a showpiece for Cardin and his environment concept, manufacturers came running. Soon he had Pierre Cardin printed linens, 'Tissus Environment', which retailed in the US for $13 a yard; Cardin's French chocolates were shaped as pyramids, while a Japanese version contained chocolate jigsaw-puzzle pieces. The Javellin sports cars made by American Motors Corporation were sold with PC 'designed' interiors, while the Dutch firm Bruynzeel was peddling Pierre Cardin kitchens. Through the streets of Tokyo pedallers shelled out money for PC's collapsible bicycle. It was an explosion. 'I want to design everything,' he said. 'Swimming pools, pyjamas, shoes, but I haven't time.'

Shortly after Espace opened, Cardin went for a walk to pick up the evening newspaper. He noticed a woman staring at an Espace poster. 'That Cardin. The next thing you know he'll have his name on a Camembert box,' she mumbled. He tapped her on the shoulder. 'Nothing would please me more,' he said.

Cardin was signing licences with both hands. Reported sales of Pierre Cardin products at wholesale reached $22 million in 1970. That figure had more than doubled three years later. By 1973 he was earning $3.7 million in royalties on nearly $50 million in PC turnover.

Cardin's success inspired stinging attacks from his competitors. 'Designing chocolates!' sniffed an anonymous power at Yves Saint Laurent. 'The next thing you know he will be designing cheese.' And at the other end France's leading industrial designer, Roger Tallon, was sharpening his quills: 'Cardin is exploiting his name to death. Those who surround him have created a Cardin myth. To me, it is simply a bag of wind.' In many ways they were right. The grab-bag of products had little to do with Cardin other than carrying his name. But the public did not know that. And they were eager to spend the extra francs, yen, dollars, pounds and cruzeiros for his name. Cardin, too, was never concerned about what his competitors thought. He respected only one person's opinion – his own. 'When I did ready-to-wear twelve years ago,' he responded, 'they thought I was ridiculous. But they all followed. They will follow in design, too.'

And they did.

PIERRE CARDIN

•   •   •   •

When, a decade earlier, Cardin had signed his first, historic ready-to-wear licensing deal, another visionary was busy at work. About the same time historian Daniel J. Boorstin, a Rhodes scholar, was kicking around ideas about American society with his wife. In 1963, in a slim volume called *The Decline of Radicalism*, Boorstin first articulated the notion of what he called 'Consumption Communities'. By the time he expanded his theories in his Pulitzer Prize-winning trilogy, *The Americans*, Boorstin's premise had become widely accepted – that people asserted their identity through the brands they consumed.

According to his theory, in the last 100 years retailing had radically changed. Although the department store was really born in Europe, the most notable example being Bon Marché in Paris, the stores were refined in the US. After the Civil War grand new 'consumer palaces' opened in American cities. They were centrally located, sold huge volume and offered a wide range of merchandise, including dry goods, home furnishings, clothing and household wares. Unlike the elegant but forbidding shops of Europe, the American department store was palatial, public, inviting. The cast-iron fronts, slender columns and show windows allowed the beautiful multi-coloured merchandise to be explored in the sunlight. Sweeping staircases and modern elevators seduced hundreds of thousands of ladies into stores like John Wanamaker in Philadelphia; Field, Leiter & Co. (later Marshall Field & Co.) in Chicago; R.H. Macy's and Lord & Taylor in New York. As Émile Zola observed, the department store 'democ-ratized luxury'. And the chain store began to take hold, offering lower prices that came from economies of scale. By 1912 the Great Atlantic & Pacific Tea Company (A&P) had nearly 500 stores nationwide; during the following three years a new A&P store opened every three days. Even though the chain store was a low-cost supplier of goods, it still offered services such as charge accounts and free delivery.

F.W.Woolworth, meanwhile, had ushered in the era of the 'five and ten-cent store'. The concept was simple. In a world where haggling was a social pastime, brave new entrepreneurs like Woolworth tried to induce consumers to buy an item simply because of the low price, not because they necessarily needed the item. The emphasis was not on the quality or function of the product but on its price. In a small dry-goods store in Watertown, New York, young Woolworth set up a five-cent counter of crochet needles, button-hooks, thimbles, soaps and harmonicas. Everything sold the first day. By 1900 he owned fifty-nine stores with a volume exceeding $5 million.

No longer was there a need for salesmanship. These large stores instituted the lowest possible fixed prices and the products sold themselves. How different from the traditional old-world shop where the best products were only brought out in front of the wealthiest customers, and where prices were dictated by what the customer could pay and what the salesman could push. With the birth of the modern department and chain stores a good deal no longer depended upon bargaining abilities. Even a child could be trusted to acquire the best possible deal. Wrote Boorstin: 'An urban shopper now could stroll through the world of actual goods as casually as a farmer soon could be leafing through the mail order catalogue.'

In 1872 Aaron Montgomery Ward, in his 12 by 14-foot loft, produced a single price sheet that listed a handful of items for sale and explained how to order. By eliminating the middlemen, Ward promised savings of 40 per cent on items like fans, parasols, cutlery, trunks and needles. Ten years later Ward's catalogue was 240 pages long and listed nearly 10,000 products. Richard Warren Sears was another entrepreneur who built a mail-order empire. With promises of 'satisfaction or your money back', Sears, Roebuck and Company reported sales of $53.2 million in the fiscal year ending 30 July 1907, just twenty years after he had begun his business.

Within just one or two generations shopping had gone from a personalized social event to this brave new world where millions of dispersed customers who would never meet bought identical, national-brand products. With the simultaneous developments in mass production – most notably the perfection of ready-to-wear clothes – a subtle but profound change had occurred in US society: uniform products with uniform prices were being distributed nationally.

Enter advertising. Again, advertising did not originate in the US but it was in turn-of-the-century America that the business was reworked and refined in ingenious ways. In the early nineteenth century the Agate rule required that advertisements in the influential East coast papers be printed only in minute type. Robert Bonner, who advertised his own paper, the *New York Ledger*, in other publications, battled against the Agate rule. He created an advertising sensation in 1856 when he took out a full page and repeated his advertisement 600 hundred times. It was called 'iteration copy', the effective and ingenious repeating of a commonplace message, such as 'Don't go home without the *New York Ledger*'.

In 1879 Philadelphia's Wanamaker store placed the first full-page retail newspaper advertisement in the US. 'Goods suitable for the millionaire,' read an R.H. Macy advertisement in 1887, 'at prices in reach of millions.' The advertising war was on. The Sears or Ward mail-order catalogues played their part in early advertising too – the original catalogues of wood engravings were replaced in the early twentieth century by slick linotype and four-colour printing. 'While the salesman persuaded the customer that the item was peculiarly suited to his unique needs, the advertisement persuaded groups of buyers that the item was well suited to the needs of all persons in the group,' wrote Boorstin.

In 1867 Americans spent $50 million on advertising; by 1900 that sum had increased tenfold. By the start of the First World War consumers were asking for national brands of chewing gum, watches, hats, breakfast food, razor blades and pianos. Agencies specializing in giving advertising advice appeared. One such firm, N.W. Ayer of Philadelphia, pioneered the method of building brand loyalty. In January 1899 it launched the National Biscuit Company's 'Uneeda Biscuit' campaign. An airtight package with a distinctive trademark and brandname had the desired result after Ayer pushed the product in newspapers, magazines, street-cars, posters and painted signs. Overnight and all over the country consumers rushed to stores demanding the Uneeda Biscuit.

Advertising created nationally recognized brand-names. The media aggressively defined and reinforced the identity and quality of the product. And also, most importantly, of its purchaser.

The combination of these three factors – mass production, mass distribution and mass advertising – created a phenomenon unique to the twentieth century. Boorstin called it the birth of the 'Consumption Community' – large groups of people owning an identical product with an identical image. Consumption communities, in turn, radically shook up how we viewed ourselves. Traditionally people identified themselves in ethnic, religious or political terms. Example: 'I am a Catholic Democrat of Italian descent.' Or: 'I am a middle-western Lutheran of Norwegian heritage.' And so on. Those identifying labels, of course, remained important; but Boorstin recognized a new form of identity growing out of the new consumer age. Example: 'I am a Cadillac-driving, Johnny Walker Black Label-drinking, Davidoff cigar-smoker.' The products consumed gave identity to the purchaser. Radio, and later the omnipresent television, visualized, articulated and reinforced the product and its community even more so.

All feelings of community, even if superficial, produce positive side effects. A consumption community, wrote Boorstin, 'consists of people who have a feeling of shared well-being, shared risks, common interests and common concerns that come from consuming the same kinds of objects'. The man driving a convertible Volkswagen down a country road, spotting another man driving the same car in the opposite direction, will often wave spontaneously. As members of the convertible Volkswagen community they both have a natural affinity. Consumption communities were democratic, race and colour were unimportant, the only membership condition being the ability to pay for the product. They were simply a family of people willing to 'walk a mile for a Camel'.

It is unlikely that Cardin ever read Boorstin's brilliant thesis. And yet he had arrived at the same conclusion by clawing up from his humble background into the glittering world of couture and notoriety. Indeed, precisely because of his humble origins, Cardin grasped the psychological needs of the lower and middle classes. He understood their aspirations.

At the age of 37, when he ushered in the designer-label era Cardin pioneered one of the most profound changes in modern-day consumption communities. The designer label offered the consumer a unique new form of identity. 'Designer labels have the aura of celebrity that distinguish them from other labels, and the celebrity value overshadows the functional value of the product,' explained Boorstin. 'But celebrity value is also a function. It gives psychological and emotional income to the purchaser.' In other words, when the consumer bought a Pierre Cardin product a bit of his notoriety rubbed off on the consumer. The buyer, perhaps mired in a mundane suburban life, was suddenly elevated into a more glamorous world: he was a privileged member of an international group, all of whom, of course, had exceptionally good taste and shared Cardin's fame.

As his fashion flame fizzled, Cardin spent his considerable energy wringing his designer label for all it was worth. The timing was perfect, for in the quaalude-and-disco 1970s the designer label became the most coveted of purchases. He was always a step or two ahead of his competitors, alone fully grasping the voracious worldwide appetite for signed merchandise.

Cardin flew into New York. Bellest's associate, Andrew Wargo, picked him up in a limousine and they rolled down Seventh Avenue potholes to the showroom of the women's knitwear licensee, Belldoch. A pile of simple, Italian-manufactured quality T-shirts with the PC logo were part of the products the company president, Gene Hochfelder, was showing. Cardin asked how much he charged for the T-shirt. Hochfelder told him the price, which was in the neighbourhood of $15 wholesale, $30 retail. 'Uh-huh,' grunted Cardin.

On he went to other products. The tour was drawing to a close, but again he asked the price of the T-shirts. He thanked Hochfelder for the tour and Wargo opened the door of the limousine for Cardin to climb in the back. The black car pulled into the traffic of knotted New York cabbies. Cardin sat pensive.

'You know, I have a boutique in Milan and we buy from the same manufacturer. I know what he pays,' said Cardin in quiet awe. He turned to Wargo. 'See, Andrew, see how much people have the need to dream.'

Explained Boorstin: 'It is a mistake to assume that the main value from a product is its actual physical functioning value. We buy things for all sorts of reasons. When I buy a Pierre Cardin pan I'm counting on the fact that you're going to be impressed I bought it. Call it the imperial power of prestige.

PIERRE CARDIN

Economists have long said that psychological satisfaction has to be counted into a product's market value. The appeal of a designer product is much vaguer, but no less valid. That's not bad, getting more satisfaction.'

•   •   •   •

Already by 1975 the press was gasping at his reach. 'It is now theoretically possible for a man to wake between Cardin sheets, walk on a Cardin carpet to his Cardin-designed kitchen and make coffee in a Cardin coffee pot,' wrote the *Los Angeles Times*. 'He could then light up with a Cardin lighter, shower with Cardin soap, blot with a Cardin towel. Moving along, the hypothetical man could don his Cardin shoes, underwear, shirt and tie, kiss his Cardin-clad wife and children goodbye and drive in his Swiss-made $30,000 Cardin-styled auto to an office furnished by you-know-who.'

'He was still in control and he didn't have that many rivals,' said Kurt Barnard, a marketing consultant. 'He was pretty much on top of the heap which makes it easy. His supremacy was not questioned. His name was a household word. His licensees stood in line at his door because of his reputation, his marketing clout, and his seeming infallibility at the time. His name was magic.'

As the 1970s progressed the quality of the products began to become uneven. Just about any manufacturer offering enough money could buy the rights to Cardin's name. He started selling a $2.99 bottle of Bordeaux wine (red, white and rosé). It was so bad the corks used to disintegrate, said his former press officer. In 1977 came a line of furniture made by Dillingham manufacturing Co., Laurel Lamps manufacturing Co., and Scandinavian Folklore Carpets of Denmark for Ege Rya Inc. The complete line – from the 'Escargot' lamp in Swedish brass and satin glass for $75, to a Monte Carlo sectional sofa at $2,187 – was launched in the US at B. Altman & Co. The *pièce de résistance* was a wildly uncomfortable C-shaped signature chair in black wool and chromed side panels for $1,040.

To back up his commercial furniture line, in Paris and New York Cardin opened prototype furniture stores called 'Evolution', providing the same shocking publicity effects in furniture as his haute couture did in fashion. In these stores customers could buy Pierre Cardin's 'utilitarian sculpture', say, a $4,000 refrigerator which did everything but light the dinner candles, or a clamshell-shaped leather couch with a canopy encrusted with thirty-six giant tortoise shells for $130,000.

Planes and cars followed. In 1978 a vice-president of Atlantic Aviation, Roger Ritchie, wanted to 'sprinkle a little stardust' on an executive jet called the Westward I. He turned to the designer who, at the time, had the strongest presence in the male world. Cardin was paid a $25,000 fee for his name and design input. (It was painted with the same black-on-white stripes that covered his line of pots and pans.) Cars were another thing. He had designed his prototype Simca a few years earlier. Then came the 4-cylinder 'Shark', another prototype by Switzerland's Sbarro, which boasted a maximum speed of 210 km/h. But now a car for the masses was needed.

Andrew Wargo in New York, assigned to develop the 'environment' line there, found a little Florida-based marketing company which put together a Pierre Cardin car kit. The company was called Standard Motors, and it put together a package by which dealerships could spruce up their brand-new Cadillac with a $2,500 kit which included an air cushion, co-ordinated fur carpeting, a set of matched luggage, a highway emergency kit, one year's free membership in the Pierre Cardin Motor Club, and the Cardin signature in 24-carat gold plate.

All was going well until the press conference, when someone explained that Standard Motors was hardly General Motors. And then Cardin got cold feet. He simply stood up and told them he had nothing to do with the deal. Standard Motors executives were apoplectic. Cardin found another exit. A new car company, headed by a New York businessman called Mel Reaume, bought out Standard Motors' licence for Cardin and started negotiating another car deal. This arrangement was different. Cadillacs were bought and customized at a special garage. 'Evolution I' was an 18-foot long-nosed PC Eldorado Cadillac, with Waterford crystal and pewter serving unit. The floor was graced with 100 per cent English virgin wool carpets, advertised as 'Mouton', while in the back a Sony-Betamax system was ready for use. The steering wheel was mahogany and the interior was trimmed with 22-carat gold plate. It was a V-8 car that was available in colours ranging from Pinot-Noir (Black Cherry) to Warm Cognac (Golden Brown), all hand-applied and rubber-lacquered in thirty coats of paint. The 'Evolution I' retailed for $52,000. Enough Americans seemed interested at first. But then the company went under during the recession of the late 1970s.

Cardin couldn't stop. He had to keep pushing, pushing. Next came 'prototypes for living'. There was a Pierre Cardin camper to be dragged off the road on holidays, or ceramic igloos for hot climates. 'The house will be entirely covered with mosaic and faience, inside and out – it's so easy to sponge down and keep clean,' Cardin rhapsodized to *Connoisseur* magazine. 'Each room will be different, decorated with designs in relief, sculptures coming right out of the wall.'

And then came a flood of knick-knacks. Skis, dolls, alarm clocks, vinyl luggage. Umbrellas covered in little PC's were so tacky that even the US press attaché, Arnold Linsman, was too embarrassed to give them to the press. Then came Pierre Cardin Electronique. It sold hair-dryers that wholesaled for $5.75, portable clip-on reading lamps for $2.95, solar calculators for $5.47. 'Cardin doesn't have any class, but he has great ideas,' said Sala.

•   •   •   •

'My name is more important than myself,' Cardin once said to Alain Carré. It was a sad and shocking admission. 'I think he is a man who is less happy with himself than he is with the accomplishments of his work,' said his friend Robert Green. 'Don't you get the feeling all workaholics, and he is that, are people who really don't want to stop and face themselves? What they see is not so amusing or interesting or there exists a level of unhappiness they don't want to face. I felt this of Pierre even twenty-five years ago. There was this enormous drive, with so little time and so much to do. He was always racing against time and the goals and responsibilities he placed upon himself.'

He was changing. As his empire grew, so did his sense of self. Already back in the late 1950s Cardin had started talking about himself in the third person. By the 1970s his identification with his persona had become, to some, alarming. Cardin was becoming a label.

Moses Pendleton recalled watching Cardin circulate at a cocktail party. 'I noticed he would not say how he was, but he'd say how his name was,' said Pendleton. 'We'd hear him say, "My name is big in Buenos Aires, but not so big in Caracas." He'd tell you where his name was and where it was going, but not where he was going. And it was as if . . . when he came into a place it would be the man, who maybe no-one really knew, and the name, which he would walk along and introduce to you.'

Everyone, to some degree or other, defines himself as the sum total of family, reputation, work, house, car, and so on. But sometimes identification with the external elements of life becomes excessive, and the man is swallowed by the public image. 'We have sensed that when the rich man winced at the loss of a few dollars or the businessman agonized over a trivial reverse, it was not the loss of the money that mattered but the loss of a certain amount of Self,' wrote economist Robert L. Heilbroner in his book, *The Quest for Wealth*.

That was Cardin. His employees softened towards him when they noticed that the man seemed to get lost somewhere in the Pierre Cardin label. 'I recall one evening two or three days before Christmas,' said Sala. 'I was having dinner with friends, around 10 at night, and we looked out of the window. It was very cold and we saw Cardin walking with his hands in his pockets, walking by alone. He was walking down the street, kind of abandoned by everybody a couple of nights before Christmas, blown around by the wind. At such times he would stop all night in the store and start moving everything around, all the pants, just changing everything around the store.'

The orphan-like loneliness that emanated from Cardin appeared to make him run. 'The only rendezvous he probably has missed was love,' wrote magazine writer Edgar Schneider. 'And that possibly explains the rest.' But Cardin scorned sympathy. 'Family life does not interest me,' he said. 'But I have no emptiness in my life. I have my business affairs, my trips.' Cardin was trapped between two worlds: a celebrity, which he adored being, and a simple man, which he also was. Between the two he raged, between arrogance and humility.

Cardin was often being honoured by various groups. He won three Golden Thimbles, the Oscars of Paris's fashion world; was made Chevalier de la Légion d'Honneur. When he travelled he was treated like royalty or a head of state. Jean Manusardi recalled a time when Cardin had just come back from an overseas trip. 'It's ridiculous, Manusardi,' he said. 'I've done some things, to be sure. There are reasons for me to be well known. But after all, when I hear people say . . . honestly . . . that I am France. No, that's really too much.'

That humility, however, was offset by equal amounts of egomania. There was the famous, often repeated story of the time when Cardin's accountant, Genevieve, nervously shadowed him as he stalked the halls of his office in a foul mood. She was trying to get his signature on a cheque for one of his agents. Cardin simply did not feel like signing it.

'But Mr Cardin, this is for our trademark . . . They have been waiting for a long time . . .'

'Trademarks! This is just like lawyers or doctors or notaries . . . Listen, Genevieve, if you open a telephone directory, you'll find pages full of lawyers. There are hundreds, thousands of them. Whereas Pierre Cardin . . . Do you know how many Pierre Cardins there are? Hey! Do you know how many there are? Well, I'm going to tell you how many there are. There is one.' He pointed his finger at his heart. 'And it's me.' (Other employees heard a similar speech as well, although it was often banks and bankers that prompted the tirade.)

S. Miller Harris, the extremely successful shirtmaker, also noticed the two faces of Cardin. The two men were alone, going over the forthcoming shirt line. Cardin was overwhelmed with a desire to help Harris. He just ran around and around the atelier collecting fabrics, dashing back to Harris to show a cuff idea. 'What do you think of this?' Cardin asked, almost thumping his tail. On another occasion he drove Harris and his wife to dinner near Notre Dame. It was his favourite restaurant, Le Voltaire. He hadn't made reservations and while they sat in the car he dashed out in the pouring rain to ask the waiters if there was a table for three.

'He's very unpretentious, almost humble, one on one,' explained Harris. 'But in front of a crowd he makes an ass of himself.' ('I am the greatest,' Cardin told *Women's Wear Daily* in 1970. 'I have become a public phenomenon, like Charlie Chaplin or Brigitte Bardot,' he told *Newsweek* in 1972.)

'Cardin's charm was that he would drive this 7- or 8-year-old Peugeot by himself. He didn't like chauffeurs,' said Wargo. 'I think it's because he likes to keep things simple in his life. He always has to play Pierre Cardin. There must be a point in his life where he is just himself. Otherwise he'd go cuckoo.'

The place where he hid from the demands of his label was his town house. After the opening of Espace in 1970 Cardin moved into a new home. He bought, reputedly for $1 million, 18 Rue de l'Élysée, next to the palace and two minutes from the office. It was a pockmarked, spooky house with black cast-iron columns and a black door. Tall, skinny, eighteenth-century windows had little iron lattice-work balconies. The curious were kept at bay by old-fashioned, cheap-looking curtains. (He kept his Anatole France apartment, but from then on used it rarely.)

It was the simple Italian life of Saint-Etienne that he recreated at 18 Rue de l'Élysée. There he lived in almost complete solitude, alone with his sister Janine, twenty years his senior. 'She is his surrogate mother,' said his cousin, Tino Cardin. There was no femme de ménage, no cook, no secretary. Janine was his housekeeper, ironing his shirts, straightening the house, occasionally running a duster over the hodge-podge of furniture; (today, nearly 90, she still runs the house). The two rattled through the house, amongst the plastic bric-à-brac and Boulle furniture. Janine cooked the simple steak and salad he ate almost every night. She was, by all accounts, refreshingly uncomplicated and straight. She helped calm her hyperactive brother.

Cardin's apartment in the house was often a mess. In one part he had modernistic furniture, not terribly expensive-looking; in other corners, ornate and beautiful antiques, the gold and black of Boulle furniture. 'It was very dark, completely messed,' recalled Kornblith of a rare occasion when he was invited into the house. It appeared as if a year's worth of unopened mail was sitting there, 'He could have had contracts from a licensee in Bangladesh and he would never have known it.' Others noticed that framed drawings had slipped in their mounts. And for years the house never seemed completely furnished. 'His town house was typical of Cardin,' recalled Dryansky. 'He never finished anything, nothing was ever done to perfection – not even his couture. It's part of his complexity.'

In the summer he woke at 5 a.m. He made his own bed. If his sister was at her own house in Avignon he ground his own coffee, rinsed his cup. 'Within a few minutes, he has repaired to the ground-floor study lined with antique bookcases and seated himself behind a massive desk. There, like an old-fashioned notaire, he pores over the leather-bound ledgers that contain the accounts of his far-flung empire, checking them against the previous day's fluctuations in the dollar, yen, mark,' wrote William H. Meyers for the *New York Times Magazine.*

Cardin usually worked at home till about 10 in the morning. If it was a day to move furniture he put on a tweed jacket and dreary white shirt. Then he was off to his office a few minutes away, where he ran through his hectic day, jumping from sewing buttons to producing a play to meeting a journalist to visiting a boutique to signing contracts to charming licensees to threatening an employee. He ran through his day but was never where he was supposed to be. Unexpectedly he would materialize and quiz an employee as to what he or she was doing; rarely did he give them instructions. His day might end at 7 or 8 or 9 p.m., but Cardin, ever restless, always found something else to do. He often called up an employee and insisted they cancel their plans and have dinner with him, or else he dashed over to Espace to catch a show. He never personally threw parties any more. Nicole Alphand or André Oliver did. On occasion they forced him to go, but he always seemed uncomfortable, his mind elsewhere, and wanted to leave as soon as he could. 'I am as ambitious as I ever was, but I am not the same,' he said in a rare moment of reflection. 'Now I want to be alone more. When I was young I wanted to learn as much as I could and that meant meeting a great deal of people. Now I just try to keep my private life very private. It can be done.' 'Pierre is finally very lonely,' said Kim Moltzer. 'He could be surrounded by people, being very charming, but he is essentially alone.'

To unwind before bed he drank Badoit or a beer and read the evening paper, *France-Soir.* If his stomach was upset he drank a Fernet Branca and then drifted into a brief sleep in his wool-jersey pyjamas. 'He only needs a few hours sleep,' said Sala. 'Even when he went to bed very late at night, the next morning he was absolutely fresh.'

Cardin did not use his fortune to prop himself up in a Louis XIV life-style. Quite the opposite: it took so little to entertain him. He was often picked up at his house by a workman in a van. 'I like bumping around in a big vehicle,' he once confessed. But sometimes the outside world invaded his Rue de l'Élysée mansion. Cardin was absolutely terrible about appearing at prearranged meetings. He rebelled. 'He is a preoccupied man, who has a sense of his own omnipotence,' said his friend Robert L. Green. 'People who have that sense don't conform to the usual values. They keep people waiting for hours or cancel appointments at the last moment. There is a selfishness. But I think it's part and parcel with the intensity of the way he works and the enormity of his empire.'

Alain Carré rang the doorbell at 18 Rue de l'Élysée early one morning. He had not been working at the house long, and he was there to pick Cardin up for a very important meeting in the south of France at a licensee's factory. The meeting had been in preparation for months. After ringing the doorbell Carré was let into the house. He waited. Finally, Cardin appeared at the top of the staircase. He was in his pyjamas. 'I'm not coming,' he shrieked from the landing. 'I won't come.' The 27-year-old Carré, who looked much younger, got on the train by himself. He was met at the other end by the company's chairman and some ten managers. Carré stammered out some excuse to the company officials that Cardin was ill. They never said anything, but courteously took Carré on a tour of the factory and discussed the details of the contract with him. 'Cardin always played tricks like that,' recalled Carré. 'It was his greatest failing. Pierre is really very self-destructive. He's an hysteric.'

Said Cardin to a British journalist: 'I never analyse myself.'

THE SELF PROMOTER

'You have to understand one thing, and that is the most important thing,' explained Daniel Fallot, leaning urgently over the coffee table. 'There are around Pierre Cardin a number of people who have helped develop his name. But as far as public relations was concerned, the most important person in the whole house was Pierre Cardin himself. He taught himself how to talk to journalists.'

Celebrityhood was the magic behind the successful designer label. And celebrityhood, of course, was a product of the media. Cardin realized early on that if he could garner enough publicity, manufacturers willing to pay for his name would come fluttering to him like moths to a flame. He told *Women's Wear Daily* in 1979 that the only thing he was truly interested in was the press. 'It transmits the image of one's label,' he said. 'I have always given a great importance to the media. I make four or five trips a year around the world just to do radio, television and interviews. I love it passionately.'

'Cardin wants all the notoriety and publicity that he can get,' said Arnold Linsman, the American-based publicity officer during the 1970s. 'He's like one of those people who says I don't care what they say as long as they correctly spell my name . . . Cardin, as a public relations performer, is sensational.'

PIERRE CARDIN

In an effort to combat runaway inflation in the late 1970s, the French government announced several draconian price freezes. Many retailers were caught circumventing the order, Cardin's stores among them. But unlike his couturier colleagues who quietly paid the fines, Cardin turned the embarrassment to his advantage. He refused the services of his lawyer and cancelled an 'extremely important' lunch to appear in person before the judge of the 11th Correctional Chamber. The press followed. 'Morally, I am innocent,' he told the judge. The court was unimpressed and fined him the equivalent of $10,000. It was of no consequence because he walked away with more than $10,000 worth of publicity. 'He's an actor,' snorted Max Bellest, 'a fantastic actor.'

And yet one could never simply dismiss Cardin as a shameless self-promoter, for his actions were always grounded in sincerity. Shrewd journalists backed away from hucksters; he was no huckster. No, a good deal of Cardin's outrage in the 11th Correctional Chamber was authentic. 'To understand all this and to come up with an impression of Cardin as a cynical, calculating businessman would be a mistake,' wrote G. Y. Dryansky in *Women's Wear Daily* in 1973. 'No one who has known Pierre Cardin will tell you that he is a phony.'

His media sense, like all his talents, was intuitive. 'He has an ability to read people's minds,' said Carré. 'Cardin could guess among 400 people who was the one really important journalist. For her he would do an incredible show, receiving her like a princess. One day I was with him in Milan. When we arrived at his boutique we saw an old man, obviously not satisfied, coming out of the shop. Cardin asked him what was wrong and the man immediately recognized Cardin. This old man – slovenly, fat, impossible to dress – told Cardin that he couldn't find anything in the boutique. Cardin made him come in, and they both went downstairs and stayed for an hour. Cardin changed everything around, and the man, delighted, left with ten suits. Cardin had guessed the man was a millionaire. He was that way with journalists, too.'

Robert L. Green, the fashion director for *Playboy*, recalled Cardin at work. 'Cardin was the great courtesan as far as the press was concerned. He made each editor feel that he or she was the most important person in the world. And the approach would be: "Oh, I need your advice, I need your help, I want to hear what you have to say. I admire and respect you so much." It's hard for people not to respond to that. And because he's a man of considerable intelligence it was not just obsequiousness or a bore. No, he was very skilled at doing that. He's very charming. He has an elf-like quality.' And he pampered them. 'You'd arrive in Paris and there'd be wonderful flowers, and a box of extraordinary cheeses and maybe a little caviare. And because he knew that I had a sweet tooth, there was always some absolutely delicious candy in the hotel room,' said Green. 'Or if he discovered that you had a room, he might up it to a suite with a word to the management.'

In 1971 Jean Manusardi pulled off a modest coup in Yugoslavia. He convinced the communist authorities that the nation's millions of Western tourists would snap up the competitively priced Yugoslavian-made Cardin products, earning the nation sorely-needed hard currency. Cardin was delighted, because it was another first for a Parisian fashion designer. In three years the house of Cardin signed ten Yugoslavian licensing agreements, including small leather goods, men's shirts, trousers, jackets, sweaters, scarves, sheets and purses. All he needed was the magic push of the press. So he invited some ten Yugoslav journalists to his house for lunch. 'They went absolutely mad,' recalled Manusardi. 'Can't you imagine them going back to their towns in Yugoslavia, telling everyone they had lunch with Pierre Cardin in his private house?'

Fashion designers, of course, were tailor-made for celebrityhood because four times a year some 1000 journalists and photographers descended on Paris to review their collections. But most fashion designers were rather dull. Either they were painfully shy, or else they could only talk about work, endlessly droning on about mounting sleeves or some superficial philosophy about beauty. Not Cardin. 'One can like Cardin or not,' he told *Newsweek* in 1972, 'but I am always interesting.'

That he was. He started his interviews outrageously and ended them outrageously. 'Pierre Cardin is the most accomplished designer in the world,' he often said, jumping out of his seat a few dozen times, zigzagging across the room as the astounded writer took notes. Most journalists could not believe what they saw, what they heard. Who was this guy, his frayed suit two sizes too big, talking about himself in the third person? 'I have been brilliantly successful,' he continued in his nasal, whining voice. And then came the Cardinisms: 'The chair of the future may look exactly like a rock,' or 'I have thought of all the women from violence to purity,' or 'Why am I bad if I sell a frying pan?' Sometimes he even produced very lovely, very poetic comments, like 'good taste should walk in the streets, on the bodies of anonymous women'. His social visions – 'fashion should serve the masses' – were rich and broad and deep. Said Green: 'You were dealing with a person who had a great sociological sense and psychological sense rather than just design sense.'

The outrageous statements that annoyed associates were actually brilliant public relations. His outlandish comments gave the journalist a terrific springboard for an article. He knew what journalists wanted and he delivered into their hands sensational headlines, much as he gave the photographer a cover photo when he sprinkled throughout his collections preposterous bat-wing and hula-hoop outfits. It did not matter if the article was heavy with sarcasm. 'His monologues were unbelievable. They completely lacked a grounding in reality,' recalled Dryansky. 'His claims about himself were just so funny, you couldn't believe he was getting away with it. It was an absurdity.'

There were times when his media monologues backfired. In the late 1960s there was a brief rage for wearing white turtle-necks with tuxedos. Just after he signed a new tie contract with a French manufacturer, Cardin announced to the world's press that there was no future in ties. Ties were dead. 'What is a tie? It is only two strings hanging,' he said. His French tie licensee went berserk and the house executives had quite a time trying to clean up the mess.

Cardin did not mind playing with the facts. A favourite pastime was to rewrite history, naturally glorifying his own role. 'In fact, I was Dior's first employee,' Cardin confidently told London's *Evening News* in 1978. 'It was 1946 when we opened. Monsieur Dior, me and a secretary.' Cardin, in truth, was a fairly minor player. There were many other more important employees – Rouët, Carré, Luling – who were behind the opening. 'He has a lot of imagination,' said Rouët.

In other interviews Cardin and his press officers repeatedly claimed that the Chambre Syndicale threw him out of its ranks when he launched ready-to-wear. 'He was the first noted designer to show ready-to-wear . . . a revolutionary move that got him expelled from the Chambre Syndicale de la Couture Parisienne,' wrote Hébé Dorsey in the *International Herald Tribune* in 1977. That story was so often repeated that it became part of the Cardin mythology, and no journalist thought to question its accuracy. As we have seen, the facts were somewhat different. According to Denise Dubois, the Chambre Syndicale's files show that Cardin's departure was many years after his launch of ready-to-wear. His first women's licence was in 1959; in 1966 he chose to resign so that he could release photographs to the press in violation of the Chambre's rules. He rejoined again in 1974. But his version of being thrown out is, of course, much more dramatic. It makes better copy.

Another favourite exaggeration was that of his role in *La Belle et la Bête*. 'Immediately I arrived in Paris I'd met influential people in all spheres of the arts,' he informed the *Sunday Express*. 'I designed costumes for Jean Cocteau and Christian Bérard . . .' Many articles about Cardin state he single-handedly designed and made the costumes of *La Belle et la Bête*, when in fact he was a lowly sewer at the house of Paquin.

Some fashion journalists were in collusion with Cardin, collaborating in his myth-making. 'Fashion journalism has its own ground rules and its own journalistic standards. There's a general "gift karma",' said Anne Bogart, a respected free-lance journalist who worked many years for *Women's Wear Daily*.

'It's corrupt at the centre,' explained a press director at a leading haute-couture house who asked to remain anonymous.

At the lowest level, couturiers would lend garments to the poorly-paid fashion press for special functions. Reporters on salaries of $18,000, after all, could not afford the gowns needed for the parties and galas they covered. The next level of 'gift karma' was also fairly innocuous: journalists were showered with small gifts – such as flowers – each time they wrote a favourable article about a couture house.

The next stage, however, was not so innocent. The successful haute-couture houses were rumoured to have graft budgets running into hundreds of thousands of dollars. It worked like this: journalists were discreetly asked to come by and pick up any suit or purse they wanted, sometimes worth as much as $2,000. 'You're never offered a gift for a particular story, and it's up to you to pick up your graft,' said Bogart, who has turned down several such offers. 'But I've seen fashion journalists in fairly influential positions accept expensive gifts. For example, I saw one journalist accept a suit, and when I discussed it with her, she was unconvinced that accepting such gifts could influence or prejudice further dealings with that house.' (Obviously, there are many outstanding fashion journalists who never fell for the bait.)

Sometimes a journalist landed Cardin in trouble. In 1966 he made a beautiful dress, completely embroidered with the colours of the rainbow. The dress was ordered by Claude Pompidou for a gala at the Paris Opéra on 19 November. Jean-Guy Vermont, who made the embroidery, claimed that a well-known French journalist also fell in love with the gown and begged Cardin to be given it. At first he refused, but she pouted and stamped her feet and batted her eyelids until he relented. He made her promise, however, that she would not wear it to the Opéra gala, as Madame Pompidou would be wearing it. She promised. But the journalist could not resist, said Vermont, and both women wore the identical dresses to the gala.

So, when Cardin told these 'reporters' a story, they often printed it, whether it was true or not. Compromised and not overly concerned about being professional, they never checked to see if his claims were true. 'Manipulating the press is part of Cardin's forte,' said Sala. 'He's very astute, shrewd. He could always claim something was not true afterwards.'

That was how he pulled off some spectacular media hypes. In the late 1960s a thermoformed synthetic fabric was invented by a lab technician. Those who saw it said it was amazing: the laboratory seethed with hissing steam, and then out popped a brightly rippled dress, injection-moulded over a wooden dummy. It had its drawbacks: dresses could only be made in the size of the wooden dummy. Cardin, however, seized on it with all his passion for the New and pirated the fabric as 'Cardine'. A few dresses were made, some mannequins peeled on the synthetic garments, and a press conference was held. The girls stood out on the street, looking like walking orange egg-cartons, and around them dozens of photographers crouched and snapped cameras.

Executives at the house recalled that 'Cardine' was touted as spot- and iron-free; it was going to revolutionize the garment industry. The press coverage was so overwhelming that Maison Cardin received substantial orders for the revolutionary fabric, and Paris's department store, Galeries Lafayette, immediately offered 50 square metres of floor space to display the New Age material. The house measured its 'Cardine' coverage by the ton, and yet once it had been received the fabric was never used. Cardin dropped 'Cardine' as quickly as he had seized it.

In 1971 came the 'contract of the century'. Everyone wrote about it. 'His newest venture takes the breath away,' gushed the respected journalist, Serena Sinclair. 'He makes clothes in India, of local materials designed by himself, and then has them shipped to the USSR. This makes him yet once more unique, for no other couturier has succeeded in selling to this vast untouched hungry market. The twenty dresses, all in printed Indian cotton, will sell in Russia in the summer of 1973, say Cardin's associates. Although the deal was worked out by the Indian and Russian governments, using the Handwork Export Company of India, from which Cardin had already bought many fabrics in the past, he had to go to Moscow in late 1971 to finalize the details himself.' *Women's Wear Daily* reported a similar story. So did *Time* and *Newsweek*. As he often did, Cardin announced the deal after only the vaguest of talks. The India–USSR–Cardin love triangle never got past some initial discussions before bogging down in realities. No matter. The house gained column inches by the mile.

Cardin's Simca car deal was a different farce altogether. The car design deal was to be a headline grabber, the first time a Parisian designer had done such a thing. Even though he had little interest in cars, he was attracted by a generous fee and a free Chrysler. 'The night before the presentation I saw Pierre in his courtyard, sitting in the back seat of the car,' said an executive. 'With a pair of scissors and a hammer he was "modifying" the car.'

Such details could be overlooked. Cardin remained the favourite subject of many journalists; he was always good for a good quote. In April 1979 the legendary fashion editor of the *International Herald Tribune*, Hébé Dorsey, was at Le Sept for a *Vogue*-sponsored dinner closing a fashion season. The rooms were stuffed with women mad about dresses, men mad about each other. It was a fashion orgasm of bare shoulders, leather and gold chains, lace, sequins, lamé. Designer Pierre Balmain was in a black Zorro cape, while Guy Laroche sat in a satin blouson. Pierre Cardin was seated at the hostess's table.

In marched Karl Lagerfeld, fanning himself with large black feathers. His pony-tail was tied with a bow, his mouth, claimed Dorsey, touched up with lip gloss. In tow was his dear friend Anna Piaggi. Piaggi, who worked for Italian *Vogue*, was famous for her get-ups. That night she looked like a giant chandelier in storage – her head was wrapped in white gauze and she wore a lace crinoline La Scala dress so big that Neimann Marcus's president, Philip Miller, had to move to make room for her skirts. Cardin flipped out. 'A scandal, a disgrace, a shame to Paris fashions,' he was mumbling to anyone who would listen. 'Madwoman of Chaillot. I'm finishing my dessert then out, can't take it anymore . . .' (This from the man who spearheaded hula-hoops as high fashion.) But Lagerfeld was a close friend of the hostess and he sat himself and Piaggi down at the head table where Cardin was sitting. Just when everyone thought the ruckus was over, Cardin struck.

'Madame, you are a clown,' he said to Piaggi, seated across the table. Guests gasped. Forks froze in mid-air. Lagerfeld stopped fanning himself and started looking right, then left.

'And you are a monkey.'

Lagerfeld choked in his Hilditch & Key collar. 'No, is that true, monsieur?' said Lagerfeld, ready to drop his bear-like physique on Cardin. Lagerfeld's neighbour restrained him. Piaggi, very ladylike, never said a word. After the theatrics had subsided Lagerfeld pushed his plate back. 'He cut my appetite.'

Dorsey, a very good writer, dipped her sardonic quill to full effect the next day in the *International Herald Tribune*. Cardin, once again, had provided her with spectacular copy.

•   •   •   •

'The Cardin organization was loose, not terribly professional, disorganized,' said Stanley C. Gillette, a former chairman of Ship 'n Shore Inc., a US licensee. 'No, it was just frantic.'

Cardin ran his business as he ran his couture shows – sans co-ordination. The company known as SARL de Gestion Pierre Cardin had a peculiar set-up. Since the late 1950s, after he was repeatedly stolen from, Cardin had a system for maintaining control: he was the only one in the house allowed to sign licensing contracts and cheques. In principle it was a clever way of staying on top of the business, of intuiting the in- and outflows of the company. But by 1976, with just half a dozen executives, he was administering a budding global empire of 400 contracts and thousands of products. He also spent almost half the year

PIERRE CARDIN

flying from New York to Buenos Aires to Tokyo to Johannesburg to Tel Aviv to Zagreb to Bombay. So, at the end of every month he came back to Paris to sign stacks of cheques and contracts. Some of these cheques were for just a few francs, perhaps a stationery bill, and yet only he was authorized to sign. As a result, it often took days for him to sign all the documents that had piled up on his desk in great stacks.

'It happened that sometimes we didn't know where Pierre Cardin was and we absolutely needed his signature, maybe for a bank, and everything was blocked. Then he would appear from nowhere and sign,' said Daniel Fallot. 'In these kinds of situations where you have packs of cheques, drafts, promissory notes and bills to sign, you look at the first two, three, ten, but then you sign and sign. We could make him sign anything. That was the danger.'

Besides that, there was no master list of what the company had on the books. Cardin's executives could not turn to a roster or computer printout that itemized what licensees had what products in what geographic zone. In theory it was all in Pierre Cardin's head. And yet it didn't work that way. 'Cardin himself has no idea what he has,' said Sala.

Businessmen pay a price for sloppiness. Cardin was no exception. Over the years he signed exclusive deals with more than one company simultaneously. When wigs briefly became the rage in the late 1960s and early 1970s he signed two wig agreements. In New York Max Bellest had cooked up PC wigs for the US; in Paris Jean Manusardi had set up a worldwide contract. As the company was organized, of course, only Cardin could possibly have known of the overlap. Manusardi was instructed to sort out the mess, which could have cost Cardin a small fortune to settle. In good faith the parties convened in Paris to find a solution. Cardin was there, backed up by Manusardi and a lawyer. At one point during the discussions he was shown the contracts, and each page where he had initialled them.

'Monsieur Cardin,' said the wig representative, 'you initialled it. That's your signature.'

Cardin looked up. 'I don't know,' he said in his nasal voice, 'someone might have forged my signature.'

Manusardi and the lawyer blanched. How the hell were they going to get out of this one? Luckily the licensees were equally disgusted with the whole mess, and they just wanted to wash their hands of the deal. An amicable settlement was reached. ('Mistakes were never made by him,' recalled Manusardi. 'You don't say, "Someone forged my signature." This you do in front of the Almighty, the day before Judgement, not for a wig deal.')

Cardin, miraculously, often escaped unscathed from the disasters created by his chronic disorganization. 'Cardin was the boss so the licensees swallowed their pride,' said Sala. 'Business is business and they just closed their eyes to certain things.' There was an unwritten rule: if manufacturers wanted Pierre Cardin's name they had to put up with unconventional practices. S. Miller Harris, president of the US shirt firm, claimed there was overlap between another US licensee and his company: both companies were making sportswear. The infringement was ground for a lawsuit and Harris complained to the Cardin organization, repeatedly. Nothing happened. 'They probably did it because they were getting income from both sources,' claimed Harris. The net result, however, was damaging to the Cardin organization. Stores often carried both lines of sportswear and casual wear, but they bore no relation to each other and confused the consumer. Yet Harris never sued.

Cardin was not so lucky a few years later. Marvin Morse had a company in Long Island City, New York. The twenty employees at his Morse Typewriter company sold new and used typewriters. But in late 1975 he imported some Pierre Cardin cigarette lighters from the Prince Company of Japan, an Asian licensee, and started selling them at US Duty Free shops. They moved well. Thereafter Morse wanted to become the US-based licensee for lighters. Max Bellest, of course, was responsible for all US deals, but for some reason Morse was told to contact Paris directly. His contact was Hervé Duquesnoy, a somewhat inexperienced young executive who had been rapidly promoted to licensing director.

Duquesnoy and Morse entered into negotiations. They were quite far along when, in March 1977, it was discovered that cigarette lighters were actually part of the contract with Swank, Inc., Cardin's respected US licensee for men's jewellery, cuff-links and a host of other accessories. Although no final contract had yet been signed, Morse sued Pierre Cardin claiming that an agreement was in place and that he had suffered loss of profits. Some four years later the case came to rest. Pierre Cardin had to fork over a staggering $594,968.80 to the little typewriter company under the Long Island City bridge.

The Morse case ran counter to the public relations image Cardin had established as a successful businessman. A constant source of mystery revolved around how much he could retain in his head and stay on top of. No-one, for example, ever saw a budget, yet he seemed to have a handle on expenses. Nor did Cardin like to write letters; his executives had to write the letters he signed. And as to reading his mail, it was an unwritten rule that letters over a few paragraphs were immediately passed on. He did not have the patience to read long letters. 'It is extraordinary that [the company could grow so big without formal organization],' said Linsman. 'It has in fact happened in the head of one person. I don't think he ever wrote a damn thing down.' The scale of the operation also awed his fellow designers. 'What remains an absolute mystery is how Cardin can control all that himself and be such a businessman,' said Kenzo. 'He is an artist and an extraordinary businessman at the same time.'

What emerged from a careful reading of the Morse case, however, was a picture far from this idealistic image of Cardin. He had an intuitive sense of what was going on but he did not have real control. The Cardin empire was a giant fungus with its own independent life. Spores of independent licensees grew in the dark and crept into every corner of the earth, fertilized by a steady supply of superb public relations. Sometimes, one would have to think, the empire grew in spite of Cardin.

'When the licences are filed, are they filed alphabetically or by product or are they segregated in any way?' Morse's lawyers asked Cardin in the US court case. 'Do you know, Mr Cardin, if your office has any system for filing licences?'

'No, I don't know,' responded Cardin. 'System?'

'Yes, a system for filing a licence, such as filing it by product or country or alphabetically or chronologically, any such system?'

'No.'

Well, there was some sort of a filing system, even if Cardin did not know it. The young executive, Hervé Duquesnoy, said that he helped set it up. But apparently these files, the most rudimentary tool to organize a business, were in a state of shambles. In this case the all-important Swank agreement of 1967 that included the cigarette lighters, and would have told Duquesnoy he could not authorize Morse to sell them, was missing. Even though, mind you, this was one of the most important US licensees, earning Cardin nearly $800,000 in royalties a year, and listing some forty products. Perhaps compounding the confusion was the fact Cardin was continually making everyone move from office to office. 'Sometimes we move,' Duquesnoy told the lawyers. 'We did not keep the same offices during this time.' That was an understatement.

At one point the opposing lawyers asked Cardin whether he remembered discussing Morse with Duquesnoy. 'It is impossible for me to say yes or no,' said the man who worked fifteen hours a day. 'I don't remember. We meet so many, many people, many, many things, every day, every day. If I have every day, if I have the same story, I have 1,000 stories in my life, you know.'

'He does not remember,' translated Cardin's lawyer.

But this exhausting image of Cardin trying to retain '1,000 stories' every day was perhaps the most accurate description of what the life of Pierre Cardin must be like. In Paris he often attended three lunches simultaneously, running from table to table discussing differing aspects of his far-flung empire. 'I don't follow everything, because my head is not so big, you know,' he explained in his nasal voice. 'I have more than 400 licensees and to follow everything in every country is impossible for me.'

But the trouble was self-inflicted. Many of the company's problems could have been avoided with some rudimentary organization. But Cardin had a real aversion to even the mildest form of organization. He ran his fast-growing international empire like a mom and pop grocery store at best. Traditional planning meetings were barred at the house and executives were dissuaded from talking to each other. No one could pin him down to a meeting. If they wanted to see Cardin, executives said, they sometimes ambushed him in the hall or staircase as he was rushing to the airport. 'You can't put Cardin around a table and discuss philosophy or strategy,' said Sala. 'He doesn't know what he wants but he wants it right away . . . Pierre Cardin has a violent sense of business.'

'There was no structure,' said Alain Carré. 'One day I sent a note organizing a meeting with Manusardi, Sala, and Pierre Cardin. It seemed to me quite natural. Cardin called me and said, "Meetings? What for? You'd better work." There have never been any meetings. To see him, I had to invite him for lunch at the Espace Pierre Cardin. He ate; I did not. When he was in a good mood, I would talk with him about important things. When he was not, I ignored his answers. Sometimes with important news I would wait outside his office for two hours.'

•   •   •   •

When the 1,000 stories in Cardin's life became too much he turned to his favourite releases. Like some housewife in need of therapy, he compulsively swept and straightened up and redecorated at the most inopportune moments. He indulged himself equally in great shopping binges. 'He'd buy anything,' said Manusardi. 'Textiles, furniture, mustard.' Most of his shopping jaunts were supposedly for his boutiques. These were all fairly small shops, showcases really for all of Cardin's products. Or that was the idea. The prudent policy was to buy a few samples, perhaps a hundred or so, from each of his top licensees, and then bind them together in a coherent PC look.

But that would have been too conventional. Daniel Fallot once went with Cardin to Britain. They came across Shetland cardigans in beautiful colours. There were four sizes. Cardin bought an eye-popping 7,000. 'They were still there ten years later,' recalled Fallot.

The sweaters were not Cardin's products. He did not design them; his manufacturers did not make them. And yet, said several employees, Cardin on occasion sewed his own label into products that appealed to him. 'Of course he put on his label,' said Manusardi. 'He bought them therefore they belonged to him.'

Cardin did the same in Yugoslavia, at a textile exhibition in Belgrade. 'He didn't buy one thing from our licensees. But he bought things all over the exhibit. I particularly remember the sweaters he bought from a company in Macedonia,' said Manusardi. 'It was just for the sake of buying. He was like a child.'

Arnold Linsman was also astounded when he went shopping with Cardin. While travelling in America, the two of them walked into a country Western store in Houston, decorated with a Texas-style Cadillac with steer horns. Cardin first bought ten cowboy hats. And then he tore through the store like a tornado. 'I didn't know what he was going to do with it all. He was like a kid with a bunch of toys. There was great enthusiasm over certain things. He was buying these things in quantity, and, of course, the salesmen were standing there smiling as none of this stuff was cheap. He bought three contemporary adaptations of the old saddle-bags, leather, sort of horseshoe bags. They were about $175 each and he gave me one,' said Linsman. 'He was very thoughtful in some respects, very chintzy in others.'

The same happened in Italy. 'I went with him to a furniture exhibition,' said Sala. 'I don't know what he didn't buy. Tables, chairs, sofas, anything but it had to be unusual. I never saw him use the furniture either. He must have a kind of museum storing the stuff. Or a warehouse.'

On one trip to Italy Cardin bought 2,000 men's jackets from his Italian licensee for his Parisian boutique. Bril, the French menswear licensee, was understandably upset, and the Paris staff was at a loss as to what they should do with all the jackets. The colours did not suit the French clientele. But selling the jackets was obviously not the purpose. Such driven buying must have been a pleasant release from tension, much like cleaning out a sock drawer or rearranging a row of pants.

•　　　　•　　　　•　　　　•

John Kornblith, the US menswear licensee, had lunch with Cardin at his apartment on the Seine. Kornblith was a hi-fi freak. 'I was struck by a sound system he had,' he recalled. 'The most amazing enormous, spherical Cardin-looking speakers, and with the turntable, amplifier, all the workings also built right into this big translucent sphere.'

Kornblith went back to New York and the next thing he knew the sound system arrived at his home on Central Park South. Cardin, probably inspired one afternoon by his genuine affection for Kornblith, had wrapped the stereo system himself and stuck it in the mail. 'This gigantic carton arrived,' said Kornblith. 'But the stereo was smashed into a thousand pieces.' Cardin had simply taken a carton and black tape and wrapped up the system, without using fittings or cushions. It was quintessential Cardin: a brilliant idea destroyed by sloppy execution and a lack of attention to detail. But the point was understood. He liked his licensee.

'He never got angry at the licensees,' said Sala. 'With them he was more soft. After all, they were the ones bringing in the money . . . Cardin gave his licensees a lot of freedom. He didn't expect them to make exactly what he wanted them to. Justly, every market has its own needs.'

Cardin exercised marginal control over his licensees. He never dictated a look, but allowed them a great deal of latitude for interpretation. If this hurt him in the long term, in the sense that it diffused his image, it was also an engine for growth. It was the upside of Cardin's chaos: a looseness and decentralization which granted the local manufacturer his expertise, his ability to satisfy local market tastes.

In the early days, in 1968, Kornblith could not even get designs out of Paris, the organization was so terrible. 'But I'm a practical enough merchant to think that maybe I was better off that I had more latitude to work it out for myself,' he said. He and his partner, Marvin Kirsten, took one of Cardin's Paris suits back to New York and performed a fashion autopsy. 'When I tried on a Paris-made PC suit I realized the armhole was much too small for the American market. The American had a bigger chest and wider shoulders,' said Kirsten. Intercontinental's executives designed and made a version they thought would sell in the US. It did do well, and Cardin had had little to do with its production, although he did give the suits final approval.

'If the licensees had followed what he did, his royalty cheques would have plummeted,' said Green. S. Miller Harris agreed: 'Although Cardin gave us plenty of drawings and had fashion shows, there really wasn't anything on the runways that you could market in the US.' Cardin must have known this. He gave his manufacturers space.

Bernard Wachter, a womenswear licensee in the late 1970s, recalled the conflicts he had with assistant designers sent from Paris to review the line. They were motivated by the desire to maintain a sharp, immediately recognizable Cardin image. On one occasion they stopped Wachter's production because they felt the product did not represent the PC look. In a quick-turnaround business such stoppages were deadly. 'Cardin himself came in and re-approved it,' said Wachter. 'He was interested in money and sometimes the people that he sent in would be more interested in aesthetics than money. He came a month later and said they were perfect, they were just what he wanted.'

Cardin based his relationships with licensees on pragmatism. It was terrific compensation for the disorganization. To the small or medium-sized company, incapable of spending fortunes on launching and marketing a famous brand-name, the Pierre Cardin service was of great value. Cardin provided a boiler-plate brand name to anyone willing to pay for it. It was as if any widget maker could kidnap the 'Marlboro' man for his widget sales. 'A handkerchief company on its own might have had a pretty good product, but it left a snow-flake impression,' explained James Posner, an international retail consultant. 'It didn't hit you. But the Pierre Cardin label helped make something pretty good become more legitimate. The Pierre Cardin name tied them [manufacturers] into a standard.'

A torrent of media coverage, and a pragmatic relationship with his licen-sees, kept the business growing. Combined, they were able to outrun Cardin's horrendous disorganization.

●   ●   ●   ●

There were critics.

'Pierre Cardin is like the little girl with the curl in the middle of her forehead. Sometimes he's very, very good. Sometimes he seems to be trashing fashion,' wrote Bernadine Morris of the *New York Times* in 1975. 'An example are his free-form handbags, carry-alls really. Sometimes they take the shape of buttocks or have sculpted hands extending from them. Amusing? Maybe in the 1960s, but fashion is moving down other roads.'

His critics were mainly from the traditional, old-world couture set. 'Pierre was willing to use his name to licence products all over the world, no matter what the products were,' said Green. 'Many products certainly were suspect in terms of quality. And when you start to bootleg your name in that way, it isn't the public that resents it so much, it's the press. The fashion press finds it difficult to laud and praise somebody who they feel is being a little tacky. Manufacturers who licensed the name and made it worthwhile financially were people who dealt with the mass market. And the mass market by its nature is the lowest possible taste level of any society.'

What he lost in the fashion press, however, Cardin picked up in other publications. In 1977 he launched a line of cheap-looking furniture in the US. He came for a whirlwind five-city tour in October as part of the publicity push. It started on 4 October with a champagne reception at B. Altman & Co., the New York department store launching the 'Environment for the Home Collection of furnishings'. The range went from $70 lamps to $1,375 cabinets, in glass and chrome and synthetic fibres.

Cardin had not designed the collection, as became patently obvious to anyone watching him walk through the showrooms. He twisted his spectacles around his hands and with real interest walked around inspecting 'his' lamps shaped as snails. And yet he dazzled. 'Pierre Cardin captured more attention than did his creations,' wrote *Interior Design*. 'Cardin, followed by a film crew and a dozen still photographers, wandered among the crowd receiving congratulations from total strangers, and obliging the film makers by occasionally running a hand over a table, opening a cabinet door and bouncing on the chairs and sofas. Because of the widespread recognition of the Cardin name, the affair had more of the character of a media event than the unveiling of a furniture collection.'

The New York Times, the *Philadelphia Inquirer* and the *Miami Herald* did their obligatory pieces during that whirlwind tour. But so did lesser publications, thanks to the Associated Press wire service. Cardin was splayed across papers like the *News Tribune* in Duluth, Minnesota; the *Lubbock Avalanche Journal* of Lubbock, Texas; the *Wichita Eagle* of Wichita, Kansas. Cardin had a staggering 110 articles printed about him in just two weeks. It was just another example of the effects of modern mass communications. Thanks to it middle America cottoned on to Pierre Cardin. He, meanwhile, was shrewd enough to cash in on the designer label appetite created by his publicity.

Cardin seduced the sceptics. His media genius neutered hostile members of the press. Marianne Tuteur, a public relations executive, recalled bringing to Cardin a tough nut. Mitch Bobkin, an editor at *Retailing Home Furnishings*, was seeing Cardin reluctantly. Up until that point he had studiously ignored Cardin because it was clear that the designer had little to do with the furniture line that bore his name. But Bobkin was a power at the important trade publication for home furnishings. Somehow he had to be won over.

Tuteur and Bobkin entered the Hotel Pierre in New York and made their way up to Cardin's suite. When they entered the rooms he was ensconced in the fluffy pillows of a reproduction eighteenth-century sofa, reported Bobkin. Cardin launched into his vision of the future 'environment'. To illustrate the naturalness of the life to come, he plopped down on all fours in front of the imitation Louis XVI coffee-table. 'This is a return to the natural beauty and grace of the animal,' he said, hunkering on the floor in his tightly-cut suit. 'There is nothing more beautiful than an animal in its own world. As time goes on, we will all live in a world that is comfortable, with surfaces and furniture which are as uneven and as natural as the environment of outdoors. This is where the animal of man used to live.'

Cardin was talking absolute bafflegab, not making the slightest bit of sense. No matter. Mitch Bobkin was mesmerized by Cardin. 'In that time an armchair may look like a dune or maybe a piece of wood,' explained Cardin with a straight face. 'There may be bumps in the carpet to suggest little hills. But everything will copy the natural forms, the forms of nature.' Bobkin wrote a favourable article.

KEEPING COUNT

11

'It's Cardin's big mystery. Except for a little bit of bookkeeping in the house, there was never a proper administrative office. Nobody really knew how it was being done,' said Sala about the company's financial status. 'Maybe he knew everything that was going on and maybe he had no idea. No one ever knew how big the company was, what the assets or capital were. He could be drowning in money, or he could be broke.'

Nothing fascinated Cardin-watchers more than his reputed wealth. Cardin ingeniously refused to talk about the size of his fortune, though he indirectly encouraged wild speculation. He hid the figures even from his own employees.

Because he had learned some rudimentary accounting while at the Red Cross during the war, Cardin insisted that accounts be done on old-fashioned graph paper. (Only fairly recently has he allowed a data-processing company to take over the company payroll. It used to be done by an army of accountants on eight-column pads.) His knowledge of accountancy must have been rudimentary and yet he passed himself off as an accounting wizard. Sala recalled a time when Cardin was in Milan looking over the Italian accounts. He found what he thought was a mistake. The stockholder's equity was entered on the liability side, an obligation the company had towards its shareholders. But Cardin thought it should go on the asset side of the balance sheet. Sala repeatedly explained why it was in the liability column. 'That's not true. That's not right. In our country that's different,' Cardin insisted. 'I know how it's done. I know how it's kept.' Sala recalled: 'Cardin had dismissed all the accounting rules in existence around the world.'

Publicly, Cardin and the house gave the impression that he was wealthier than he was. He was considered a brilliant real-estate investor, owning numerous apartments and offices in some of Paris's most exclusive neighbourhoods. By the 1980s, for example, his organization was working out of twelve buildings and stores around the Élysée palace. He was fond of driving American visitors madly through the streets and pointing out, 'This is mine . . . and this is mine'. Cardin picked up real estate as he picked up sweaters during shopping sprees. Clandestine residences were dotted around the world. In Milan he owned a beautiful apartment. In Venice he was reputed to have a palace near the Piazza San Marco. And there were whisperings of mysterious country estates. There were the flats above the stores: in the Vichy store he had a hideaway apartment, above Espace Cardin was another. He had a few rooms in his old Rue Richepance building. There was an apartment in New York. In Paris he had a virtual string of them. He personally didn't use many of them. He just liked hoarding them.

'He's a peasant and that's why he likes real estate,' said a friend. 'He isn't a speculator. He is a very good negotiator as peasants can be when they want to see the real stuff. But he would never go into something like junk bonds.' Said a former employee, 'He's totally international in his vision, but he's a peasant. He's the kind who keeps his money under his mattress.'

Cardin was restless during a vacation in Port-la-Galère, a town on the Riviera, so, as the story was spread to the press, he bought the town. In Port-la-Galère he picked up a string of harbour-front shops, plus a stone villa complete with swimming pool and tower. In this summer house Cardin drank thyme infusions, cleaned paths, weeded, hefted stones backwards and forwards, pruned trees, lopped the shrubs away, put seed in his dovecote. 'He relaxes by looking at his past through thousands of photos. He brought them from Paris in order to organize his archives while on vacation. Thousands of photographs where he poses with all the celebrities . . .' recorded Janie Samet in *Le Figaro* after she visited him. During the summer, with his entourage in tow, Cardin could be seen careering wildly down the winding Riviera roads to the vegetable markets.

'Whenever property has been for sale in the quartier ["at the right price," he adds] he has snapped it up. Now his writ runs over more cubic metres of the

Élysée section of Paris than the president can call on,' wrote the *Sunday Times* of London. Although Cardin owned the odd house, store and apartment outright, he did not and does not own nearly the amount of real estate that journalists have credited him with. He owns only an estimated 20 or 30 per cent of the properties he uses. The rest are held on long-term leases.

Occasionally he has been very hard up for cash. At such times he has quietly sold the rights to his name. Since 1966 he has repeatedly sold and bought back the rights to his name in perfume. In the 1980s he sold off the worldwide rights to his name in several categories of marginal products, such as tobacco and writing materials.

In 1973, after sinking his fortune into the risky Espace Pierre Cardin, he sold the rights to his name in Argentina. South America has always been difficult for businessmen. In the 1960s and 1970s, with its burgeoning bourgeoisie, it was an attractive place for Cardin to do business. But many of the countries had arcane foreign exchange controls which meant that he could not get his money out. 'I negotiated the sale of his name in Argentina,' said Manusardi. 'I knew he needed cash, and on the other hand I knew he wasn't going to see one dollar of royalties. It was a cash deal and the fellows also agreed to pay him several years of royalties out of accounts in the US. The sale and goodwill money helped him buy the building on Avenue Marigny.'

Brazil was another problem. No such deal was agreed there. 'I'm sure Cardin is a multimillionaire in Brazilian cruzeiros,' said Manusardi. 'He owns sugar-fields, cattle fields and real estate. He can't get the money out. He could retire in Brazil.'

If Cardin was not as wealthy as he appeared, he was still adequately rich. In 1978, 370 licensees worldwide were selling some $250 million at wholesale, the equivalent of about $13 million in annual income to the low-overhead Maison Cardin.

●   ●   ●   ●

Cardin's relationship to money was complicated. He had just left Milan when, the following morning, Mario Sala called Paris to see if he had arrived safely. Sala couldn't find anyone who knew whether Cardin had arrived or not until he got Cardin's accountant. 'He must be here,' she said, 'because when I opened the safe this morning the money was all gone.' The accountant had put the cash from Cardin's Paris boutiques into the safe. She had a key, as did he. 'Cardin wanted to see the store money with his own eyes,' explained Sala, 'touch it with his hands. It was his fetish, despite all the money he had, the millions. He just liked to see his money.'

PIERRE CARDIN

Every season an Asian sock licensee sent a batch of socks for Cardin to approve. 'He would keep every sock for himself, he wouldn't even give them away,' said a former employee. 'They would pile up in his house. Piles of chocolates and socks and glasses. They were just dumped and warehoused in his beautiful house.'

In the early 1970s, while Jean Manusardi was in the room, Cardin was scrutinizing the sums pouring into the coffers from the US. In particular, he was examining how much Max Bellest, André Oliver and Nicole Alphand were earning. In the mid-1960s, when he had nothing, Cardin had agreed to pay Bellest 10 per cent of his US royalties, with another 9 per cent each going to Alphand and Oliver. He was happy to do so when there was no money involved, but by the mid-1970s they were picking up some $300,000 each annually. Cardin was livid.

'We did Max's contract together, Monsieur Cardin,' retorted Manusardi. 'He's your employee, you never paid him anything, and in the beginning he spent his own money. I think it's a natural reward. About Nicole and André, you never asked my advice, you never ask anybody's advice, you did it by yourself. So if you want to reduce it, why don't you discuss it with them. But not with me. I don't get a penny from the States.'

At that thought Cardin cackled with pleasure. He paid his employees terribly. Executives lucky enough to work on a commission basis tied to his royalties did well, but the others were underpaid. There were perks, of course. Business and entertainment expenses were never questioned. Sometimes, in fact, Cardin encouraged people to travel more. And the younger, single employees were often housed in one of the many apartments Cardin leased. But he also held salaries low, sometimes not giving a raise for several years.

Cardin had an extremely low overhead. He was surrounded by just a half-dozen executives; the offices were tattered and sparse; a handful of accountants and designers backed up the worldwide organization. He refused even to buy theft or fire insurance for his boutiques. There were no in-house lawyers, no chief financial officers, no layers of bureaucrats. It was a lean operation. Sydney Schwartz, Cardin's American lawyer, explained to the US courts: 'Mr Cardin is the gérant, which means president, director, managing agent, everything.'

The only real expenses Cardin had were his money-losing haute-couture and Espace Cardin indulgences. And his travelling. And even there he stood apart from the traditional designer crowd. 'If Halston took a trip he took an entourage of forty-two people with a line-up of limousines, with enough luggage to leave the country . . . This would be a trip to New Jersey,' said Robert Green. 'Whereas Cardin always seemed to function almost as a classic businessman. He travels lightly. He'll eat at a coffee shop counter if that's convenient.'

He did travel lightly. On one trip John Kornblith was dashing after Cardin. 'I remember walking, running really, because Cardin runs, from our Intercontinental office on Seventh Avenue to a meeting at Bloomingdale's,' said Kornblith. 'Suddenly Cardin looked at me and said, "Isn't it funny we sell suits, and I can go all over the world with just three outfits. A blue blazer and grey flannel pants, a grey flannel suit, and black tie." '

Cardin was very economical, and in that sense was truly the superb business mogul his publicity said he was. He did not even pay for the staging of publicity events, since his contracts shrewdly stipulated that licensees had to contribute 2.5 per cent of their net sales to a marketing budget. 'He is an extremely tough businessman and I remember seeing that he turned off the lights every night,' said Bernard Wachter. 'I just think he is a super, super businessman. Maybe he doesn't like to spend enough money on paying management people, on having enough management. But he just likes doing everything himself.'

The few bills Cardin did have, he often paid late. Part of the problem, as we have seen, was due to his arcane system of control, whereby he was the only one allowed to sign the cheques. But a simple reluctance to part with his cash was also at the root of his slow response time. Barbara Ligeti, one of his former US press officers, recalled a time when he invited a large group of people to a restaurant when he was touring the US. When the bill came he signed it with a flourish of his famous signature and then walked out of the restaurant. Ligeti said she had to reassure the puzzled restaurant management that they should send the bill to her office.

'Cardin is very stingy, it's one of his characteristics,' said Alain Carré. 'When Pierre Cardin goes to a restaurant he signs the bill and then he leaves. Since people recognize him they don't dare say anything. If someone asks him, he says, "Just send it to me." And it works. What they don't know is that they will have to ask ten times before being paid.'

Some small businesses that worked with Maison Cardin had similar experiences. 'Pierre just cannot pay. He can't. I don't know why,' said the photographer, Roland de Vassal. 'He doesn't like giving money to other people. He takes you out to lunch and dinner, but if you tell him, "Pierre, you owe me 200 francs," he says, "No. No." Who knows why?'

Throughout the 1970s Cardin used the services of André Lemarié, a specialist in providing feathers and artificial flowers to couturiers. For ten years the atelier of creaky, warped wooden floors in Paris's porno district executed orders for Cardin and André Oliver. Then it abruptly stopped. 'He thought we were too expensive,' said Lemarié. 'He just doesn't like to pay. He thinks that's normal. Although he made a lot of money, he doesn't believe in the same principle for others.' In this case he was exercising the frugality which is a commendable quality in a businessman.

But shrewd business practices were not always at the root of his cavalier attitude towards paying bills. Alain Carré said that he tried to protect unsuspecting small businessmen from Cardin's bad habits. 'I thought it was really disgusting when it concerned artists,' he said. 'I once saw an engraver show one of his engravings to Pierre Cardin. Cardin found it marvellous and asked the man to do a 15-metre-long reproduction of it for the "rotonde" at Espace Cardin. The person did it on Pierre Cardin's word, without an order sheet or anything else. He invested in copper. He spent hours on it. When the work was finished he came by with his huge engraving. Cardin said, "What is this? It looks awful." Some people could have gone bankrupt like that.'

Another employee, who insisted on anonymity, said he too tried to protect small businesses from Cardin. This executive went with Cardin to a Milanese furniture and design exhibition. Cardin saw an armchair he liked and compulsively ordered fifty. The Italian salesmen went wild. Cardin left, but later the executive doubled back to the stall. He told the Italians to send only two, and that the house would confirm the rest. 'At that time he couldn't even fit a tie into the boutiques, they were so stuffed,' said the executive.

Cardin was also extremely suspicious. He employed, clothed and educated young street toughs. 'Some were real gangsters,' said an employee. A stream of these young, handsome men repaid Cardin's generosity by stealing from him. One of the more innovative of Cardin's thieves was a former driver promoted to be manager of the men's shop. He shook down Cardin's licensees for years, forcing them to pay him under the table for prime space in the store. This sort of constant petty thieving around the house fed into Cardin's paranoia. 'I think he's suspicious of everyone,' said Wachter. 'He's like a king surrounded by a court, who doesn't know who to trust and who not to trust. He has a great fear, I think, of being taken advantage of.'

In the mid-1970s one of Cardin's close business associates was discussing a garment with him. It soon became clear that Cardin was afraid to leave the room. 'He thought I was going to take the outfit and have it made elsewhere. He didn't trust me,' recalled the businessman. 'It was one of the greatest humiliations I have ever suffered.'

Cardin did have some good reasons to be cautious. Periodically unethical licensees and crooked employees took advantage of his slipshod organization and poor management controls. What was curious, however, was that he rarely seemed to accuse the real culprits, but on the contrary those employees who were utterly loyal. 'He once accused me,' said de Vassal. 'All that money you must have stolen from me,' he said. I told him, "Pierre, I never stole money from you. You never paid me." '

Yet on the flip side Cardin was rooted deeply in the Italian tradition of the patriarch. He might one minute accuse a loyal associate of theft but in the next moment, if the employee was ever in real trouble, Cardin could be generous like very few modern employers. When Roland de Vassal had a terrible car accident, Cardin was a true friend well beyond the call of duty. He paid part of de Vassal's hospital bill. 'And when I left the hospital he arranged for me to live in André Oliver's private house. André and Pierre really took care of me. But he does have a problem. Paying up is a genuine problem. I don't know why.'

None of his former employees, even the most bitter, ever doubted that he would help them if they were in true distress. 'Cardin may be hard on his employees, but he loves them,' said one of his former photographers, Michel Boutefeu. 'Every time one of them had a problem he sent flowers and gave money. I think there is more good to say about Cardin than there is bad.' When his mannequins married, he treated them like family and spent like some Sicilian padrone, often paying for a grand wedding or honeymoon. If an employee was ill or hospitalized, Cardin moved in quickly and picked up the tab. Mila Parély, the actress from *La Belle et la Bête*, fell on hard times in the late 1960s and appealed to Cardin for help. No questions asked, Cardin graciously and generously hired her in London. 'He's always there when you need a friend,' said Parély.

'He could get really angry over ten francs, have a real fight,' said Sala, 'and then spend a lot more on something else.' Alain Carré was equally puzzled. 'The way he relates to money should be analysed by a psychiatrist,' he said. Personally Cardin indulged in shopping sprees and his voracious appetite for redecorating. He spared no expense when interior decorating, and often wasted fortunes ripping pipes out, putting them back in, ripping them out again. 'It's my money,' he was fond of saying. 'It's all mine and I can do with it as I like.'

However, when an employee once ordered 100 plastic pens for supplies, Cardin promptly rang her up in hysterics. In the depths of winter in Paris, executives at Maison Cardin often shivered in their offices because Cardin was reluctant to pay for central heating. And the offices were often dingy, in need of a paint job, the carpets tattered and threadbare. 'On the other hand,' said Arnold Linsman, 'how do you figure a guy who says to me, "I want you to come over to Paris because I'm introducing my environment collection, and I want you to come on the Concorde because you should have that experience." He flew me to Paris and back, not on the licensee's expense, but at his, just so I could have the pleasure of flying the Concorde.'

His rage over people taking advantage of him bubbled to the fore in 1977. He had just moved his office around the corner from 118 Faubourg Saint-Honoré, where he became known in the late 1950s, to 27 Avenue de Marigny, above the stores in which he had launched his Peacock Revolution. Abruptly he decided that any outsider wanting to see his couture collection had to pay 50 francs and book in advance. 'Why', he asked in a rage, 'should anybody walk into a couture house for free? Why should they ruin my rugs, take up my salesladies' time and steal my ideas? After all, if you go to a movie or a café you have to pay for it.' He went as far as announcing his plans to the press.

His executives rolled their eyes heavenward and sighed, but luckily the idea never went very far. Shortly thereafter, however, Saks Fifth Avenue wanted to do a television advertising campaign with Cardin and had asked him to New York for a meeting. The store wanted Cardin to contribute to the advertising campaign but Max Bellest, recalled Bernard Wachter, simply told Cardin that the president and chairman of Saks wanted to discuss advertising. Wachter, Bellest and Cardin were ushered into the room where the gods of retailing sat. 'They proceeded to talk about everything being wonderful with the business and the entire discussion was held in English,' said Wachter. 'And then all of a sudden the [president of Saks] turned around to Mr Cardin and said, "We would like $50,000 for your contribution towards this ad." Mr Cardin did not speak a word of English after that comment. And he pulled it off. He just made believe he didn't know what they were talking about. He proceeded in French and turned around to Max and said, "Why did you bring me here to this?" We left. We never gave the $50,000.'

•   •   •   •

'Pierre would sign anything as long as interesting sums of money were offered,' said Carré. 'Lots of people asking for the PC licence wanted the name only. They thought it was all they needed to help them sell more and at a higher price. But I fought them. I thought we had to create things that were all in the same spirit. Cardin never understood that a coherent policy on brand image and a spontaneous recognition were necessary to preserve the name.'

At his peak Carré was working with some hundred PC licensees, assisting them with their designs. With all these new Pierre Cardin products – from bidets to boxes of tissues – Carré thought maintaining a distinct and recognizable image was absolutely paramount to the long-term health of the company. Not that PC china manufactured in Brazil need be exactly the same as china manufactured in Italy, but there should be a common design thread that could immediately identify them as Pierre Cardin products. Otherwise the explosion of unrelated products diffused and blurred the valuable image.

Manusardi, Alphand, Sala, Bellest and even Fallot agreed with that principle. Cardin did not.

In the mid–1970s, with so many licensees pounding at their door, Cardin's licensing directors found they could run in any direction they wanted. But they did not know which direction that should be. Sometimes he pushed them to sign any kind of a deal just for the sake of hauling in money. Other times he would rant and rave that the products were not reflecting his image, that they were not good enough. On one occasion in New York, said US executives, Cardin threw the collection of one of his licensees out of the window, in a fit of rage. The garments fluttered down into the Seventh Avenue fashion district.

What did Cardin really want? Cash or prestige? To put an end to the confusing messages Manusardi cornered his maître. 'Monsieur Cardin, we'd like to know precisely what you want – in order not to make mistakes, and in order to be in accordance with your wishes,' started Manusardi, clearing his throat. 'Let's put it this way. You have three choices. One is to make a few billion francs quickly by exploiting the name aggressively for a few years, then closing shop and going fishing. Or do you want the house to survive ten years, make more and more money, but salvaging the image somewhat? Some sort of a balance. The third way is you want Pierre Cardin to be a monument lasting for ever, and in that case we believe you should stop licensing. In fact we think you should cut down and perhaps start again rebuilding.'

'So you think my life is a failure?'

Manusardi was flabbergasted. He didn't know how to respond. Nor could he get anything more out of him. 'If you're happy, everybody's happy,' Manusardi ventured.

Cardin's executives also encouraged him to hire a staff to travel the world policing his licensees. There was virtually no-one spot-checking products at the source, in the stores, maintaining quality control. Cardin, perhaps believing in his own publicity, claimed that he knew what his licensees were up to. He said he had control, but he did not.

The stores that sold Pierre Cardin products greatly affected the overall image of the label. If Pierre Cardin watches were sold in, say, the New York stores Tourneau or Saks Fifth Avenue for $250 each, the image remained prestigious. If, however, the products showed up for $50 in suburban outlets like K-Mart, as they did in the 1980s, the Pierre Cardin image suffered terribly. All Cardin's contracts stipulated that he had the right to approve the points of distribution, and yet he never hired the staff to enforce the prestige rule. He refused to grow up with his empire, to delegate. 'He runs the empire very much like a stationery store,' said Andrew Wargo. The consequence was to be expected. Many licensees took advantage of the huge gap in management.

PIERRE CARDIN

'There was a lot of cheating going on and Pierre Cardin was showing up in a lot of discount stores,' recalled Stanley C. Gillette, a former PC licensee. 'That hurt everyone except the people making money off the higher volume. We called our counsel to try and get the Cardin organization to enforce the distribution rules. I think they [Cardin's executives] were incredibly naive about that. I know for a fact that they tended to believe whatever their licensees told them. For example, the Cardin people inspected collections every six months, but the licensees didn't actually show the stuff they were selling.' Said S. Miller Harris, 'The organization was simply unable to control the number of licensees and the distribution.'

In the US, as early as 1972, Pierre Cardin ties, which normally retailed for $12.00, were sold for just a few dollars at a discount store, Chifora, on West 32nd Street in New York. At Loehmann's, another well-known discount chain in New York, sunglasses designed to sell at $12.50 and $15.00 per pair were sold under the Cardin label, in bags carrying the Cardin name, for $2.98 and $3.98. In one court case a former licensee claimed that Pierre Cardin products were being sold in 'flea markets'. By the 1980s the situation had gone from bad to worse. PC products were everywhere. Inexpensive European PC watches began showing up in the US markets, despite the fact that an American company, Continental Time Corporation, had an exclusive US watch licence. And then another company, Pierre Cardin Électronique, was also given a licence for alarm clocks. The result was a free-for-all, complete with acrimonious lawsuits. At a store called Buffums, Pierre Cardin watches were dumped for $49.99 during distress sales.

Any pretence at maintaining a prestige front had collapsed. In September 1988 any tourist speeding across the channel between Dover and Calais on the hovercraft was forced to leave his car in the vessel's bowels and take a seat upstairs in the lounge. On the seats, under protective plastic antimacassars, the Hoverspeed Duty Free advertisements for the 1988/9 season featured 'exclusive Pierre Cardin jewellery'. Shoppers could purchase Pierre Cardin's 18-carat gold-plated necklace for £5.55 and seven pairs of earrings for £10.85. The gold-plated earrings included little sparkling chips with a diamond-like appearance.

In November, in Paris's 5th arrondissement, on the Rue Monge near the Sorbonne, a discount store with about twelve square metres of retail space was having a Pierre Cardin special. Amongst the boxes — Taiwanese key-chains in the shape of the Zodiac, Smurf pencils, orange day-glow erasers — students were drawn to banana-yellow PC sweatshirts selling for 65 francs. A Parisian woman in a grey overcoat and fox collar hunting for bargains ran her arthritic hands over the Pierre Cardin sweatshirts, and then passed on.

A few months later, in New York in February 1989, Bloomingdale's ran an ad in the *New York Times* for its luggage clearance. Customers could save 50 per cent on 'clearance and discontinued' totes, pullmans, duffles and carry-ons. Top of the list were items from 'Pierre Cardin Jet Stream'. By this time Pierre Cardin's luggage licensee was one of the top American performers; it was particularly successful moving merchandise through a direct-mail campaign with American Express. In 1989 American Express bombarded its cardholders with 50 million pieces of PC advertising. Cardholders were able to purchase a six-piece set of lightweight Pierre Cardin luggage for $99.99. 'Pierre Cardin is probably as large in volume as all other designer luggage in the US combined,' claimed Pierre Cardin Luggage's president, David Katz. In 1982, said Katz, the company was selling about $200,000 a year of luggage at wholesale. 'There are now substantial numbers of weeks that we do more than that per week,' he said.

The relentless exploitation of Cardin's name is frowned on by traditional marketing gurus. 'It's really emptying the glass of the last dregs,' said Kurt Barnard. 'The Pierre Cardin name has an enviable recognition factor but it's threadbare around the edges. There is no distinctive individuality. Its image is blurred, diffused.'

Historian Daniel J. Boorstin, meanwhile, called Cardin's marketing success a 'pyrrhic victory'. 'All great advertising victories are pyrrhic victories,' he explained. 'If designer labels are really successful, and reach larger and larger markets, they become so democratized that everybody wears them. And then they become franchised for hamburgers and everything else. People want to benefit from the prestige of the Cardin label, but of course the prestige quality has been destroyed. The destruction comes not because no-one wants the Cardin name, but because everybody wants the Cardin name.'

•   •   •   •

'I've always felt that Cardin operates on the basis of being rather like the head schoolmistress whom everybody fears,' said Green. 'There was always an element of tension because it was a little like the princess in the palace. What is her mood today? Is it going to be off with our heads or not?' Bernard Wachter noticed the tension at Maison Cardin as well: 'He ran his business on a great deal of fear. The people surrounding Mr Cardin were afraid of him.'

Some managers would call Cardin's method of motivation 'creative tension'. In 1980 Cardin appointed Bernard Danillon de Cazella as his press officer, a very friendly man who knew how to massage and work journalists. Charles-Efflam Heidsieck, however, was a young employee responsible for public relations in Cardin's latter-day restaurant business. If Heidsieck arranged an interview, Cardin showed up at Danillon's office. 'Look, I don't need you. The press comes without you,' Cardin said. One employee described his management technique as 'divide and conquer'. 'He knows how to elevate people, and how to pull them down,' he said. 'He tells you, "You are nothing, I am everything. If you don't work for me you will see you are not as powerful as you are now." '

'You never see Cardin,' said Michel Boutefeu. 'He is everywhere, but actually never anywhere to be seen . . . until he shows up by surprise.' When Cardin did show up, he did not give guidance or instructions, but instead assaulted his employees with a barrage of questions. 'Those guys, did they come back? What are they doing? What do they want? Did we get a letter? When are they coming back?' The staff was always on edge, waiting for Cardin to swoop down.

'There were very few women at the house, and most of the men were homosexuals,' said a female employee. 'The funniest thing, and also the most unbearable, was the bickering amongst all these guys for his attention. They were ready to do anything for him. I saw some of the most ridiculous behaviour. In particular there was one guy, a window decorator, who roamed around talking to everybody, having coffee. But he also knew the approximate time when Cardin would come to the office, and then at that hour he would be there doing the most [work] . . . draping things. And this would get the other guys very upset. You would see all these butterflies come out. It was like a harem when the emperor walked along. If the emperor had a favourite it was like the Chinese court.'

The rivalry was staggering. 'You always had to show Cardin your work yourself, because if you didn't no one else would. They would only show your mistakes,' said another employee. 'People working for him liked to hit out at each other. If they had the chance to do something mean they would never miss it. But there was one area where none of them lied. That was, was he in a good mood? They always answered that correctly. You know, he always has people waiting in line in the lobby, waiting for their turn to see him. Some of them have very important things to discuss with him. Never mind, you have to get in line and wait your turn. Sometimes, however, after the fourth one, he would get nervous and angry. Pfft, everyone disappeared.'

Cardin found it nearly impossible to delegate authority. 'Cardin wants to do everything himself,' recalled Sala. 'But obviously he didn't have time to do it all. Consequently there was confusion.' The business cards of Cardin employees were always very impressive. Fresh-faced 24-year-old men held the title of director or manager. 'He made his staff appear more important than they were to the outside,' said an employee, 'but inside there was only one person.'

Roland de Vassal recalled an appointment he had with Cardin at 2 p.m. Predictably, at the expected time Cardin was not to be found. At 5 p.m., after waiting three hours, de Vassal gave up. As he was leaving the building he bumped into Cardin. The chairman of a billion-dollar empire was covered in plaster, as if he had just come from replastering a wall somewhere.

'What on earth are you doing, Pierre?'

'You know, if I didn't do everything myself, nothing would get done.' Cardin was holding the keys to the central heating.

He held every key in the house and there was no drawer or door that he would not investigate. An element of paranoia pulsed through the house. One employee said that she often had the feeling that Cardin riffled through her drawers when she was absent. 'One day Cardin came to ask me something and found I was locked inside the lab,' said the photographer, Boutefeu. 'He probably thought this was suspicious, so he started banging on the lab door and threatened to force it in. It was not until I explained to him that opening the door would ruin a few thousand francs worth of photos that he decided to leave.'

Remarkable as it sounds, Cardin also exhibited signs of jealousy towards his employees. Sala, as Cardin's Italian representative, was well known by the Italian licensees. When Cardin started a line of furniture in Italy the two men met up at the exhibitions. Cardin noticed the licensees fussing over Sala.

'You're very well known here, aren't you?' he said coldly.

'He was Pierre Cardin. We weren't,' recalled Sala. 'There was no reason why he should feel that way. But he was always jealous. The only person he ever really trusted was his sister.' Maybe Yoshi Takata and André Oliver belonged to this short list also.

When Cardin's suspicions and jealousy became acute he took employees down a few notches. 'Cardin always undermined his employees,' said Harris, who thought Pierre Cardin's boutiques were terrible, an eclectic hodge-podge of rag-tag products. 'His retail stores were truly atrocious,' he said. 'They were unbelievably badly merchandised, with no point of view. You go into Polo you know what Polo is; you go into Tiffany, you know what Tiffany is; you go into Cardin and you don't know what it is.' His store on the Boulevard Saint-Germain, for example, jumped from women's clothes to sportswear to men's clothes to ski and knitwear, and then back to women's clothes before closing for good. Cardin constantly changed his mind, constantly lost interest, constantly spent his weekends reshuffling merchandise.

These stores sorely needed professional management. As his career at the house was drawing to an end, Jean Manusardi began negotiating with Bril a clever lease-back agreement. Bril, a smart retailer, would take control of the stores while paying Cardin rent and a royalty on the turnover. A clever deal, and the stores might start coming together. Cardin let Manusardi work out an agreement, but as the deal was coming to a head he said, 'It isn't me,' and walked out.

Such behaviour was common. Cardin's employees carefully negotiated deals with his approval and at the eleventh hour, when the contract was to be signed, he cut them off at the knees by walking out. They were left alone in the room trying to explain what had just happened to the enraged manufacturer who might have flown all the way to Paris for the meeting. It was, of course, extremely embarrassing for the employees. Worse, however, was that it hurt their credibility with the licensees and damaged their ability to impose discipline.

One of the most dramatic cases of Cardin undermining his employees involved Max Bellest in New York. In the 1970s America was developing extremely well, largely thanks to Bellest. 'Max is a man with incredibly high standards,' said John Kornblith. 'He had a long view. He would never purposely give licences to less than prestigious quality manufacturers, or he would not, simply for money, have any of his licensees sell at cheap stores.'

That was why he started having trouble with Sheridane Designs Inc. Sheridane did not work well with other licensees. 'We worked very well with Intercontinental [menswear], co-ordinating swatches, but neither of us could get any co-operation out of Sheridane for ties,' said Harris. 'If someone wanted to put together a Cardin outfit, they couldn't. Either the ties were not in the stores that carried the suits and the shirts, because the stores did not like the [tie] quality or the pattern, or else they were there but they didn't work with the shirts because there was no intercommunication between our company and theirs, despite the fact we gave them swatches long before.' Said Kornblith, 'The tie maker was of inferior quality.'

The tie company was Pierre Cardin's first US licensee, signed in April 1967. Cravat Pierre Ltd, later to become Sheridane Designs Ltd, Inc., was allowed to manufacture and market Pierre Cardin men's neckwear, scarves, ascots, handkerchief, bibs and cummerbunds. For that Sheridane was required to pay a 5 per cent royalty on net sales, plus, like all other US licensees, another 2.5 per cent of net sales for a group advertising budget. The company's two co-chairmen were Michael T. Kellerman and Morton H. Spar.

In the early 1970s Bellest claimed Sheridane was hurting the Pierre Cardin image. Other PC licensees were selling at Saks Fifth Avenue, Bonwit Teller, Lord & Taylor's, Altmans and Bloomingdale's. At that time, for reasons of prestige, Macy's, Gimbles and other Herald Square stores in New York were absolutely out of bounds to the US licensees. Altmans had dropped the Sheridane tie line, said Bellest, while Barneys and Lord & Taylor's salesman were grousing to him that the Sheridane line was too busy, too loud. Bellest was not happy.

The Sheridane management was equally not enamoured of Bellest. 'Max was difficult,' said Morty Spar. 'He was an erratic person.' In January 1973 Mike Kellerman dropped out of the American PC licensees' public relations programme, stating in his resignation letter that he preferred to advertise directly and independently of the group. A month later Kellerman went to Paris to see Jean Manusardi, Nicole Alphand and Pierre Cardin, all in an attempt to bypass Bellest who was hell-bent on disciplining what he perceived as a renegade licensee. Kellerman wanted Paris to let him sell at the forbidden Macy's.

In March Bellest asked Sheridane to submit swatches and designs for prior approval, as stipulated in the licensing contract, in an effort to improve the quality of the ties. Kellerman claimed it was impractical to work that way and invited Bellest to Europe, as he had done on previous occasions, to see the fabric houses he ordered the material from. In the meantime Bellest had ordered the accounting firm Herbert H. Levess & Co. to audit the books of Sheridane. Arguments flew between the two parties. After initially refusing to show its books, Sheridane finally let the accountants audit a period restricted from 1 May 1971 to 31 January 1973. The accountants found, according to Cardin's lawyer Sydney J. Schwartz, that Sheridane had underpaid royalties to the extent of $10,000. Schwartz sent letters terminating the licensing agreement.

Kellerman sued for an injunction forbidding SA Pierre Cardin from terminating the licensing agreement. He made several allegations; Bellest and SA Pierre Cardin made counter-allegations. As the case started, Kellerman tried to bypass Bellest and Schwartz again by appealing directly to Cardin himself for a settlement. 'I am absolutely astonished that you allowed your "Napoleonic" agent to get between our friendship and mutual respect,' Kellerman wrote in a handwritten note. 'I was the first licensee you had in America and I have always been honest, fair and ethical with you. These lawsuits can only be damaging to both of us. I think you and I should meet privately at your convenience to see what can be salvaged. Please understand that this request should not be viewed as a sign of weakness on my part but comes instead from our long friendship and my personal respect and understanding and admiration for you. Kindly cable me at once if you want me to come to see you.'

In return a note was sent to Kellerman, signed by Cardin, which simply said, 'Talk to my New York lawyers.' Eventually all the charges and counter-charges were dropped or settled. But it was costly and messy. In one case the courts decided that the Cardin organization could not cancel the licence as the termination notices sent earlier by Schwartz were 'insufficient and of no legal effect'. The Cardin organization had technically not executed its cancellation correctly. New cases languished in the courts. In the meantime, rather than send a note Kellerman flew directly to Paris to woo Cardin. It worked. He walked away with a contract that stipulated Sheridane could bypass Bellest. Bellest could no longer screen Sheridane's customers, nor approve the tie line. 'He undermined Max,' said Spar. 'I don't know why he did it.'

Bellest was badly hurt. His authority in the US was irrevocably damaged, as was his ability to maintain the prestige of the label. From then on licensees could do pretty much what they wanted, provided they paid homage to the maître in Paris. Cardin was reminding them who was boss.

•   •   •   •

In 1968 Claude Lanzmann, the great television journalist, interviewed Pierre Cardin for a French television programme called *Dim Dam Dom*. 'I am a very sensitive person and I am very close to people, people from all social backgrounds,' Cardin told Lanzmann. 'I always put myself in other people's state of mind, and I think my employees . . . I am equal to a workwoman as well as to Mrs so and so. At least I don't think my personality changes. No, I am very true.'

Not all of Cardin's employees agreed with this account of himself. On a Monday morning in 1973 Jean Manusardi trundled up the steps to his office. He was in for a surprise. Without a word Cardin had installed another desk in Manusardi's office and behind it was a hawkish, very thin young man in his twenties. 'On the Friday before I never knew that Edouard Saint Bris existed. He fell from heaven,' said Manusardi. Was this a message that he was no longer in favour? 'Not at all. Edouard wouldn't have been in my office if I had been in the cellar. I was supposed to train him.'

As one young man was coming in, an old pro was being squeezed out. It was Mario Sala in Italy. Sala had done a fine job developing Italy and Cardin seemed to be favourably impressed by him. Shortly before the trouble hit, Cardin asked Sala's wife whether she would mind moving to Paris as he wanted her husband to manage the head office. 'I always had a good relationship with Cardin,' insisted Sala. In 1975 Cardin called up Sala and said he was coming to Italy with a new man. He was a Uruguayan in his early thirties, with pale skin and slicked-back hair. Cardin set him up in his Milan apartment and told Sala he wanted the newcomer to run the men's division of the Milan boutique. In no time he was in control of the whole store.

'He tried to take possession of all of Italy. He certainly wasn't qualified,' said Sala. 'I don't know if Cardin promised it to him. These are private things that no one will ever know.' Said Manusardi, who watched it unfold from Paris, 'I always thought he needed a reason to kill Sala to put this Uruguayan in his chair.' (If that was the reason for the mess that followed, it was all in vain. The

Uruguayan disappeared as quickly as he came. He was a flash of lightning, not even lasting a year.)

The Uruguayan immediately started fighting with the Italian accountant, who in turn was fighting a losing battle with cancer. Suddenly Cardin showed up in Sala's office. Always suspicious of his employees, and perhaps poisoned by the whisperings of the young man living in his Milan flat, Cardin accused the accountant of dishonesty. Sala defended the accountant, who was a friend, and told Cardin that the man was dying of cancer.

'It's not true. He is not honest,' Cardin snapped back. 'According to me he does not have cancer. He wants to hide behind the excuse of cancer.'

Sala, a lawyer, rarely lost his temper; yelling was not his style. But he was now frothing. 'I really don't know what it was about,' he recalled. 'Maybe he was doubting my honesty.' To Sala, a concentration camp survivor, freedom and honesty were two things worth dying for. No-one – not even the great Pierre Cardin – was going to get away with maligning a good man's reputation with baseless accusations. Sala threw Cardin out of his office.

The accountant died a few months afterwards. 'On the outside Pierre is very pleasant,' said Sala. 'Inside he is Jekyll and Hyde.' He never wanted to work for Cardin again. He wrote to him asking to go separate ways. For building up Italy, Sala was paid a 10 per cent fee on all Cardin's Italian royalties, which were around 150 million lire at the time. The accountant had paid Sala directly but that had stopped once he became too ill to work. Sala was owed several million lire and in his letter of resignation he asked to be paid the sums owed him.

One letter. Several letters. No response. Instead Sala received a letter from an Italian lawyer hired by Cardin. The letter, said Sala, had one message: 'You say you worked for Cardin. We have no record of that, therefore we don't owe you any money.' It was ludicrous. Sala filed suit.

'Cardin's lawyer came to my office and I had a table full of correspondence related to my work with Cardin. I gave him a photocopy of everything that was essential,' said Sala. 'Next the judge asked for the two parties to convene in court. I went. Cardin didn't.' Cardin's 'case' collapsed before it started and his Italian attorney settled with Sala. 'I had nothing against Cardin once he paid me,' he said.

The Sala case had repercussions in Paris. 'That was the end for me,' said Manusardi. 'I couldn't respect Cardin any more, not enough to live off of his money. He would have to do impossible things to kill my admiration for him – he's quite a guy – but I don't hold him in esteem any more.' Manusardi resigned in 1976 after ten years on the designer's payroll. (As a parting gift Cardin gave Manusardi a fat bonus, although he need not have done so under French law. It was a tacit and generous acknowledgement that Manusardi had done good work for him. Even after all the capriciousness, the yelling, the suspicion, Cardin knew that Manusardi had had his best interests at heart.)

At one full swoop two of Cardin's best employees were gone. 'I've always sensed in Pierre that touch of the paranoid,' said Green. 'He doesn't like very strong people because they stand up to him. He wants to run things and he wants people to understand that, you know, "I control this". His attitude is, "Without me there is nothing here." '

An era was ending. Pérou had died a few years earlier. Alain Carré had also had enough. 'I could not bear the people and the atmosphere at Cardin's,' said Carré, who left in 1975 to start his own design firm. 'It was like the Vatican, poisoned.'

And then Cardin took aim at Nicole Alphand. 'He always knows when someone has finished his time. Pierre senses, "He has done what he can do, he can't do anything further",' said Max Bellest. Said another employee, 'He squeezes you like a lemon and then throws you away.'

By the late 1970s Nicole Alphand was pulling in nearly $400,000 a year and her interest was limited to the US market where her hefty salary was coming from. Understandably that irked Cardin. In 1975, in an effort to rekindle his sagging fashion reputation, he took a 25-year fashion retrospective of his work on a tour of the US. Robert Green was hired to be the master of ceremonies and commentator. During that trip Cardin's dissatisfaction with Alphand bubbled up to the surface. 'I think by the time we went on tour he was very disenchanted with her,' recalled Green. 'He felt saddled by her and he wasn't in a position where he could fire her without creating enormous problems.' During the tour Cardin sat next to Green on the plane. 'Oh, I love you dearly,' said Cardin, whispering in the ear of his confidant, 'but one of the rewards of having you here is that I don't have to sit with her.'

'He was dying to wedge her out of the American operations,' remembered Linsman. But firing was another matter. Cardin, in all his years as a business mogul, rarely fired anybody. In France employees enjoyed a great deal of legal protection and it cost employers a small fortune to fire anyone. His preferred method was just to let the employee atrophy with menial tasks; or, by publicly slighting and undermining them, he created such an unbearable atmosphere that they often chose to leave. On any up-front nastiness, Cardin usually sent in hatchet men to do the job for him. (He once asked Daniel Fallot to fire Manusardi, and then later asked Manusardi to fire Fallot. Both refused, so no-one wound up getting fired.)

Cardin's desire to be rid of Nicole Alphand took care of itself. At first she had trouble swallowing. Then she had an operation on her throat. Six weeks later, in February 1979, she died of cancer. She had never been ill before. As she lay in her bed during the final days, she repeatedly told her husband she was travelling to China with Cardin. 'She kept on obsessing about going to China,' recalled Hervé Alphand.

Nicole Alphand helped make Cardin into what he is today. 'She was responsible for launching Cardin in the US,' said Harris. 'I don't know how much longer it would have taken without her – years and years longer.' Everyone sincerely sang her praises. 'She had personality that would win anyone over, and yet she was fiery,' said Kornblith. 'Nicole was a marvellous woman. I miss her,' said Bellest. 'If she hadn't been at the house, the house would not be what it is today. She could pull Pierre's rein. She had a marvellous mind and a marvellous heart.' She could also be extremely arrogant, infuriating, snobbish. And yet most people forgave her because she got things done. 'When Nicole was alive those ladies showed up at the fashion shows,' recalled Linsman. 'She turned out the people.'

'A week after Nicole Alphand died Pierre was badmouthing her,' said S. Miller Harris. 'I really found it shocking. He talked as if she really hadn't done anything for him. That she had hurt the house of Cardin and that he wouldn't – maybe it was false bravado – that he wouldn't miss her.'

André Oliver and many of the couture old-timers still quietly did their thing unmolested. Of the old business executives, however, only Max Bellest remained. The ageing Bellest had a lifelong contract so he was an untouchable, but Cardin eroded his hold on the US market. He installed a younger man, Nicholas J. DeMarco, who took over many of the day-to-day duties in New York. The fiery Bellest and Cardin were going to bang heads later.

With all the departures, voluntary or not, Cardin needed replacements. He passed over seasoned professionals from outside and instead turned to the inexpensive young men he had recently hired. Edouard Saint Bris, whom Manusardi had trained, immediately stepped into the void. The other choice was unexpected. Cardin turned to Hervé Duquesnoy, a handsome, soft-spoken young man he had installed in his office in November 1975. Cardin had a professional and long-suffering secretary, but Duquesnoy was also listed as his secretary. Still in his twenties and rather inexperienced, Duquesnoy was rapidly promoted into Manusardi's job of licensing manager. (Duquesnoy's inexperience cost Cardin dearly in the Morse case. He would in time, however, grow into the job and become valuable to the organization.) At the end of the 1970s, these two young men were Cardin's principal Paris executives, overseeing a worldwide network of nearly 400 licences, thousands of products.

Some of the outspoken experienced executives who were pushed aside today complain bitterly that they were replaced by sycophants. Fame had warped Cardin's judgement, they said, and he could no longer tolerate anyone questioning his decisions. Instead, they maintained, Cardin surrounded himself with inexpensive, weak men who blindly jumped at his voice. Perhaps. Cardin did treat many of his older employees shabbily, and he certainly could not tolerate dissent. And yet, to some extent, he also re-energized his sagging organization in the late 1970s with fresh blood. The winners in the 1970s house purge were a new generation of loyal, highly motivated younger men appreciative of their unique opportunities.

They rallied to Cardin's defence. 'I like Cardin very much. I know all his faults, but I refute them,' said Charles-Efflam Heidsieck, an employee who started work at the age of 24 in the 1980s. 'For one reason, I learned a lot from him. I received a business education that was tremendous . . . When I started working with him I always [talked directly]. Today I work at two or three levels. I know how to manipulate in business.'

Cardin was going to need such soldiers for his next big move.

COMRADE CARDIN

12

The blue-and-white 'Spirit of '76' touched down on the dusty Peking tarmac on 21 February 1972. Out stepped US President Richard Nixon and his wife Pat. The thick, black glasses of the wire-haired Henry Kissinger appeared at the top of the steps; Secretary of State William Rogers followed. Awaiting the American visitors at the bottom, elegant and bean-thin, was the Chinese premier, Chou En-Lai. Nixon reached out, pumped Chou's hand. The opening of China's doors had begun.

At first the reception was low-key, even austere. After inspecting the honour guards of the Liberation Army, Navy and Air Force, President Nixon and his entourage were bundled into a line of black limousines and whizzed over to their government-approved lodgings. As the presidential party passed the stadium-sized Tiananmen Square in front of the Forbidden City, the Chinese public went about their business on bicycles as if nothing was happening. In comparison, Nicolae Ceausescu of Romania had been welcomed by hundreds of thousands of singing and flag-waving families just a few months earlier.

Shortly after arriving, however, Nixon and Kissinger were hustled into Mao Tse-Tung's private study for an unscheduled meeting. They sat in cream-coloured armchairs, Mao's Buddha-belly pulling at his buttons, little side tables piled untidily high with books and papers. In the presence of Chairman Mao, President Nixon was uncharacteristically awed and humbled. Mao made earthy jokes.

The thaw had started. The Chinese visibly relaxed with Nixon after Mao had signalled his approval of détente. What followed was a banquet in the Great Hall of the People. The room buzzed with jovial conversation, and Nixon went from table to table determined, it seemed, to toast every Chinaman in the room. Chou fed Pat Nixon tasty morsels of unrecognizable food. Nixon made a speech, cleverly borrowing Mao's famous expression, 'Seize the day, seize the hour.'

'Let us, in these five days, start a long march together, not in lock step, but on different roads leading to the same goal . . .'

• • • •

'While Paris was fighting over who was in, Cardin was travelling the world,' explained his director, Edouard Saint Bris. In the 1970s Cardin licensed his way across the globe. 'He is the king of licensors, and practically invented the word,' said Diana Vreeland, the matriarch of fashion editors. 'His name is known because of his persistence in projecting it into the farthest corners of the world.' While the rarefied élite in Paris, London and New York considered him passé, the middle classes in Rio de Janeiro, Johannesburg and Akron, Ohio, still thought he was a class act.

Shortly after the fall of Saigon, the town hall in San Biagio di Callalta, Italy, received a phone call from Cardin's secretary. She wanted to know if Monsieur Cardin could, after all these years, get an Italian passport. Cardin wanted the passport, the Italian officials were told, so he could do business in Vietnam. The implication was that the new communist authorities would not do business with a Frenchman – the French being the previous occupiers of Indo-China – so Cardin needed an Italian passport. He did not get one.

The prudent question, however, was what businessman would possibly want to do business in war-ravaged communist Vietnam? And Cardin wasn't selling high-tension cables but designer clothes, the archetypal symbol of decadent capitalism. And yet that was how he worked, brilliantly. Years and years ahead of anyone else in his determination to open up new markets, Cardin made his fortune over thirty years by licensing his name in obscure countries, no matter what the politics. It started with Japan in the late 1950s; by the late 1970s he was operating in countries like Venezuela, Cyprus and Indonesia. As these countries grew, he grew. Most other Paris designers were locked into their little world; had no idea these markets even existed. Cardin was, in this sense, a risk-taker and contrarian extraordinaire, a businessman of rare vision. 'I never go where oil has already been discovered,' he told *Forbes* magazine in 1988.

But by the late 1970s he seemed to have reached a plateau. He had licensed his way into the most important capitalist countries in the world; it was difficult to - find a product category that did not carry his name. 'I had come to the end of my - tether. I felt useless,' he finally admitted. Others observed it too. Wrote the *Sunday Times* of London: 'As he returns he looks suddenly brittle, as if decades of pursuing his vocation of chic have consumed inner juices and left him mummified.'

In 1977, Cardin was invited by a French television station to visit La Tour-du-Pin where he had spent the early years of his childhood. He stood in the school - courtyard, children mobbing him under the trees. 'What do you want to be?' he asked the children, as they jostled awkwardly under school satchels and wind-breakers and sweaters. They screamed professions at him, trying to catch his attention. He looked tired. Cardin glanced at the old gym where as a child he had - admired the older boys working out on the parallel bars. 'He didn't seem inclined to talk about his childhood,' recalled the school principal. 'But he seemed very moved.'

'I'd be very happy if I could be twenty again, starting over, without the name Pierre Cardin,' he told a journalist. He had peaked, and that was terror. 'If he sensed that his empire was slipping, or he was slipping, he would be very depressed,' said his friend Robert Green.

•   •   •   •

What had he not done?

It was during this momentary pause of the late 1970s, when he fished around for inspiration, that Cardin seized upon two projects staggering in their scope and audacity.

The first ambition, of course, involved his love of travel. As was his wont, when he felt uninspired and drained Cardin packed his bags and hit the road. This time he headed for China. On 28 November 1978, he boarded a plane with eight staff members and a fleet of reporters from *Paris Match* and Germany's *Stern*. At Peking airport Cardin ran up to a giant poster of Mao. 'Only Mao is better than I am,' he told the press corps, 'he dressed 900 million people.'

The wooing had begun. Cardin was the first Western designer invited to China. The Chinese had been exporting inexpensive T-shirts and such to the Third World and the West, but they were now ready to upgrade. They needed hard currency, and to that end wanted to adopt Western design cachet so that they could export added-value goods. 'They need steel works and factories, and for that they need hard currencies,' Cardin told *Stern*. 'And that is what, with my ideas, I will get them. I am the best in my field.'

PIERRE CARDIN

Wonderful, said Wong Ming-Juin, the general manager of China's clothing industry. During the customary round-table banquet, Wong Ming toasted the idea nineteen times with Mao-Tai, the sharp Chinese firewater. 'Gan Be [empty glasses],' Cardin said, one of the few expressions he had learned. By the end his cheeks were quite red and glowing. 'The things I can give all these people,' he told the crowd of journalists. But he was also thinking about his own empire. 'If I can produce one button for every Chinese,' he began telling people during that trip, 'that's 900 million buttons.'

He toured nine textile factories in Tientsin, Hangchow, Peking and Shanghai. Ever curious, he pored over a single silkworm thread drawn from cocoons submerged in trays of water; he pumped the delicate hand of a white-goateed artisan with Trotsky spectacles who made ethereal, birdlike silk sculptures; and with Mao-capped young men he draped down-soft cashmere around his neck and inspected the quality through his bifocals. Cameramen snapped his every move, watching him as he dashed from room to room in PC hiking boots and flannel pants, always a few yards ahead of the official delegation. He fingered material, inspected the sewing and buttonholes, sipped countless cups of green tea, ran his hand over the head of a seamstress telling her she had done 'clean work'. And he invited everybody he met to Paris. 'If you happen to be in Paris, why don't you come by,' he said. (Not that he had to fear hordes of Chinese would take him up on his offer.)

At the end of the trip, ten days later, Cardin spontaneously decided to produce a fashion show in Shanghai. He co-opted a secretary and a typist – this was the workers' paradise, after all – put their heads in curlers, draped them in Cardin creations of Chinese cloth and unleashed them on communist officials clad in drab Mao suits. They were shocked into silence. A few grinned. They invited him back the next year, in March.

Cardin got back to the West and played his China card masterfully. Since Nixon's historic trip a few years earlier the West was starved for information about the Middle Kingdom and the creaky opening of its great doors. Cardin picked up pages in *Paris Match*; a lead story in *Le Figaro*; a page of *Time* magazine; pages in *Look* and *Life*. Even *The New York Times* fell. In its prestigious Business People section, its 8 January 1979 lead showed Cardin meditatively clutching his chin. 'China Names Cardin as Fashion Consultant,' trumpeted the paper. 'Under the agreement with Peking, Mr Cardin will advise the Chinese on how to style their textile products to make them more saleable in the West.' Cardin told *The New York Times* a Chinese ready-to-wear line made to his specifications would eventually be sold under the Cardin label, with royalties paid in high-quality silks and cashmeres. 'The agreement in China, Mr Cardin said, also foresees training a number of Chinese technicians in Cardin workshops in France.'

The announcement was, as usual, premature. Irate high-ranking Chinese officials were soon making it clear that not only had no deal been signed, but they didn't expect to sign one either. And unlike many other occasions where Cardin's hype went by undetected, this time he was forced to back-pedal hard. He finally had to admit publicly, as he did to *Women's Wear Daily* in February 1979, that 'nothing has been realized, finalized or decided'.

But he had a second chance. He flew back to China in March 1979, this time bringing all his artillery, including some 300 outfits and a gaggle of French and Japanese models. He spent a small fortune on the trip. Disco music blared from the large Hall of Nationalities Palace on Chang An Avenue, a few blocks from Chairman Mao Tse-Tung's mausoleum. A white stage and fashion ramp was plastered with Cardin's name in Chinese characters. This was a closed-door affair. Some 300 Chinese textile workers and sellers were the only people invited to see what the world of Western fashions was like. No-one from the press was given an invitation and Chinese strongmen stood at the door to make sure only the invited appeared.

'What the Chinese hadn't figured on was Cardin's own love of press coverage, nor how ferocious and courageous the Chinese [foreign] press corps can be,' observed John Fraser of Toronto's *Globe & Mail*. For fifteen minutes pandemonium reigned at the entrance gates, with journalists trading insults and threats with fierce-looking Chinese bouncers. Cardin was in the middle, trying to shoo in the press corps with much arm-waving. At one point during the crush he himself was barred from entering because he could not produce an invitation. At that moment, however, the Japanese press corps arrived in a solid phalanx and, with Tokyo rush-hour subway skills, propelled the entire mass irreversibly forward with a momentum that could have poured through the Great Wall.

The packed hall finally settled down. To pounding disco music the Chinese saw a parade of see-through blouses, thigh-slashed skirts, pagoda shoulder pads, and men clad in Space Age tight-fitting pants. The foreign residents of Peking were appalled at this display of Western decadence, of materialism at its most trivial. The Chinese, however, accustomed to evaluating clothes by the number of cotton coupons they required, loved it. At first they were mostly silent, staring in amazement. But many of them immediately and shrewdly separated Cardin's outlandish headline-generating outfits from the immensely wearable and decorous dresses that were modelled on the Asian mannequins. It was a deft and sensitive touch by Cardin – possibly, noted journalist Fraser, 'aimed at a future market no other fashion designer would even dream of scratching'.

It was an extraordinary event, and even the bleary-eyed Peking hands were impressed by Cardin's stroke of genius. Observed Fraser: 'There have been some wild sights in China during the past year, as this country reaches out to the West to see what's going on, but it will be hard to beat the front row of comrades of both sexes in their blue cotton pants and jackets on top of two layers of long underwear watching a slinky model from Paris swish by sans brassière.'

Again Cardin's extraordinary intuition had caught a movement before anyone else knew what was going on. 'What the Chinese wanted', he observed shrewdly, 'was Paris and nothing else.' A decade later *Forbes* magazine's editor, James W. Michaels, articulated what Cardin somehow – intuitively, mysteriously – knew well in advance. 'In a world of mass communications and rapidly expanding affluence, commonalities of taste that any good socialist would have decried as bourgeois and decadent are transcending politics and nationality.' Socialists, as well as capitalists, had a psychological need to express themselves through the products they consumed. Even the masses needed glamour. It was a truism of late twentieth-century life that swept away ideologies, boundaries, politicians.

'He doesn't know anything about market research,' said one of Cardin's old Parisian associates, 'yet he is ten years ahead of it.' S. Miller Harris marvelled, 'His sense of timing, throughout his life, has been exquisite.'

●   ●   ●   ●

In 1979 John Kornblith, the American menswear manufacturer, decided to pack it in. Intercontinental Apparel Inc. had stumbled, and Kornblith's attention was pulled towards his hugely successful McDonald's interests. Perhaps Kornblith also sensed that Cardin's influence as a men's designer was waning. He put the company up on the block and the giant Hart Schaffner & Marx agreed to buy it for $2,925,000 plus the assumption of some $11 million in obligations.

The deal was already signed when the Hart Schaffner & Marx lawyers suddenly insisted they needed another change in the wording. Kornblith was up very early the next morning trying to work out the problem. He had to get the new documents to Cardin, yet he couldn't make it to Paris himself. Cardin was suspicious of everyone else. Kornblith's wife, Dorothy, awoke at 7 a.m. He smiled at her. 'Guess who's going to Paris? You're the only one Pierre will trust.'

Dorothy caught the evening flight. She arrived in Paris, whisked through customs, and was off to Cardin's office. By 10 a.m. he had signed all four copies of the deal.

'When do you return?' asked Cardin.

'The one o'clock flight,' replied Dorothy.

'Come.'

Cardin bundled Dorothy into his rickety little car and started driving madly through the streets of Paris. 'And this is mine,' he said, starting a tour of everything he owned. In an hour and a half he showed her every boutique he operated. 'My head was spinning,' recalled Dorothy. Then his secretary jumped in his car and took Dorothy back to Charles de Gaulle airport.

The deal was done. Cardin flew to New York to meet his new menswear licensee. As usual he stayed at the Hotel Pierre. Kornblith came by the hotel at 7 a.m. In the sombrely rich hotel lobby of cream and grey Cardin was curled up, dead asleep on a couch. Kornblith could not figure out whether he had come down early and nodded off, or whether he just had not gone to sleep the night before. It was well known that when he was in New York Cardin often disappeared into the bowels of Greenwich Village. He was wearing, it appeared to Kornblith, the previous night's suit. 'I was dressed to the nines,' said Kornblith. 'He was dressed in that rumpled way he looked so often – the suits too large; the scuffed, unshined brown shoes.'

He woke Cardin up. The two went to the airport and got on the plane to Chicago for the luncheon with HS&M's chief executive officer, Jerome S. Gore, and a dozen buttoned-down, straight-laced mid-Western executives. HS&M hired private rooms in one of the sky clubs where, through the bird-proof windows, Chicago's black towers and windy concrete canyons were laid out. Before they sat down a good wine was passed around. Gore cleared his throat and started making a toast to the man they were honouring. Pierre Cardin. Pierre . . .

He had disappeared.

Kornblith ran into the restaurant entrance, frantically looking for Cardin amongst the potted plants and glass and fast-moving businessmen. He couldn't find him. Finally he spotted the designer in a public phone booth. Of course, Cardin did not have a credit card or change or anything. And yet he was demanding the operator connect him with his Paris office. 'This is Pierre Cardin . . .' his nasal voice lashed the operator.

●   ●   ●   ●

Cardin again flew into New York for a three-day visit in October 1980, fresh from opening two doomed boutiques in Sofia, Bulgaria; a four-day wool promotion in Australia where he was almost crushed by 4,000 sheep; and a trip to Italy to approve a furniture line. In New York he was opening an art exhibition and his new five-storey US headquarters on 57th Street; attending a dinner at Luchows after a fashion retrospective at the Fashion Institute of Technology; and, as a highlight, showing a 30-year retrospective of his career, followed by a black-tie dinner in the Metropolitan Museum of Art. The Metropolitan? 'It is extraordinary, no?' Cardin told a *Women's Wear Daily* journalist, his eyes widening with childish wonder. 'The first time fashion has been honoured in such a way. It is simply magnificent.'

The Metropolitan was not exactly honouring Cardin. He was honouring himself. The cash-starved museum accepted a $25,000 'gift' and he spent another $225,000 on the fête. It was the beginning of the rent-a-temple-at-the-Met hysteria which swept 1980s New York society.

André Oliver was put in charge of organizing the party, and like everything he touched it was breathtakingly elegant. A string and woodwind ensemble wearing kimonos delicately played Satie and Stravinsky as they sat on grass mats; tables were covered in tender rosy-beige cloths that matched the temple stone; and some 200 candles, palm fronds and white dendrobium orchids glistened in reflecting pools.

The celebrities were out in force. Pat Lawford Kennedy worked the room in sequinned shoulders; Diana Vreeland chatted while four young men each weighing about 110 pounds followed her every move. William S. Paley, Jerome Robbins, Betsy Bloomingdale. The list was long. Even Norman Mailer was there. 'I have been known to wear a shirt of his once in a while,' Mailer said a tad defensively to a curious *New York Times* journalist. Meanwhile Andy Warhol created an impromptu artwork by smashing chocolate truffles inside the evening's souvenir book and signing his name.

Standing discreetly to Cardin's side was Didier Heye. He was one of Cardin's new executives who had shot up to the top. 'It's strange to see such a young man like that floating around with Cardin at every moment,' said Arnold Linsman. 'On the other hand he served reasonably well as a translator and knew an awful lot about Cardin's business. For someone as young as he was he had an awful good grasp of reality and never-never land.'

Didier Heye was kind, a gentleman. And, astoundingly, Cardin seemed to trust him – one of the very few people he has ever trusted. 'Didier was not overseeing anything,' explained an insider, 'he was just with Pierre Cardin. But he was very much appreciated.' Licensees claimed that when they had a particularly important point to get across to Cardin they told it to Heye, who alone could convince Cardin of the merits of a case. 'He was a good influence,' said Max Bellest. 'Very discreet, perfect manners, and with a good mind.' And he alone could temper Cardin's abusive moods.

The day after the Metropolitan extravaganza Cardin held another fashion show. A model noticed she had her dress on inside-out. 'What do you think this is? Fashion? This is the stage,' Cardin roared. And with those philosophical words he shoved her on to the runway.

•   •   •   •

In 1979 the New York garment manufacturer, Bernard Wachter, started using Chinese factories, particularly around Shanghai, to produce items for his prestigious, up-market women's line. China's low labour costs were extremely attractive to Wachter, as was the abundant high-quality silk. He hired Chinese embroiderers, skilled in a labour-intensive art largely lost in the West, to stitch-and-bead classic designs into silks which were then shipped to Hong Kong for finishing. Although lucrative, the experience was not problem-free. 'There were tremendous delays in delivery, sometimes six months to a year,' said Wachter. The reason: garments from backwoods factories were transported by river boats or oxen.

In 1980 Wachter became a Cardin licensee, producing a successful expensive womenswear line. Three years later Cardin invited Wachter and some 200 other licensees to Peking. Cardin, with immense cunning, had manufactured his designs in dozens of factories all over the country. The samples covered complete men's and women's collections.

'The licensees were invited into this hall,' recalled Wachter. 'There was this huge fashion show, with Chinese models, and all the designs Cardin had made in China were shown the audience. After that we all went into another hall – his licensees from around the world – and the Chinese tried to sell us the Cardin designs.' Banks of tables, rows and rows stretching seemingly for ever, were open for business. And all were selling Cardin products. 'I would say it was the best-laid plan that any designer has ever had. Cardin had opened up entire China to his licensees. It was an absolute genius plan.'

Yet it failed. The 200 licensees swarmed into the hall and headed for the tables exploding in colour – camel-hair overcoats, silk shirts, cashmere sweaters. Wachter went to the table of a Shanghai manufacturer of silk blouses, a group he had been doing business with for several years. He asked for the prices. They quoted him a price several multiples of what he had been paying in the past. Wachter, in shock, began questioning the Chinese as to why they were quoting such prohibitively high prices. 'Because it is Pierre Cardin,' they responded.

'They quoted outrageously high prices, no matter what category, to everyone in the hall. There was a kind of murmur, and then an uproar,' recalled Wachter. The brilliant plan was botched, not by Cardin but by the Chinese. Apparently the communist bureaucrats could not figure out how to price the Cardin merchandise. 'They sent a high delegation to Paris to look at the couture shops. They looked at a blouse, say for $200, and figured: "If he sells a shirt for $200, then the wholesale cost is $100, the manufacturer's first cost is $50, and we want to give them a break, so we'll give it to them for $40.'' And I had previously been paying $10. They thought that what they saw in the Paris couture store was the Cardin price range, and then they worked their way backwards.' The trouble with that reasoning, of course, was that the licensees dealt in the competitively priced mass market, not the expensive, poorly selling couture market, and could not work with the prices the Chinese had set. Cardin's executives tried to explain to the Chinese why their pricing was all wrong. The language barrier, however, proved too great.

The following night the Cardin licensees were treated to an evening of Chinese delicacies, a dinner of camel hump and bears' paws.

●   ●   ●   ●

Cardin travelled, jumped on plane after plane. Before most knew that Korea was a potentially lucrative market, with its 40 million people and growing middle classes, he was in Seoul peddling PC. An interesting statistic told the whole story: only 20 per cent of South Korea's 40 million people bought ready-to-wear, compared to 75 per cent in Japan where Cardin had blazed the trail thirty years earlier.

Korea was becoming increasingly sophisticated as it geared up for the 1988 Summer Olympics. Its exports were growing vigorously on the back of its energetic textile industry, but to reach new growth targets the government fished around for means to import Western technology and design cachet. They turned to the adaptable business tool, the licensing agreement.

In 1982 they finally gave approval to the first licensing deal, with 'recommended' royalty limits of 5 per cent. In 1983 Cardin signed a men's suits, coats and accessories contract; then a swimwear contract. The partner was Korea's industrial giant Samsung, and it reportedly guaranteed Cardin a minimum royalty of $315,000 over three years.

But Cardin's hunger was not sated. He wanted the forbidden market. Ever since he first travelled to the Soviet Union in 1964 he had fantasized about seducing the last great commercial frontier: Communist Russia. In the early 1970s he announced with much ballyhoo the India–USSR deal that never existed. But in the early 1980s he pulled out all the stops. After all, the French and the Russians had a long history together. In Moscow's back streets dressmakers still occupied stores on streets called 'Atelye', a corruption of the word 'atelier' and a throwback to the days of the French-speaking aristocracy.

Cardin began his wooing under Andropov. Then Andropov and his successor Chernenko died, and up rose the relatively unknown Mikhail S. Gorbachev.

The new Soviet First Lady was not the customary potato with warts, but an educated, stylish and petite woman. Cardin had a Soviet fantasy that included everything from a Moscow Maxim's to a Soviet-manufactured perfume. He established offices at the Sovincentr Hotel complex – 'The Trump Tower of Russia', as he called it – and hired Jeff Knipper, an odd man with hair swept up and back like a porcupine, to be his Paris–Moscow liaison. But first Cardin had to spend money in the USSR, much as he was doing in China, in order to win loyalty. His love-making required a reach into his deep pockets.

On 31 October 1983, Cardin, his entourage and some fourteen French journalists huddled at Charles de Gaulle airport waiting to board their plane. Art journalists from the conservative *Le Figaro* to the communist *Humanité* were on the junket. 'Why is Pierre giving us Moscow?' whispered one perplexed journalist.

The reason was *Junon and Avos*. Cardin was importing intact to Espace Pierre Cardin the first Soviet rock opera, complete with a cast of sixty, constant smoke-letting, and Broadway-like dance routines. The plot revolved around a love story between a Soviet count and a 16-year-old Spanish girl from San Francisco. Mythic prototypes – from rope-twirling cowboys to shadowy monks – combined with erotic dance routines. The music swung violently from liturgical chants to harsh, gravelly rock. 'It hit me like that,' Cardin said, striking his chest. And that was why the fourteen journalists were in Moscow.

Cardin started gabbing and immediately his language took flight into little poesies. He proudly announced he was launching a 'diplomatic concept – to make peace with art and fashion'. The journalists were fed hot dog-sized cold sausages and canned peas for breakfast, and then dragged through the Moscow streets. Autumn had hit Moscow with a thud. Columns of smoke from factories poured into the leaden November sky. Moscow's river was charcoal and the crumbling, high-rise apartment buildings swallowed the unsmiling ham-thick bodies in long underwear and overcoats.

'They have wonderful mass production here,' Cardin told the journalists. They nearly choked, but Cardin's propaganda was paving the way for future deals. 'It is not a poor country. In the USSR they have money to spend on clothes. Everybody is working. And the rent, the medicine, is paid for by the government,' he told them. His comments were preposterous – right from the pages of pre-Glasnost Soviet doublespeak. In case any journalist did not know that he greatly admired the Soviets, he set the record straight: 'Such a concentration of will, such discipline.'

By the end the group was preparing for its trip back to the Moscow airport with the honeycombed industrial ceilings. Cardin was chatting to the journalists about his plans for the next two weeks: first to India to meet with

PIERRE CARDIN

Mrs Indira Gandhi and discuss the possibility of a restaurant in Bombay; then on to Osaka, New York and Rio. As he talked he absent-mindedly pulled out of his pocket a wad of money that contained bills from three countries.

That trip helped liberate Russian caviare and vodka for the Maxim's label. The big break, however, came in October 1985 when the Gorbachevs arrived in Paris for a three-day visit. Gorbachev was doing his own wooing. *Le Monde* called it 'Operation Seduction'; French President François Mitterrand called it a 'charm offensive'; a Reagan administration official called it 'more Gucci diplomacy'. In such jockeying for advantage, one undisputed winner turned out to be Pierre Cardin.

His arch rival, Pierre Bergé at Yves Saint Laurent, announced that Mrs Raisa Gorbachev was visiting the YSL salon on Thursday at 5 p.m. sharp. At the last moment, however, Raisa cancelled her visit to Yves Saint Laurent, rescheduling it for Friday, and instead went for a private showing at Pierre Cardin. The clucking in Paris was practically heard in Vladivostok.

The moment Raisa Gorbachev stepped out of the Aeroflot Il–62 jetliner, beady fashion eyes bore into her. Millions scrutinized her stylish haircut, her flat-heeled shoes. 'Not since President John Kennedy jokingly referred to himself in 1961 as "the man who accompanied Jackie Kennedy to Paris" has a travelling First Lady generated as much excitement and curiosity as Raisa Maksimovna Gorbachev,' editorialized *Time* magazine. French fashion journalists concluded she was elegant but not chic. She was meanly sniped at for wearing the same pin-stripe suit twice in the same trip. 'Princess Diana of England wears the same dress twice in public, but at least she waits two years,' said Odile Pouget of Monte Carlo radio. A brown chiffon gold-striped pleated evening dress for dinner at the Élysée Palace was dismissed as a 'Muscovite gown'. 'She has to support the one Moscow couture house and apparently they are having a season of stripes,' was the catty observation of the influential Nathalie Mont-Servan of *Le Monde*.

But the clothes she wore for the visit to Maison Pierre Cardin were praised. In a sturdy grey herring-bone suit and metallic silver stockings, the 51-year-old red-head sat poker-faced through the collection of some fifty gowns, including a lavender-sequined evening gown for $3,750. Raisa sat on Cardin's Espace egg-type chairs and told him his styles were 'not commercial, but I respect them as works of art'. Some thirty-five minutes later Cardin kissed Raisa's pearly-pink, well-manicured hand and helped her into the limousine. 'She told me she hoped we'd succeed in developing a commercial rapport,' he told the press clamouring at the kerbside. 'She said, "I would like to help you. If you need me, call me." ' And then he released to the world her measurements, which were 90 centimetres around the bust, 70 waist, 96 around the hips. 'She is a woman of great charm, of style, and most of all of intelligence and culture,' he said. 'She is a formidable woman.' (At Yves Saint Laurent she was shown a sable-lined raincoat and satin ball-gowns. Saint Laurent gave her a bottle of his 'Paris' perfume. She wanted 'Opium', however, and was given that as well.)

The Soviet Union needed design and manufacturing assistance. Your basic grey had been in season for the last sixty-eight years in Moscow. The spike-haired Soviet fashion designer with the Italian-style men's handbag, Slava Zaitsev, was making expensive and well-crafted clothes for Moscow's élite under the Republican Ministries of Services. But the masses were clothed by the thick-set men who ran the Ministry of Light Industry. Their designs were little different from the days of Stalin – outdated factories clanked out clothes with poor cuts in scratchy, colourless materials. Lingerie was mostly of the wire-reinforced type. The customary queue often bypassed the Muscovite clothing shops. 'Nobody would buy their old-fashioned rubbish,' an art student explained to a British journalist. 'It is poorly cut and often so badly made it falls apart within weeks, while the materials feel horrible and the colours clash.' Muscovites instead preferred to spend hours queuing up for a scrap of imported Indian cloth at Dom Tkani (House of Cloth), so they could make their own clothes. The consumers' desires were an infinitely stronger urge than any shame that came from charges of being 'bourgeois' and 'decadent'. 'There is tremendous interest in this kind of clothing,' Slava Zaitsev told *The New York Times* in 1986. 'More and more people want to show their individuality through the clothes they wear.'

Fortunately the new Soviet leadership had a more realistic view of its people and 'Perestroika' was launched. Because of Raisa Gorbachev's fascination with fashion, one of the first industries to get to work was the Ministry of Light Industry. Cardin saw the opening and he moved like lightning. It was reported he dined tête-à-tête with the Soviet First Lady at the Gorbachev's snow-wrapped dacha outside Moscow, just two months after he had kissed her hand in Paris. Practically the next day Cardin signed a historic memorandum of understanding with Ivan Gritsenko, Soviet Deputy Minister for Light Industries. Cardin was to design twenty-one different products, including men's, women's and children's wear, made from Soviet-produced fabrics in thirty-two factories scattered throughout the Soviet Union. Some of the Soviets were to be trained in Paris. Cardin's label would be on all the clothes, and, of course, he was to receive royalties. At a Moscow press conference in late December 1985, Cardin looked the part of French designer in a dapper blue blazer with a purple silk foulard. 'The Soviet Union has an ideal image in Mrs Gorbachev, who is beautiful, elegant and wears fashion divinely,' he said.

In April 1986 the deal was inked. It was all so surreal, foreshadowing the political changes in the Eastern Bloc. On that trip Cardin and his aides, including his press officer Bernard Danillon de Cazella, swept into the Foreign Trade Bank in Moscow. Soviets stared in awe and horror at Danillon, clad in black leather pants, green shirt, tasselled loafers and ankle-length cashmere overcoat. Meanwhile Jeff Knipper, Cardin's Soviet liaison, was implying in conversations that Cardin would never dare fire him because he had mysterious protection in the Kremlin.

Over the years, including his Moscow office and producing the rock opera, Cardin sank some $10 million dollars into cultivating the Soviet market. It did not go smoothly. He prematurely announced plans for a Pierre Cardin superstore which never materialized; instead the Soviet-made PC garments were peddled in the traditional department stores. The Cardin suits sold for between 100 and 400 roubles; Soviets earned roughly 200 to 300 roubles a month. Cardin pooh-poohed the problem, claiming that Soviets had huge forced savings because there were no products to buy on the shelves. To help move the merchandise, the Soviets did an unheard-of thing, airing a Soviet-style advertisement of the Pierre Cardin clothes line on national television. Even so, Western journalists grilled him about the Soviet reputation for shoddy quality. 'Oh, please,' he said in a huff, 'a country that can send a rocket to the moon can also make a jacket.'

Cardin's gamble paid off. By 1988 the Soviets were paying him some $180,000 a quarter in royalties. Other designers followed. Clothing manufacturers in France were granted contracts to help modernize Soviet plants, and Pierre Bergé of Yves Saint Laurent was soon negotiating with the Soviet officials. But Cardin, as usual, was first.

'I think the essence of Cardin is that he is a person who is impatient,' said Robert Green. 'People bore him easily and he needs the stimulus of a new project. He needs the enormity of the challenge of all of China, of all of Russia. He needs a sense of the dramatic.'

•   •   •   •

China, the big hope, washed out. No-one expected that the Soviets would make the plunge before the Chinese. Cardin had a few Chinese plants manufacturing merchandise for export – beautiful men's cashmere coats with high collars and throat belts, for example – but he was not selling clothing to the Chinese masses as he dreamed.

Yet it remained an obsession. Max Bellest recalled how Cardin's younger co-ordinator in America, Nicholas DeMarco, had organized a beautiful lunch with the US licensees in the New York office. The luncheon was charming and everyone was relaxed. Then Cardin got up to make a speech. The mood immediately soured. 'My name, my name . . .' he went on interminably, telling them how famous he was. 'Look, look, China!' Cardin spent the whole time talking about the Soviets and China, markets the Americans were not overly concerned with. 'Can you imagine what I could make?' he asked his US licensees. 'Imagine if I sold one toothbrush to every person.' Eyes rolled. Disenchanted, the American licensees broke up the party. They had been hoping Cardin was going to announce plans to galvanize the US market which was starting to stagnate.

By the late 1980s Cardin's name was fairly well known inside China, but he still had no means to cash in on the recognition. The answer came from Turin, Italy, where Gruppo GFT hung its hat. Gruppo GFT was one of the country's most respected and successful ready-to-wear manufacturers. It was the backer and manufacturer of Giorgio Armani, Emanuel Ungaro and Valentino. Since the 1960s it had been Pierre Cardin's Mexican licensee, and from 1987 on it was producing clothes in Tsien-Tsin, 150 kilometres outside Peking. In January 1988, GFT joined forces with Cardin to create Pierre Cardin China Ltd.

Shrewdly, GFT was given complete management control of the venture. The company, financed initially with $1 million, was 60 per cent owned by Cardin and GFT, while CITIC (the Peking-based China International Trust and Investment Corporation) and Natcan International Trade Financing Co. Ltd of Hong Kong each owned 20 per cent. This was a start-up in the fullest sense of the word. The joint venture's purpose was to produce and distribute clothing, accessories and shoes for men, women and children. And later Pierre Cardin home furnishings and leather goods. But since modern distribution or retailing channels did not exist in China, the logistics of this assignment was daunting. Everything was to start from scratch. 'We will open 4,000 Pierre Cardin stores all over China,' Cardin ran around telling the press.

It was Arnaud de la Motte who negotiated the Gruppo GFT contract for Maison Cardin. He looked as if he was barely out of his twenties. 'Pierre wanted to develop a complete line for the Chinese people,' said de la Motte. 'We didn't want to put a label on Chinese fabrics. The costs were low but so was the quality. We wanted, absolutely, to get occidental standards on products.'

But in the early days of June 1989 the bottom fell out of the great Chinese experiment. On 2 June, some 5,000 troops attempted the first crush of the pro-democracy students protesting in mighty Tiananmen Square. The manoeuvre ended in disarray when 100,000 students and Peking residents blocked the paths of the army trucks. By the early hours of Sunday morning, the Chinese government had lost its patience. At 1.30 a.m. gunfire could be heard to the south-west of the square; parallel lines of fire lit the north of the square. And then gunfire was coming from in the square. By 2.15 panic was raging and the streets were filled with men and women running, cycling, with cries of 'retreat, retreat'. After rows and rows of students and workers were shot the lights in the square were switched off and the students started screaming in terror. Forty minutes later the lights went on again and loudspeakers warned the students to leave the square or suffer the consequence. Reported the London *Times*: 'An immediate vote was taken and the students decided to leave. Holding hands, they processed to the south, where they were allowed to pass out of the square. Then they were shot at.'

MAXIM'S: POTS FLY

13

In 1890, at 3 Rue Royale, seven wrought-iron tables with marble tops lined the front of Maison Imoda, an Italian ice-cream parlour. Waiters, holding metal trays aloft, came dashing out of the café door, their starched white aprons flapping just above their ankles. They wore smart, tight-fitting black jackets with white dickies and bow-ties, and took orders for vanilla ice with backs ram-rod straight. Next door the horses of delivery carriages clattered their hooves across the cobblestones as they pulled into the courtyard. Over the café, a careless resident had forgotten to secure the shutters and they banged gently in the breeze.

Three years later the café was taken over by a waiter, Maxime Gaillard, who, caught up in the English rage of the time, called his establishment by the anglicized version of his name, Maxim's. As soon as Gaillard's bar opened on 23 April 1893, it swelled with a motley crew of newcomers and low-lifes, of Parisian snobs slumming for the evening.

Gaillard died in January 1895 and left the restaurant to his cook and head waiter, who within four years called in the decorator Louis Marnez to update the interior. The pavement in front of the bar was packed with cane chairs and heavy iron tables. Streetlamps were crowned with twisting iron hats. In the

207

summer the red awning was lowered for shade, and the stylized Belle Époque handwriting announcing the 'Maxim's' establishment caught the breeze and flapped. Flush against the darkened window, steamy palm-trees promised delights exotic and raunchy.

Maxim's reputation was naughty and permissive. English aristocrats brought their Parisian whores there after dressing them at Paquin or Worth. Orchid-like women in white flowing gowns leaned across the linen tables, whispering into the ears of white-haired, red-faced gentlemen in evening dress. The lighting was dark, the carpeting red and lush, and on the walls unbridled eroticism stimulated the appetite: in peach and orange pastels voluptuous women dipped their naked bodies into cool lakes; they reclined invitingly on crimson poppies, cupping ripe fruit, their nipples hard. In this cosy, champagne-filled atmosphere, the naughty were safe. It was their club, and it filled with the likes of le Prince de Sagan, le Baron Lepic, le Comte de Montesquieu. It was at Maxim's, it was said, that the future King Edward VII drank champagne from a dancer's slipper.

Maxim's became so popular with the British aristocrats that in 1907 they bought the restaurant and listed it on the London stock exchange (where it was publicly traded until the 1980s). In the restaurant, meanwhile, roast pheasant and quails' eggs and magnums of Moët et Chandon kept the clientele sated. They danced the Argentine tango. 'Its décor was the most glittery, its women the most ravishing, its top-drawer scandals the most toothsome,' observed a news magazine. 'Until about 1930 – the year when one might say it underwent a moral face-lifting – Maxim's was a place where women were seen but never ladies,' observed the Comtesse de Toulouse-Lautrec.

In 1931 the Frenchman Octave Vaudable bought the majority of the shares and the famous Albert, prince of maîtres d'hôtel, took charge. In the darkened entrance the huge, red-faced Monsieur Albert ruled with Swiss efficiency. He had the right to keep the restaurant empty if he deemed no-one was acceptable enough to enter. In a little cage above the entrance hall, the hat-check girl stared down on guests timidly making their way down the long darkened corridor. 'Between the two of them they would scare the bejesus out of anybody,' said Maggi Nolan, a society columnist. If Albert seated a customer on the right side of the room they were banished to what was known as 'Siberia'. If they were seated on the left, however, their social standing was high; the left-corner table was always reserved for royalty.

Max Bellest recalled the sparkling days of Maxim's in the 1930s. An assistant to Albert welcomed him as 'Monsieur le Comte' one evening. 'I am not a comte,' said Bellest, a little testy. 'Is this a restaurant where when you forget the name of your customers you call them comte?'

The waiter laughed. 'Oh, Monsieur Bellest,' he said, 'it is of no importance and it is so good for the house.'

'In that case I am very offended,' responded Bellest, 'because I think I look good enough to be called Monsieur le Duc.' From then on Albert always called Bellest 'Monsieur le Duc'.

During the Nazi occupation German officers, many of them old habitués, took over Maxim's as their own club, and any Frenchman entering its mahogany vestibule was considered a collaborator. After the German surrender, when it was briefly seized by the British, it once again opened its doors with a roar. It was a favourite for gossip columnists, such as Maggi Nolan of the *International Herald Tribune* who would write her columns simply by reconstructing the room in her mind while back in front of the typewriter. On the right, just before Siberia, there was a corner table reserved for the White Russians. Rosy-faced bon vivants with white, twirling moustaches turned their champagne bottles upside down in the bucket before the last glass was emptied. The Aga Khan, and later his son Aly, dined with beautiful women. Rita Hayworth sat near the Duke and Duchess of Windsor, who of course occupied the royal table. Across the room Aristotle Onassis and Maria Callas ate olives. Visiting Hollywood stars sat near oil magnates; New York industrialists dined across the room from Indian maharajahs. It was the club of the Who's Who.

By the 1970s life, and Maxim's, had changed. Élitism and formality were relegated to the shelves; democracy and informality tyrannized the day. Albert's successor, Roger Viard, was running the show under the eyes of the owner, Louis Vaudable (Octave's son), and his charming wife Maggie. On the surface it remained much the same. If one looked closely, however, one could notice that the carpet had become threadbare. The Vaudables had dabbled in side businesses to earn better returns. With partners they had opened versions of Maxim's in Tokyo, Chicago and Mexico City; offered five-week sessions of cooking lessons; participated in additional restaurants at the Paris airports, Orly and Roissy—Charles de Gaulle. And yet Maxim's heyday was over. By the end of the 1970s the restaurant's revenues had stagnated at around $4.6 million, with profits a meagre $56,900. The papers reported that the *Guide Michelin* was preparing to drop a star, and Louis Vaudable requested that the food guide drop Maxim's listing altogether. Something had to change.

In January 1977, Cardin was dining with Maggie and Louis Vaudable. An odder trio would be hard to imagine. Cardin, brash and flash; the Vaudables élitist and obsessed with good taste. Somewhere amongst the scalloped terrine and roast pheasant the conversation withered. So Vaudable broached the subject. How could he cash in on Maxim's glory? They had tried with their own catering and franchising ventures, but with no great success. 'Besides, it's not our kind of business,' he said.

Cardin was intrigued. 'You know, you have a formidable name . . .' And as Maxim's strolling violinist serenaded the room, as knives plunged into the grilled duck and truffles, Cardin, the man with a million and one ideas, painted a grand licensing vision of restaurants, hotels, perfumes, cocktail nuts.

The Vaudables and Cardin went their separate ways, but the seeds were planted. Phone calls followed. It wasn't long before Cardin and Vaudable had agreed to form a joint venture to exploit the Maxim's name. Cardin was going to manage the venture, sink his own money into it even, while the royalty fees would be split evenly between the two parties. Maxim's was the beginning of his new life. This was a project on the scope of penetrating China; the potential was enormous. It was almost as good as being twenty and having to start all over again.

●   ●   ●   ●

Cardin sank $4 million of his own money into the Maxim's venture, taking over leases and spending heavily on legal fees to secure worldwide trademark rights. Licensees were hunted down. In October 1977 La Boutique Maxim's opened, a stone's-throw from his Avenue Marigny headquarters. Deli-style billy-bi (creamed mussel soup), foie gras, pheasant, duck, and coquilles St Jacques were peddled in porcelain dishes embossed with the stylized initial 'M'. There were Maxim's teas, jams, cognacs, champagnes, and magnums of whisky. A Maxim's tin of sardines was available for 9.50 francs. Upstairs, browsers could pick up handbags and luggage and Limoges china with the 'M' in gold or burgundy art nouveau script.

A year later the joint venture launched Maxim's line of evening wear, 'L'Homme de la Nuit'. It was sold from a boutique next to the deli. The complete line went from alpaca dinner tails to polished black shoes and black-tie accessories. To promote the opening Cardin and the Vaudables hosted a $60,000 dinner at Maxim's. Oeufs du caille au caviar (quails' eggs with caviare), barbue farcie (brill), rack of lamb, puréed vegetables, and glaces the shade of honey. Cardin, for ever obsessed with youth, invited some fifty young couples who circled with the bombed-out, punk hair-dos through the pearl-choker crowd. To show off the Maxim's evening look, he flew in blond models from the US so that they could stand around in tails looking beautiful, similar to the silhouette made famous by Maxim's waiters. A samba orchestra of bronzed, muscular boys and girls snapped their bodies like rubber-bands. The din and the roar finally ended at 10.30 the following morning.

Cardin followed up with Maxim's fruits. Then a Maxim's flower shop opened; it sold a mature orchid in a Maxim's hatbox for $240. By this time the 'M' products included ceramic swans, key chains and lobster bibs. That was too tasteless, decided the Vaudables, and the honeymoon ended. The two parties began to squabble over the direction the development was taking. Cardin was itching to have Maxim's explode all over the world.

Louis Vaudable was 78, and his son, François, had little interest in following his father's footsteps as a restaurateur. It soon became clear that the only way to resolve the situation was for Cardin to buy out the Vaudables completely. Hervé Duquesnoy, who had grown into his job after learning from early mistakes, began the tedious negotiations. Some ten months later, in May 1981, the deal was completed. Cardin bought out the Vaudables' 67 per cent share in Maxim's Ltd for, claimed the house, $20 million. Pierre Cardin's acquisition was splashed across all the papers. It was expensive, but the price included minority interests in other projects, plus a royalty on the future income stream from Maxim's licensees, and, of course, the worldwide rights to the name. And there was no one better in the world at understanding the value of a name than Pierre Cardin.

Not everyone saw the logic. 'Why put all that pressure on you? It's self-destructive,' said Andrew Wargo. 'You'd think there was enough around his name to protect and worship, but Pierre just runs into another direction.' The designer's retort: 'I prefer to pay for my own errors than someone else's. It's my money.'

Paris's élite were not pleased. Nothing was more sacrosanct to Parisians than this restaurant. By the time Cardin took over, its interior of nymphs and stained glass and its curlicue lamps were protected as historic monuments, but the carpets leading upstairs were soiled and threadbare. Yet the long-time customers fretted in their over-stuffed living-rooms about the future of the rack of lamb Maria Callas, the icy magnums of Moët et Chandon, and Roger Viard, the famous maître who turned people away if they weren't socially or sartorially acceptable. This was the place to be seen. Had been since before the war. And now this Venetian trader, this tacky promoter of plastic and pop culture, was taking it over? Not without a squawk. 'It's a monument like the Louvre and therefore quite unassailable,' sniffed Robert Coutrine, food critic for *Le Monde*. 'If Maxim's becomes anything like Cardin's dresses, then I hate to think of the effect. I certainly wouldn't eat there, with people dressed in Cardin's clothes. It would spoil my appetite.'

Cardin was very conciliatory, telling the fretting French that he would do nothing to it but make it more glamorous. And, at first, he did. He earned high marks for pumping vast sums into a new, modern kitchen, abandoning the ancient one in the basement (although it produced wonderful food it was rumoured to be encrusted with grime). Then he redid the plush scarlet carpets, and made overdue technical improvements.

Cardin's associates said he never really liked Maxim's until he owned it. Nicole Alphand had always adored it, but if he had to eat out he preferred La Tour d'Argent or Le Voltaire. A good part of Maxim's reputation was based on its service, a ballet really whose performance needed heavy food with many sauces. Cardin's eating habits were diametrically opposed to Maxim's truffles and gout. Said a waiter who served him for years, 'All he ate was a grilled côte d'agneau and a green salad. He never ate anything else. It was a regime all year. He is a man who couldn't tell you whether a sauce was good or not.'

But once the restaurant was his and the hoopla had settled Cardin became restless. He put in more tables, and then installed upstairs a 'Chambre d'Amour', an art nouveau suite for $1,000 a night. 'It's a petite folie,' Cardin explained. Was the restaurant in its decline? 'Not at all,' he told Hebe Dorsey of the *International Herald Tribune*. 'The food has not changed and will not. I'm not a restaurateur, and I don't see why I should meddle with something that's doing fine.'

Of course, he thought he was a great restaurateur. And of course he began to meddle behind the scenes. He used to tell everyone about eating with the great culinary family, the Escoffiers. 'Because he ate one time with Escoffier, or I don't know who, he thinks he is the greatest restaurateur in the world. He isn't. He ruined Maxim's. He thinks he is a God and never asked the professionals how to run the restaurant,' said Franco Gentileschi, the director of the well-known L'Espadon restaurant at the Ritz Hotel, but formerly a head waiter at Maxim's between 1972 and 1984.

Cardin moved in with a heavy hand. As with everything he ran, he wanted absolute control. He didn't want to delegate; he wanted to greet every guest, seat them, cook their meal, serve them and collect their money. If only he could. Immediately he went after Roger Viard, the director of Maxim's and an institution in his own right. In the last years Louis Vaudable collected the money but let the reliable Monsieur Roger run the shop. White-haired, elegant and bean-thin, Roger knew all the clients by name, knew their special demands, where they liked to be seated. He personified that special service which had made Maxim's famous over the years. He was charming, but behind the scenes he ran a no-nonsense operation obsessed with perfection.

Viard was too strong and independent for the likes of the new boss. Cardin wanted him out. Just a few days after he had taken control of the restaurant, Cardin and Viard banged heads. Employees said Cardin began usurping Viard's job of greeting and seating the guests. Viard fought back. 'I am sorry, but I have been here forty-five years now, that means it is my rôle to

receive the clients. It is your job to go to the office. After dinner you can drop
by their tables if you like,' was the kind of message Viard repeatedly delivered
to Cardin. Cardin, understandably, did not like that. It was his restaurant, after
all, and he could do what he liked. As sparks flew between the two, the whole
staff began to suffer.

Maxim's was a well-oiled machine. Viard had given each of his head
waiters a task for which they had absolute control. One might be responsible
for just the silver, for example, another for all the china or crystal. It was up
to these head waiters to maintain the highest standards and if Viard detected
any lapses he moved in quickly and disciplined the offender. In this way, the
staff of over 100 all knew their assignments and executed their responsibilities
with the minimum of fuss. In short, by delegating and clearly delineating
responsibility, Viard had a professional and harmonious operation in place.
Service was sublime.

But this was Pierre Cardin's place now. 'When I was there with the Vaudables
I knew who the patron was,' said Gentileschi. 'It was Monsieur Roger. But
afterwards everyone gave orders. Monsieur Cardin gave one order. Monsieur
Roger gave another. The manager inside would give a third order. Four or five
people were commanding the ship at the same time. It was impossible to work
there afterwards. The disharmony. There were orders, counter-orders, orders
and counter-orders all day.'

Cardin made sure they knew who was boss. 'It's my money,' he told the
shocked staff. 'I can do with it as I like.' All Maxim's supplies had to be
approved by him, down to the number of pens, and if they were not he called
from Avenue Marigny and screamed on the phone. If a piece of equipment in
the kitchen burned out, or the boiler collapsed, the staff had to track him down
and ask permission to replace the equipment. Sometimes they had to call him in
Indonesia, or some other remote country, to get the necessary approval. Not the
most efficient way to run a restaurant. Morale plummeted. Other employees,
too afraid to talk on the record, also tell of the chronic suspicion with which
he attacked the staff. He accused them of stealing. He thought that employees
were pinching sticks of butter and legs of lamb from the larder. Even when
his attention was drawn to the detailed inventory he was not convinced. The
inventory, he responded, was too good to be true.

The next thing he did was squeeze out the plump, white-haired professionals. He didn't fire them outright, just created an unbearable atmosphere;
they flocked towards the retirement exit. 'He replaced them with beautiful
young men with blue eyes and blond hair,' recalled Gentileschi. 'He didn't care
whether they had any certificates or where they had worked. The only concern
was how they looked. It was a mistake.'

PIERRE CARDIN

Chaos was compounded by Cardin's obsession for moving furniture. He often arrived at Maxim's at 6 a.m. with a van and two or three young men as movers. He rearranged the furniture so that when the employees arrived at 9 or 10 to prepare for lunch they found a different restaurant. 'If we touched something, a wall, moved a table or a chair, we had to ask his permission,' said Gentileschi. It was an absolute repeat of how he ran Espace Cardin or his office. But it was also more than just amusing, it created real operational problems. On one decorating binge Cardin ran around ordering his men to 'take that and that'. He eyed a very large pot that offended him. It was gone. Then there was a large fish-platter. Gone. Finally he was finished and the van began its pilgrimage to a storage centre some 25 kilometres outside Paris. The chef, in all innocence, arrived at around 8 a.m. with a large salmon. He searched high and low for his fish-platter and his 'casserole' – to no avail. The staff finally located the badly-needed pot and platter, but it took two days for them to be returned. 'This is not normal,' said a perplexed employee.

Cardin was intent on increasing revenue and cutting overheads – a noble business objective – but set about the task as if Maxim's was some bistro in Saint-Etienne. He added tables. Then he turned off the central heating, said employees, and installed space-heaters instead. This was Maxim's, where richness and lushness and abundance were part of the mystique. That was what people were paying for. 'People ate with their coats on. It was terribly cold,' said Gentileschi. During the summer an air-conditioning unit was installed, hidden in an armoire. It rattled, making conversation at one particular table a matter of decibels. Another employee claimed that during the winter months, in the back of the restaurant, the staff's hands became numb with cold. Coats were normally hung in a hallway near the back entrance, but when it got very cold anyone working behind the dining-room's swinging doors eventually put their coats on to keep warm; on one particularly cold day, when they went to grab their coats, the coats, swore this employee, had actually frozen stiff.

Cardin also tried to cut costs by switching champagnes. The house champagne under the Vaudables, tailored to Maxim's specifications of blending and dryness by Moët et Chandon, retailed at $11 a glass. To boost his profit margin Cardin decided to replace Moët et Chandon with a cheaper champagne. Maxim's traditional clientele, however, knew their champagne and there was an uproar. They practically spat it out. 'This isn't champagne,' they snapped at embarrassed waiters. Cardin had to back down. He found another more up-market champagne, although still not Moët et Chandon.

Cardin's attitude towards Maxim's undermined the quiet, snobbish air of élitism that had made the restaurant famous. It was in a way a type of revenge on Paris's upper classes; but it was also self-destructive. When the Vaudables owned the restaurant they had always been in the background. In fact, although they were famous, very few people actually knew what they looked like. Not that the Vaudables were not sophisticated – they were, but they always considered themselves servants of Maxim's reputation. Their customers were first, first and first. Cardin, on the other hand, viewed Maxim's as his canteen; he had first rights. This is what distressed Roger Viard the most. A regular occurrence: at 10.30 in the morning Cardin's secretary called the restaurant and reserved the room royale for him for the same day. The tables, however, were reserved months in advance by long-standing customers. Monsieur Roger, a consummate professional, died a thousand deaths. All he could do was call up every customer, beg his apologies, and inform them Monsieur Cardin was taking over the room.

Cardin did this frequently, particularly on Friday, which was the most damaging as it was also the most popular night, when black tie was required. Long-standing American customers, who had called from overseas months in advance, were sometimes turned away at the door. 'It was terrible. This was not a banquet hall. He blocked the use of the restaurant. Sometimes he reserved thirty tables and we had to tell people at the door, who had been coming for over thirty years, they could not come in,' recalled Gentileschi, his face reddening with embarrassment at the thought. 'He ruined the house.'

To Cardin, Maxim's was also a vehicle for enhancing his celebrityhood and garnering publicity. It was the final straw to many refined French customers who had been going there for years. Thickly inked headlines in French papers suddenly screeched Cardin's new motto: 'Maxim's c'est moi'. Around silver tea-urns and bone china polite society shivered. To get his point across, a solitary Cardin posed in the empty restaurant amongst a sea of tables, with an army of waiters standing to his attention alone. In the American magazine *People* he posed in top hat and tails.

Not that he was without his defenders. His loyal young staff rushed to his protection. 'When he bought Maxim's the whole staff was frightened of him,' said Charles-Efflam Heidsieck, a young executive at the Maxim's empire. 'They reacted very badly. When he went to Maxim's they didn't make him feel involved, he did not feel at home. He said, after all, "It is my place, it is my money, and if you don't like me, you leave, because you are in my house".' It was a classic clash of cultures. A staff accustomed to a great deal of independence had been acquired by a hands-on manager. The trouble was compounded by the fact that they did not, for good reason, respect his management abilities.

In May 1985 Cardin threw a party at Maxim's to interest stars in his newest obsession, a remake of *The Merry Widow* with Maxim's as the centrepiece. The idea never went anywhere, but the party was fun. Placido Domingo was the main attraction. According to the attendant press, Texas socialite Lynn Wyatt asked for ice cubes in her champagne, while Placido Domingo Jr aged 15, declared that 'opera is a dying art form'. At the end of the party a large wooden screen fell on the back of Cardin's head. 'They are trying to kill the boss,' he laughed.

There was, however, one Cardin protégé the whole staff loved. Didier Heye frequently ate at Maxim's; he adored the restaurant. 'He was the best man around Monsieur Cardin,' said Gentileschi. 'He was lovely. Gentle, polite, elegant, discreet, educated. He was the opposite of Monsieur Cardin, and around Didier Cardin behaved.' Another employee recalled how one evening Heye was celebrating at the restaurant with a small group of friends. Cardin arrived very late. Immediately, however, he became angry and agitated. He was, said this employee, very upset that there were no women at Heye's table. It was in bad taste, indiscreet. This was Maxim's, after all. Perhaps it was just a matter of a generation gap between Cardin and Heye.

The inevitable began to happen. French society started bowing out and Maxim's was dropped from short lists. It was no longer natural to go there after a film or a play, or to have an intimate dinner for eight, as it had been for decades. 'I don't go there much any more,' said Bettina Graziani. 'It's completely different from what it was like in the 1950s and 1960s. But life is like that. It's more open to other people, which has changed the atmosphere. It's a different clientele, less sophisticated.' Cardin democratized the restaurant just as he had democratized haute couture with ready-to-wear. Many criticized him; others applauded his business realism. 'The problem with the French people is they'll say, "Maxim's is great," but they don't mind if it doesn't [make any money],' said the patrician Charles-Efflam Heidsieck. 'Cardin doesn't work for French snobs. And if you are in business you can't think that way. If you don't progress, you die.' And that was why, undoubtedly, he opened Minim's – a fast-food knock-off of the great restaurant which sold $10 sandwiches on black plastic table-tops.

Cardin and his supporters were undoubtedly correct – up to a point. How to modernize and expand, however, was where they stumbled. It was not necessary to downgrade the restaurant quite to the extent that they did. Many prestigious businesses managed to maintain an old-world, élitist image and yet grew in leaps and bounds during the 1980s. His old rival, the house of Chanel, was a spectacular case in point.

Whichever side of the argument Parisians came down on, one fact was indisputable: the days when faces from the society pages sat at each and every table were over. The restaurant was soon stuffed with Japanese tourists giggling from too much champagne. There might be an elegant elderly couple from Oregon; a table of platinum blondes and thick-necked men looking like the Corsican mafia, celebrating some occasion. The prices, of course, were never democratized; if anything they had risen. Dinner for two, with a moderate wine, cost $400. An asparagus hors d'oeuvre – in season – alone cost $35.

The *Wall Street Journal*'s saucy middle column was devoted to the Maxim's empire in November 1984:

'Celebrities still patronize the place, but today Maxim's caters to a largely different clientele. "We had a choice of four restaurants for tonight, but we had always heard so much about Maxim's that we figured, by golly, we're going there," says an Ohio Chevrolet dealer on a tour for winners of a sales contest.

'A waiter tries unsuccessfully to talk the dealer's wife out of ordering Coca-Cola as an aperitif. "It's terrible for your stomach," he says. The car dealer asks the wine steward if the cellar has any California wines "Not yet, sir," the steward answers politely. "OK, just bring me something that tastes good," the Ohioan replies. The onion soup, he says, "is as good as any restaurant in Cincinnati serves".'

Cardin, the publicity hound, loved the article. Waving the clip with each reference to Maxim's dutifully underlined by a press attaché, he ran around boasting that the *Wall Street Journal* had mentioned the restaurant no less than sixty-four times.

But despite the high prices, the extra tables, the cost-cutting, Maxim's still could not justify the price Cardin had paid for it. 'Maxim's was the same as high fashion thirty years ago,' explained Hervé Duquesnoy. 'If you didn't have ready-to-wear, or accessories, you were killed. The restaurant's break-even is very high. It's the reason why for such a name you need diversification to earn some returns.'

Cardin had a global vision for the restaurant: to open a replica of Maxim's in every major city in the world. The restaurants established the prestige image, the trademark, in a local market. It was, of course, an expensive and risky proposition. The locations had to be perfect; quality control and strong management were vital; and hefty capital investment in décor and staff were needed. But afterwards Cardin planned to cash in on the Maxim's image, vividly established by the new restaurants, by licensing popularly priced products in the local market. Perfume, frozen foods, chinaware, spirits, clothes: these products would be the equivalent of ready-to-wear. He would do this all over the world.

The Vaudables had previously opened up Maxim's in Chicago, Tokyo and Mexico City. Cardin closed Chicago, but then struck with a speed that was truly staggering. The year after he had taken control a Maxim's opened in Brussels. Then in 1983 he inaugurated Maxim's in Rio de Janeiro with a black-tie dinner which included an Arabian prince and Rio's governor, Leonel Brizola. Sources said he did not own the restaurant outright but had some mysterious Middle Eastern backers. It cost some 600 million cruzeiros to build and was operated by a company called La Belle Tour. (Perhaps it served the purpose of sopping up some of the PC cash Cardin could never get out of Brazil.)

Then there was Maxim's in London, also opened in 1983. This was purely a licensing deal with Kennedy Brookes, a catering and restaurant management firm. The restaurant opened on Panton Street, near Leicester Square, the disco and Chinese restaurant tourist centre. It had photos of the interior outside, lit up to attract strolling browsers. In the Maxim's bar-café attached to the restaurant, modestly-priced nouvelle cuisine could be ordered. A group of pimply teenagers in white aprons served the food, which sometimes took an hour to arrive cold. And yet at its official inauguration, in December 1983, the cloakroom had to be insured for £1 million. The princess of Jordan, Prince Adyn Aga Khan, the Duke and Duchess of Marlborough, Baron Eduard de Rothschild, Faye Dunaway, Charlotte Rampling and Mark Thatcher appeared, reported *The Times*.

Not without some hitches. Cardin's luggage was lost on the flight over. Clad in a safari suit he moseyed over to Panton Street to find crowds fighting to catch a glimpse of the designer. Horrified, he dashed back to the Ritz Hotel and dragged its manager, Julian Payne, out of the shower. Payne parted with his dinner-suit, some alterations were made, and Cardin pulled off the transformation. The next day he stuffed the stitched-up suit in a plastic bag and deposited it outside Payne's door – 'with a note, and not a monetary one'. (Payne recalled: 'He was a loved and respected client, but not one to parade in front of the other clients. I remember he used to wear this tie, which was more akin to a woven two-foot ruler than a gentleman's tie.')

That same year Cardin opened a Maxim's in Peking. Everyone thought he was mad. He sent some fifteen Chinese to train in Paris for three months. They returned to Peking along with sixteen Frenchmen, including three chefs. Chandeliers and eleven tons of merchandise were flown in to redecorate the drab building in East Qianmen Street. The reproduction, right down to belle époque-style lamps and hand-painted garlands between smoked-glass ceilings, recalled the Rue Royale. The decoration ran way over budget, with hundreds of French, Japanese and Chinese craftsmen at work. When it finally opened the cost of a lunch was $100 for two, which was about how much the average Chinese worker earned in three months. It was clearly for Westerners stationed in China and hungry for some European cooking. Cardin opened a fast-food joint, a Parisian bakery that sold croissants, to help pick up business from the man in the street.

As usual, Cardin was very flighty when it came to answering questions of ownership. According to the *Los Angeles Times*, however, the restaurant was a joint venture with the Peking Municipal Catering Service Corporation, an operator of about 1,800 noodle shops. The eight-year agreement called for alternating management every two years, and, it was reported, Cardin was fighting for a 50-50 share of the profits even though he had spent a fortune building it. 'The restaurant is really my gift to the Chinese people,' he said. The point was not to make a profit, but to establish locally the fame of Pierre Cardin and recognition of the Maxim's trademark. That it did. Baggy-trousered Chinese with leeks and cabbages stopped at newspaper boards to read about the mad Frenchman who had opened a Maxim's in Peking. Meanwhile, in tatty conference rooms in Paris black volumes of Chinese clippings filled a small library. Cardin could be patient.

Young men were sent to fill the ranks of Maxim's. Frédéric La Combe, with chiselled jaw and dark, deep eyes, graduated from college in June 1985. He had studied Chinese and wanted to live in China, so he asked Cardin for a job. He served a two-month apprenticeship at Maxim's in Paris before being sent to Peking without a job title. As it turned out, the previous manager had been sent to assist in the opening of the New York restaurant. The 20-year-old La Combe found he was temporarily in charge of day-to-day supervision. 'You can get a job here you'd never get at home,' he told the *Chicago Tribune*.

Lunacy and brilliance. It was Cardin's unique way of working. 'Monsieur Cardin doesn't proceed with precise evaluations. He just invests on impulse,' said Hervé Duquesnoy, grappling for the words to explain Cardin's methodology. 'Instead of losing time on two-year studies, which cost a lot, he prefers to do it directly and see if it works. He thinks that time and being first in the market is the most important thing. Some people say it's not the correct way to work. But Cardin is Cardin.'

Invest he did. He opened a Maxim's in New York, on Madison and 61st Street. Gentileschi, who was originally supposed to direct it, until he left in disgust, said that it was delayed by construction problems. In 1985, however, and some $8 million later, the restaurant opened. The heavy New Zealand wool carpet alone cost $40,000. Bronze wall-mountings and lighting fixtures from India cost $500,000. Upstairs, l'Omnibus housed a bistro-style restaurant for 150; downstairs in the Grand Salon 225 could be seated. Dinner was a $65 prix fixe, but the menu was also loaded up with supplementary charges. The quails' eggs and caviare, for example, cost an extra $25; a side order of green beans another $7. Champagne started at $55 a bottle. This was not for the budget- and calorie-conscious. No spritzers and grilled swordfish here.

'I scratch my head about Cardin,' said John Kornblith. 'You could say he's lucky, but so much has turned out so well for him that I don't think it's luck. He has a magic touch of sorts. He had no business buying Maxim's, and there was no reason to believe that Maxim's could operate a great restaurant under his direction. And I don't think it is a great restaurant, but it certainly is great drama.'

'Think of our business as a pyramid,' waxed the New York restaurant's director, Monty Zullo, to *Forbes* magazine. 'At the top is the right image – luxury, elegance, style. Then you develop the correct product lines – champagne, caviare, smoked salmon. Finally there are more restaurants, hotels, other licensees. To think of Maxim's as only a restaurant is to miss the point. You must understand the whole philosophy.'

Hotels came next. Jack A. Pratt was a sun-belt promoter who ran the $200 million revenue Pratt Hotel Corporation. He made his fortune in the mass market and wanted to break into the glitzy niche of superluxury international hotels. He couldn't afford the Ritz but he could afford Maxim's. The two men signed a deal whereby Cardin was to receive a $100,000 advance against each hotel, and 1.5 per cent of gross revenues. A spectacular deal for Cardin since he carried none of the risk.

The first hotel to open was in Palm Springs, California, in 1986, six storeys rising out of designer-boutique malls set against the San Jacinto Mountains. Like flotillas of fame Zsa Zsa Gabor and Liberace sailed around the opening party. And in the *Palm Springs Social Pictorial*, a weekly that broke news on the latest hats worn at the Polo and Country Club, the bottom of the Maxim's pyramid began to appear. Maxim's champagne was touted in a full-page ad with the catchy copy, 'Le Top of the Pops'. Albert must have turned in his grave.

Swept up with this vision of Maxim's hotels, Cardin dashed back to Paris and in December took over a long-term lease on an Avenue Gabriel mansion, a stone's-throw from Espace Pierre Cardin. How could he convince people about his Maxim's hotel chain if he didn't successfully run a prototype in Paris, explained Duquesnoy. Splattered with paint, his hair tousled, his white stubble giving him that unsavoury look, Cardin spent eighteen blissful months holed up, renovating the hotel. Out of mysterious warehouses he dragged odd pieces of furniture collected over the years. 'I wanted to give new meaning to luxury,' Cardin told William Meyers, the *New York Times Magazine* writer, in 1987.

He certainly did. Some $14 million dollars later La Résidence Maxim's opened. The sheer tackiness took people's breath away. Some rooms were Maxim's-style commercial knock-offs: bathroom murals dripping with steamy orchids, overstuffed couches in treacle colours, and festoons lashed with giant pink bows. Others were decorated with day-glow orange nylon couches from the 1970s and cheap reproductions in glass frames hung on mouse-grey wallpaper. The highlight was the 'suite Royale', a 400-square metre extravaganza with a schizophrenic sitting-room: on one side a Napoleon III-style settee, on the other a modern, armless detachable couch that ran the side of two walls.

This hodge-podge suite, designed, it was said, with oil-rich Sheikhs in mind, originally rented for $7,500 a night.

The hotel opened in 1986. That same year the Maxim's des Mers was launched, a former minesweeper converted into a floating version of the Rue Royale restaurant. Despite hints to the contrary, however, Cardin did not have his own money at stake in the yacht; this was a licensing agreement. Esther Williams was the celebrity dragged out of retirement to launch the ship. The yacht included an art deco swimming pool, sixteen luxury suites for thirty-two passengers, a piano bar, a jacuzzi, a hairdresser and a multi-lingual crew. It cost $22,000 a day to rent the yacht, to swim in the same pool Esther Williams paddled in. But of course that included meals of poulet au Calvados, gratin de citron à l'ananas, and a 1979 Château Lafite Rothschild. Management also threw in the shuffleboard free of charge.

Back in Paris, Cardin granted his customary string of interviews. Patricia McColl of W magazine saw him during that period and what she saw was really something. 'His horn-rimmed glasses are held together with a paper-clip,' she wrote. 'There's a pin in the lapel of his grey and burgundy jacket and the top button is missing. In his five-storey home opposite the presidential palace dust frosts everything . . . On the wall his Léger drawings have all slipped in their mattings and hang at drunken angles to their frames.'

A Cardin employee of the day, who asked for anonymity, described his appearance at the time: 'He always wears the same tie every day for about a year. His socks are full of holes. His shoes are never polished, and he never shaves himself very well. And his hands are fascinating. He always has some black grime under his nails. He has a worker's hands. He can't keep away from getting his hands dirty.' During the W magazine interview Cardin turned to McColl. 'I am a working man. Look at my hands,' he said proudly, holding out hands polka-dotted with pin-pricks. 'I work Saturdays and Sundays.'

Meanwhile Roger Viard, the director of the flagship restaurant, decided he had had enough and resigned after forty-seven years working at Maxim's. Cardin had won the war. At his farewell party, Paris society came to tip their hats to the 65-year-old. Marie-Helene de Rothschild, her hands swollen with arthritis, came to pay her respects; as did a string of old customers like Sao Schlumberger, the Duke and Duchess de La Rochefoucauld, Prince Jean Poniatowski. Viard's relationship with Cardin was bad to the very end. 'He totally ignored me,' Viard said. 'Too bad, because we could have done great things together.'

Cardin flew to New York. It was one year after Maxim's New York had opened and unexpectedly he showed up at the restaurant in the morning. 'I want you to double the prices, today, for lunch,' he informed the startled staff. 'I am coming for lunch, make my reservations. Same menu, double the price.' And then he left.

•   •   •   •

Shortly after the New York restaurant opened, young Charles-Efflam Heid-sieck, a member of the old French champagne family, was in a small room in the Avenue Marigny headquarters. He was applying for an entry-level management job and had been waiting for his interview with Cardin for an hour and a half. Cardin finally stuck his head in. 'I was looking to meet someone. Where is he?' Heidsieck called attention to himself. After twenty minutes Cardin opened the door, his tie flung over his shoulder, and called over his secretary in his nasal voice. She came running.

Heidsieck had the impression that Cardin's entourage of men had been trying to eavesdrop on the interview. 'Everything is fine with this young man,' Cardin droned on nasally. 'He has a good resumé. Please make everything ready. I want to sign his contract as director of public relations in New York.'

Heidsieck was in shock. He had had no idea whether Cardin liked him, or what job was expected of him. This, now, was the first Heldsieck learned of his job. 'Here's your room. You start now,' Cardin told Heidsieck. 'I'll see you in four days before you go to New York.' He was sent to an accountant, who asked him what Cardin had agreed to pay him. During the interview Heidsieck had quoted a salary requirement based on a job in Paris. But now he was going to New York. No matter. They put that figure down on the payroll as a net amount, rather than the gross it was intended to be. A good thing, too. Heidsieck, in his three years working for Cardin, was never given a raise. In February he left for New York. He was all of 24 years old.

A year later Cardin flew into New York. He had a well-known habit of going for a walk at 8 a.m. every morning. Heidsieck woke early one morning and showed up on the pavement in front of Cardin's apartment at 800 Fifth Avenue. Cardin came out.

'What are you doing here?'

'Monsieur Cardin, I know you are taking a walk, I would like to walk with you.'

'Come.'

The two began walking up Madison Avenue. Heidsieck simply wanted to get to know the mysterious man who was his maître. At such moments – relaxed, humble – Cardin was a lovely person. He was warm, treated his employees as family. He did not act as if his privacy was invaded, as many executives would have done. The two men walked past art galleries and florists, past sweater boutiques and bookstores. Garbage cans overflowed; New York Transit buses hissed as they opened their doors and released cleaning ladies on to the kerb. A woman openly defecated on the street in front of the Parisian multimillionaire. 'Look, do you see this woman . . .' Cardin said excitedly. 'Oh my God, it is disgusting.'

At the end of their walk they stopped off at a coffee shop opposite Maxim's. Waiters and waitresses bustled, taking two or three orders at a time, passing coffees and muffins and hash browns and eggs backwards and forwards. Cardin did not have any money on him, so Heidsieck treated him to a coffee. 'Look at these people,' marvelled Cardin. 'There are just three people. Look how well and hard they work. They must make more money than I make at Maxim's.'

●　　　　　●　　　　　●　　　　　●

New York was becoming very important to the Maxim's empire. Jack Pratt was putting together what he thought was going to be the jewel in Maxim's Hotel crown. The ill-fated Gotham Hotel on Fifth Avenue was changing hands, again. According to New York press reports, the 24-storey limestone building was being taken over by a group of investors led by real-estate mogul Sol Goldman, and Jack Pratt wanted in. He and his partner, the Dallas-based Southmark Corporation, ponied up for a share of the estimated $85 million needed to buy and refurbish the hotel. But the deal hit a snag. Based on projections, Pratt's deal with Cardin meant that the Parisian would pick up nearly half a million risk-free dollars the first year the hotel was in operation. According to the *New York Times Magazine*, Goldman didn't like that. Not at all. 'I'm not impressed with Maxim's,' Goldman told everyone. 'The restaurant on Madison Avenue – it's dead all the time. Who ever goes there?' The investors wanted Cardin to pick up some of the risk and a new agreement was reached. No royalty would be paid to him for the first two years unless cash flow covered debt service. The hotel opened in 1987. A single room cost from $210 to $325. The presidential suite, $2,500.

'When something is going 250 kilometres an hour, there's no way you're going to stop it,' said André Oliver, discussing his friend of thirty-five years. 'It's going to ride on to the end, and nothing will make it slow down.'

PIERRE CARDIN

•   •   •   •

Maxim's was a turning-point in Cardin's development as a businessman – a fiscal about-face. While developing the PC label, Cardin studiously avoided investing his own money. The exception – Espace Pierre Cardin – was really a personal, emotional investment which turned out to have a knock-on effect beneficial to the name as a whole. On everything else, however, he shrewdly had licensees pick up the tab.

But Maxim's was something else altogether. Investors were never really as convinced of the value of the Maxim's label as, two decades earlier, manufacturers had been convinced of the PC label. At that time Cardin had the field to himself and had no trouble finding partners. In the 1980s, however, there were so many designer labels up for grabs – largely due to his own early success – that Cardin found he had to sink his own money in projects to get them off the ground.

And he did. During the 1980s Cardin dropped $20 million in China; some $10 million in the Soviet Union; $20 million buying Maxim's, Paris; $14 million at La Résidence; $8 million at Maxim's, New York; and additional tens of millions of dollars on odds and ends like Maxim's, Rio, and a Pierre Cardin boutique in London, parties at the Metropolitan Museum, producing plays at Espace, buying a factory in France, and so on. And because Cardin abhorred banks it was all being funded by internally-generated cash. Almost all of these businesses, though they produced some $40 million in revenue, were operating at a loss, haemorrhaging even more millions of dollars every year.

Cardin could not afford these huge sums indefinitely. He instructed his accountants to route all his North American income, not to Paris, but into the Maxim's restaurant in New York. Then he pulled the plug on André Oliver's beautiful store on 57th Street, the extremely elegant men's shop of Oliver designs which Cardin had been financing – it was rumoured that the rent alone at that store was $1 million a year. And then Cardin took a swing at Max Bellest, the man who had built up America.

Max Bellest was in his late seventies. The younger Nicholas DeMarco had been appointed Pierre Cardin's co-ordinator in the late 1970s, but Bellest was still the elder statesman of the business. He still worked tirelessly on bringing in new licensees. When he joined Cardin in the 1960s he was shrewd enough to secure a lifetime contract. In the event of separation or retirement, he was to be paid 5 per cent for two years, and then 3 per cent until he died. In the early 1980s Bellest received a letter from Cardin's lawyers reducing his commission. He was still putting in a full day's work, and Cardin had never bothered to discuss his retirement with him. Now Cardin simply had his lawyers cut

Bellest's commission. Max cashed his reduced cheques and didn't say anything for a few years.

John Kornblith remained close to both Cardin and Bellest although he had cashed out. Cardin, who was hoping to launch his Minim's fast-food chain, was perhaps interested in staying in touch with Kornblith for his McDonald's connections. Bellest and Kornblith, however, were genuine friends. It soon became clear to Kornblith that a major confrontation was brewing between the fiery Max Bellest and the imperial Pierre Cardin. Bellest was incensed by the arbitrariness of Cardin's behaviour. Imagine, not even the courtesy of a phone call. 'It's a good example of Pierre being sloppy,' said Andrew Wargo, Bellest's associate. 'You never break a contract without a legal notification to cover yourself. You don't just tell a lawyer, "All right, cut Max down." That's sloppiness. Or even just the friendship thing. He should have told Max, "It's time to retire." In a letter. "Dear Max, as of a certain date, we'll reduce . . . I assume you'll agree to it, in which case I have instructed my lawyer." But he didn't. This kind of sloppiness got Cardin into a lot of trouble.'

Bellest got in touch with his lawyer. Letters flew. Bellest recalled that his lawyer informed Cardin's lawyer that Mr Cardin had no arrangement with the Bellest Corporation, the cut in commission had not been discussed, and therefore the Bellest Corporation should still have a 10 per cent commission. Furthermore, Bellest said, if we sue we're going to claim our 10 per cent retrospectively, which amounted to around $1 million. John Kornblith took Bellest's case to Cardin. 'I'm absolutely persuaded that in addition to doing a favour for Max, I did a great favour for Pierre,' recalled Kornblith. 'That was just one of the times Max was going to bring Pierre to the highest court in the land, get him on the gallows if possible.' Bellest was talking about hiring Roy Cohn, one of America's most succesful and feared lawyers.

Cardin backed down and gave Bellest a new contract. Bellest reasonably accepted the 3 per cent – he was after all 80 by this time – but Cardin also wrote strong guarantees into the contract. There was tremendous rivalry between Edouard Saint Bris and Max Bellest. Saint Bris, said Bellest, was interested in securing his number two position under Cardin. So Bellest was afraid that Saint Bris would cancel the old Bellest licensees, set up new contracts, and then cut him out of his commissions. But the new contract that Cardin had drawn up promised Bellest his 3 per cent commission on all US contracts, even if negotiated by others. Max Bellest was mollified.

After this was all over and done, Cardin was still scraping for cash to hold together his hugely expensive Maxim's experiments. For relief he turned to the past. When pressed he sold off bits of his name. In the early 1970s, for example, when the heavy investment in Espace began to threaten him, he sold his name in Argentina. Earlier, in the 1960s, he began an incredibly complicated series of deals with the perfume rights to his name. In 1966, said several executives, he sold the worldwide rights (excluding France) to the US firm Jacqueline Cochran, later to become Shulton Inc. But then Cardin indulged in his penchant for secretive asset-shuffling. According to a 1990 court case, the rights to his name for the perfume business are held in a Liechtenstein-based trust company called Picaso-Anstalt. Cardin, in turn, controls Picaso-Anstalt. On 10 October 1967 the earlier sales agreement between Picaso-Anstalt and Shulton was cancelled, and Picaso-Anstalt – that is Pierre Cardin – once again gained ownership of his name.

It did not end there. For a second time Cardin sold the rights to his name to the same party. In 1977 Picaso-Anstalt again granted Shulton the exclusive right to use the Pierre Cardin name in perfumes. It was a one-time $2 million payment for the rights, but the contract also included a $500,000 option to buy the name outright prior to the contract's expiration on 31 December 1991.

In February 1990 American Cyanamid, Shulton's parent company, put its perfume subsidiary up for sale. A prime asset, of course, was the option to buy the rights to Cardin's name in perfumes for a mere $500,000. Cardin immediately expressed interest in repurchasing his name. American Cyanamid informed him he would have to get in line with the other potential buyers and bid like everyone else. Understandably, that did not please Cardin. In late March and early April he and his lawyers sent Shulton letters terminating the 1977 contract on the basis that the company had violated it by the 'low-level, non-selective' distribution of products bearing his name. Cardin was claiming that Shulton was damaging the prestige of his name, and as such he could cancel the agreement.

Shulton responded on 12 April 1990 by exercising its purchase option, sending Picaso-Anstalt a cheque for $500,000. On the same day American Cyanamid, and its heavy-hitting counsel, filed suit in New Jersey for injunctive relief and a jury trial. In the late summer of the same year Cardin settled out of court, once again regaining the rights to his name. The undisclosed settlement, said American Cyanamid's lawyer, John C. Fricano, was 'good' for his client.

So, when in 1984 the financial strains of developing Maxim's began to surface, Cardin once again resorted to this type of secretive selling. Andrew Wargo had negotiated a PC electronics licence – alarm clocks, electric razors, hair-dryers – with a firm called Arrow Trading in New York. Around 1984 Andrew noticed he didn't receive his agent's commission. He called the manufacturer.

'Don't you know, Andrew?'

'What?'

'Pierre Cardin sold the rights to his name to another company. I now send the royalty checks to a company in Geneva.'

The company was PCL SA, a company shell with a Rue du Rhône office in Geneva. It in turn was owned by another group of silent investors. Cardin had secretly sold PCL the rights to his name in several categories besides electronics. They included tobacco products, writing products and small leather goods. This new company sold items such as plastic PC pens of the lowest quality, give-aways at hotels like Le Bristol which also inscribed their own name on them. Said Jean Manusardi, 'It represented the beginning of the end.' Andrew Wargo agreed. 'The scary thing is, what control does he have?' said Wargo. 'I don't know. They could wind up selling electronics everywhere. Why would he do it at that level, when he has so much to lose having built up his name? Why would you give someone a free hand to own your name outright? Someone probably offered him a lot of money and he said, "Hmm, who knows what tomorrow may bring." '

●   ●   ●   ●

The selling of his name to PCL SA partly explained Cardin's frenzied push of Maxim's. It was a tacit acknowledgement that the PC label was nearing the end of its life. The comet was burning out and Maxim's was his new option on life, a way to start from scratch as he had dreamed. A lot more than just his fortune was riding on Maxim's. 'I think he wanted to do it all over again, and this time maintain the standards that were not maintained the first time around,' said Kornblith.

It was not to be. Maxim's deals unravelled as quickly as they were thrown together. Maxim's in Brussels failed immediately. It was an inferior restaurant, said Maxim's staff. 'We told him, "Monsieur Cardin, you do what you want, but it is too close to Paris," ' said Gentileschi. 'He would never listen to a professional.'

According to the Brazilian press, by February 1985 the Brazilian Justice department had sealed the kitchen and locked the doors of Maxim's in Rio. La Belle Tour, the restaurant's operator, had gone under. 'It was ridiculous to try and reproduce in tropical Rio some idea that worked in Paris,' a local celebrity, Guilherme Araujo, told the magazine *Veja*. Araujo had gone to Maxim's a few times only, to find no-one else was there. 'It's not like Antonio's or Florentino's where you can see who is "in".' The food critic for the powerful *Journal do Brasil* was no fan either. 'The food is bad, super expensive and pretentious,' he wrote. The restaurant, with a capacity of 250, was empty during the week and attracted only some twenty customers on the weekend. It closed in 1985 and sat empty for years. Recently Cardin has begun throwing more money at it in an effort to resuscitate it. But it is only his own cash and determination which has opened the doors again.

London's Panton Street Maxim's closed its doors in 1989. The expected hordes of Sloane Square debutantes and playboys never materialized. Instead bored, inexperienced waiters slouched in dining-rooms with row upon row of empty tables. Kennedy Brookes, after running it at a loss, had no choice but to cancel the licence just as the catering firm was taken over by the Trusthouse Forte hotel and restaurant group.

Blood was on the streets in New York. After just one year in operation Pratt's flagship Fifth Avenue Maxim's hotel was sold to the Peninsula hotel group of Hong Kong. It was no surprise. At $210 to $325 a single, it was taking a hammering from the press. *House & Garden* featured it in its travel section and did not mince words. At the hotel restaurant, 'you pay a lot of money to look at Art Nouveau posters coyly mounted on mirror-panelled walls, next to pillars cutesied-up with Art Nouveau mouldings and a lacquer-work border wrapping the room like a bow at the chair rail line.' In the mezzanine's garden the 'faux stone' looked like 'plastic marzipan'. The large suites, meanwhile, had 'gold wallpaper that only a set designer for a Hollywood game show could love'. In November 1989 the Palm Springs hotel was sold to a Japanese golf-club chain.

The hotel in Paris, meanwhile, was empty, empty, empty. The annual occupancy rate was estimated to be around 35 per cent. Dismal. Cardin had a skeletal staff running it and yet it was still believed to be losing large sums.

However, according to Cardin Peking was near break-even in 1988, a claim that most visitors found hard to believe. The massacre at Tiananmen Square was undoubtedly a setback for all his well-laid plans. For all his dreams and hefty investment China still remained an untapped market. 'I think the Chinese used Pierre,' said Eleanor Lambert. It seems so. A modelling school opened in Xian in the spring of 1990. Catering to the dreams of young Chinese women, it is called the Xian Kadan Model Training School. Kadan is meant to sound like Cardin.

Maxim's licensees, meanwhile, had mixed results. A Maxim's perfume, launched in 1985, could be found in most drugstores in Paris, in J.C. Penney's and other lower-middle-class department stores in the US. Launched at the same time as Calvin Klein's Obsession, Maxim's perfume chalked up FF 150 million in sales in 1988. But other licensees fared less well. The Martini & Rossi Group contract to sell Maxim's cocktail nuts in Europe was cancelled after three years. 'We were pigeons,' Jean Bodnar, export manager for the group, told the *New York Times Magazine*. 'The product was a resounding failure. Maxim's is not a very well-known name.'

The Maxim's publicity never materialized. As a fashion designer, of course, Cardin received a biannual invasion of journalists which revved the PC empire like an engine. No such transmission for Maxim's. The common man in Peoria, Illinois, or Zug, Switzerland, or Kyoto, Japan, had never even heard of Maxim's. Cardin had thought that his own publicity would rub off on Maxim's. It didn't. There was very little crossover. No amount of 'Maxim's c'est moi' was going to change that.

Additionally, Cardin's development of Maxim's was slap-dash and sloppy. The sound idea of establishing a prestigious hotel or restaurant in a local market, and then moving downstream by licensing products, was never executed properly. Restless Cardin instead pushed Maxim's into a string of products – china, napkins, cognac, towels, sardines, herbs, bonbons – well before a powerful worldwide image was created. Manufacturers signed expensive licensing contracts in order to gain marketing muscle. In Maxim's case, it was flab. 'He really thinks he is Pillsbury,' said Andrew Wargo. 'He is so far from these companies, he should only know how well they are run.'

Others claimed he knew exactly what he was doing and had a grittiness that would see him through the Maxim's crash. Charles-Efflam Heidsieck pointed to an incident he witnessed at La Résidence Maxim's. That day Cardin flew into the lobby with a Japanese businessman in tow. The hotel was uncharacteristically full.

'I want to show this room,' Cardin told the concierge.

'Hello, Monsieur Cardin,' the concierge replied politely. 'I am sorry you can't visit the room because it's occupied.'

'I am in my house,' Cardin said, his voice rising. 'I want to see that room. I want to show it now.'

'Monsieur Cardin, by law I can't permit you to enter the room. It is occupied.'

He was livid. 'It's ridiculous to run the hotel in this way,' he muttered. 'I want it 75 per cent occupied and then I can show rooms.' And then he abruptly rushed out of the doors.

Cardin preferred to run the hotel a little empty and with a skeleton staff. 'Pierre is very rich and he is the only one who knows why he is doing what he is doing,' said Heidsieck. 'Maybe he wanted less staff, and less business, for tax reasons.' Maybe. But unlikely. It seems uncharacteristic that Cardin would ever willingly turn away a profit.

Others pointed to the core of the man. 'There is a dogged determination in Pierre,' said Robert Green. 'Such as, "What do you mean I can't make this work? You know I can. I will. It will work." And of course he has the funds to play some rather important games. He can gamble like crazy on giving something time to find its audience.'

PIERRE CARDIN

Could be. The buffet lunch at Espace Cardin was a case in point. Laughed at for years as a down-at-heel, greasy canteen where no one went, Espace finally became one of the hottest places to have lunch in Paris. Hordes of fashionables in Claude Montana leather coats piled sardines in olive oil and artichoke hearts in tomato basil sauce on their plates. The restaurant was crammed with people. And after losing money in his beautiful but empty Maxim's in New York, maybe the tide was changing. Initially he was too parsimonious to pay for a top chef. But that changed. In April 1989, Bryan Miller of the *New York Times* upped Maxim's to two stars and a good review after Cardin hired Marc Poidevin, a former chef of Le Cirque. 'A thriving banquet operation kept it afloat while management changed strategies. Just as it seemed that Pierre Cardin, the owner, might be forced to design a leisure line for Caldor to keep his restaurant afloat, Maxim's is coming to life,' wrote Miller. His final conclusion: 'Maxim's may yet find its way out of the doldrums.'

•   •   •   •

Cardin would undoubtedly have tirelessly worn his critics into the ground. But tragedy struck. His close associate Didier Heye fell ill in 1987. Journalists and licensees who called for him were told he was travelling. This went on for months. And then he appeared one night at his beloved Maxim's and the staff was shocked at what they saw. He was painfully thin, his baggy skin barely disguising his skeleton. That autumn he died. On 29 September 1987, *The Normal Heart* was produced at Espace Pierre Cardin. The play was about a gay New York community coming to terms with an epidemic choking it to death; about gay men saying goodbye to friends dying of AIDS.

'Heye was very much appreciated by people working for Cardin, because he was always trying to ameliorate Cardin's temper,' said a Paris employee. 'It was a good thing for Cardin. It was exciting for Cardin to work when Didier was alive. When Didier left us, Pierre changed. Didier had been like his adopted son.'

In January 1988, American Cyanamid's Shulton Group announced that it was pushing heavily into the men's fragrance arena, using the Pierre Cardin fragrances it owned as an engine. During a press conference Sheila Hopkins, a Shulton manager, was asked whether Cardin would put in personal appearances. She had her doubts. 'He is growing more reclusive these days,' she said.

Six months later Max Bellest came to Paris. He had an appointment with Cardin. The two men were old, battle-weary servants of the Pierre Cardin label. Bellest was recovering from a stroke. He waited for fifteen minutes in the salon. Then Edouard Saint Bris came out. 'Monsieur Cardin cannot come and wants you to tell me what you want,' he informed him. Bellest walked out. He waited in Paris three weeks, but he never heard a thing from Pierre Cardin, not even a phone call.

A few months later John Kornblith came to Paris. Kornblith had always stayed in touch, and every year when he came to Paris he made it a point to have lunch with Cardin. 'My relationship with him had always been perfect, as far as I'm concerned, until my last trip to Paris,' he recalled. 'But for the first time he did to me what he had done to so many other people through the years: he made a date, didn't break it, just didn't come.' Recollecting the scene, Kornblith looked out of the panoramic view of his East Side apartment. 'We probably won't be seeing each other ever again,' he said quietly.

EPILOGUE

14

It was the second meeting with Pierre Cardin. I was working on a cover story about him for *Forbes* magazine in March 1988, and Bernard Danillon had dragged Cardin back in to see me after it was clear that I was not satisfied with my first interview. I had not had any success in wangling financial details out of Cardin, and I could just imagine my New York editor's look of scorn when I passed on the house's line that figures were not revealed. Somehow, I would have to get a sense of the numbers, something that would allow me to do my own analysis.

Pierre Cardin came flapping into the conference room. He was on his way out to lunch and was wearing the most striking overcoat — a Chinese-made cashmere coat of his own design, with a belt low on the hip, very tapered, an extraordinary bat-like collar which could be lashed together with two little throat belts. I was determined not to let him off the hook this time, and as I persevered he unconsciously raised his collar, practically covering his whole face, as if protecting himself from my aggressive questioning. Finally, when he saw I wasn't going to let up, he said that others had estimated his worldwide sales at $1 billion annually.

In 1989 sales picked up strongly in the United States and Cardin sold $201 million worth of goods at wholesale in that country, on which he earned a royalty of about 4.5 per cent. The 1980s, however, were generally not as kind to Cardin as they were to many other top designers. After two decades of uninterrupted growth, according to in-house figures I have obtained, sales languished in the US during the mid-1980s at around $165 million. This in-house sales figure, compiled by certified accountants, was considerably below the official exaggeration. During this time Cardin and his executives were publicly claiming they sold $240 to $250 million worth of goods in the US.

Since then, however, the US licensees have pulled together. Based on these real sales figures, I estimate that after deducting agents' commissions Cardin is left with an estimated $7 million in annual US royalty income. And that is just a corner of his empire. He also told me he sells slightly more in Japan, slightly less in Europe, compared to America. Together these three geographic regions account for 60 per cent of his business. The remaining 40 per cent is chalked up in countries like Australia, Brazil and Indonesia.

Total worldwide sales for the Pierre Cardin and Maxim's labels must be between $900 million and $1 billion at wholesale. Included within those figures are businesses he owns outright – mostly operating at a loss – which account for about $40 million in revenue. All told, products with his labels move about $2.5 billion worth of goods at retail. Another sum: taking into consideration higher royalties in less competitive markets and volatile exchange rates, Cardin must earn between $35 and $45 million a year in royalty income worldwide. That's pure to-do-what-I-want-with cash.

An extraordinary achievement. Considering he produced those results pretty much alone, backed up by just a handful of executives and in an organization lacking all forms of recognizable structure, it really is astounding. Pierre Cardin is the businessman, if ever there was one, who personifies the 'thriving on chaos' philosophy that became the rage of management gurus during the 1980s. It makes one pause and think about the MBA factories that have poured hopeful, carbon-copy executives into the streets of Europe and America. Undoubtedly their flow-charts, growth-targets and cash-flow analysis will help them manage business empires; ultimately, however, these tools will not help them create empires. Cardin's story illustrates this as sharply as a well-cut garment: you can build an empire without administrative competence, but never without the mysterious human traits – drive, vision, intuition, conviction, grit – which are at the core of all empire builders.

Pierre Cardin is a twentieth-century phenomenon. His fortune was built on the back of rapidly changing media, which in the period of his lifetime had shrunk the world into one easily accessible market. His success could have taken place at no other time in history. He did not manufacture goods, but he manufactured an intangible marketing ether — a media by-product called celebrityhood — which sold goods.

This, now, is wealth-creation in the Information Age.

•   •   •   •

Cardin is never one to be underestimated. He still continues his monumental duties, running with the energy and determination that intimidates his younger employees. He appears vigorous, tireless, healthy. He recently made everyone move offices — again. Bernard Danillon, Edouard Saint Bris, Hervé Duquesnoy, Arnaud de la Motte, Jeff Knipper have all been moved to offices at 82 Rue du Faubourg Saint-Honoré, the address where, as a provincial arriving in Paris forty-six years before, Cardin mysteriously found Monsieur Waltener.

The old Avenue Marigny buildings have been seized for Cardin's newest idea: in the spirit of 1992, he is turning the five-storey building into a department store for European PC products. Nor is this sociological designer neglecting the other momentous political events of our time. To capitalize on the West's new-found fascination with the crumbling Communist Bloc, Cardin has resuscitated the rock opera *Junon and Avos*.

He brought the opera to New York's City Center, inviting 1,000 people to the gala in early 1990. The sharp, bitter January evening was filled with minks and cashmere. The press was there in droves, of course, and there was much popping of flashes as Annette and Oscar de la Renta climbed out of a black car; as the diminutive Arthur Schlesinger arrived in a beaver-collared overcoat. Clusters of celebrities broke off, chatted. The beatnik poet, Allen Ginsberg, looked very hip in black tie, a white silk scarf draped around his neck, pointing his fingers at Andrei Voznesensky, the Soviet poet, who listened attentively.

Among this collection of the rich and famous, amidst these international celebrities, Pierre Cardin moved about ceaselessly, his hyperactive energy exploding from every elf-like gesture, charming, the silk foulard nattily draped from his breast pocket.

•   •   •   •

Pierre Cardin ran around waving my *Forbes* story for weeks after it was published. He used it as his calling card when he visited an Asian head of state, Edouard Saint Bris told me. Charles-Efflam Heidsieck recalled he took it to La Résidence and like a little boy proudly showed it to everyone he knew at the hotel. But as soon as I mentioned to Cardin that I wanted to write a book about him the door slammed shut. Press attaché Bernard Danillon passed on my verbal requests, to no avail. I wrote a letter, sent him a photograph of his family's old house on Via Manzoni in Sant' Andrea di Barbarana. I received a note in return from Hervé Duquesnoy: 'He told me how touched and flattered he was by your project to write a book about him. However, at this time, he does not want to collaborate on the publication of such a book since he himself is thinking of possibly writing his own biography in the near future.'

After that it was hard going. Cardin tried to prevent sources from talking to me – as he had every right to do – and I went about my work. Every now and then I would get a phone call from a source after one of the house executives had pressurized him. He intended to sue me, some sources were told; an employee of his – most likely without the knowledge of Cardin – spread rather slanderous lies about me at a party in Paris. Cardin was able to block me from talking to a few important sources. And, although I interviewed well over 200 people in an attempt to be as close to the truth and accurate as possible, several would only talk on the condition of anonymity and promises of protection. They were afraid.

At one moment during my 1988 interview with Cardin I asked him straight out what would happen to the house once he passed away. He was still very fit and energetic and had many years of work left, I said, but he was also at the age where he must be thinking about his eventual death and legacy. Cardin paused and then surprised me by his response: he realized it was time to start thinking about his death, and he might sell the Pierre Cardin name completely.

I went back to my desk in London and scratched some numbers together on a pad. Without knowing the details of all his Byzantine deals, I still guessed he could sell his whole operation for well over $250 million. At the time, however, most people thought the event was very unlikely. Separate himself from his empire? Prematurely? It would be like tearing his heart from his body.

It was their comments that were premature. In the autumn of 1989 Cardin told Nicholas J. DeMarco, the US agent, that it was impossible to renew his contract for the customary three years. The reason: Cardin was negotiating the sale of his name. DeMarco said Cardin agreed to a one-year contract, with a 90-day notification of sale. That would allow DeMarco time to enter into his own negotiation with the new owners. He sent the new agreement to Paris to be signed. Cardin did not sign it. DeMarco claimed that for the next few months, whenever the two men saw each other Cardin swore he would sign the renewal shortly and reiterated that DeMarco was imperative to the US operations. Not to worry.

But the agreement was never signed. In January 1990, Cardin sent DeMarco a contract to continue as is for sixty days. Period. DeMarco did not sign it. He got on the phone, sent faxes. Dozens of attempts to reach Cardin were in vain; Cardin was not returning DeMarco's calls. In March Cardin's US lawyers called DeMarco and encouraged him to sign the 60-day document. He was told that files were open and they wanted to get this little piece of paperwork out of the way. DeMarco signed the document reluctantly. It was a mistake. A week later he got a letter of termination.

DeMarco, like earlier Cardin employees, felt he had no other choice but to contact his lawyers. In June he filed suit against Cardin for wrongful termination and breach of contract; for wrongful conversion of DeMarco's interest in Cardin's US royalties; and for fraud. DeMarco was seeking $10 million in compensatory and punitive damages. 'I have no animosity towards Cardin,' said DeMarco. 'I feel very sorry for him. He is a very lonely man right now.'

Cardin, of course, is dismissing DeMarco's case as a nuisance lawsuit. To his attorneys the case is clear cut: 'Plaintiff makes this extraordinary claim despite the fact that he executed a written employment agreement dated October 27, 1989 which explicitly provided that his employment was on an "act of will" basis subject to termination by either party or sixty (60) days notice.' As this book was going to press the case was unfolding slowly in the New York courts. The high drama continues.

But maybe not for much longer. Cardin seems to be seriously looking for a buyer. The menswear trade publication, *Daily News Record*, reported that 'sources predicted Cardin would continue his design role if he sold the company. The designer is said to be seeking a sale in order to put his full energies into design work, leaving the business details to others.'

It is not so far-fetched. At the dawn of the 1990s many young Parisian designers have begun to revisit the 1960s – above-the-knee boots; three-quarter-length sleeves; minimalism. 'Cardin is currently enjoying a revival,' wrote Lowri Turner, fashion editor for the London *Evening Standard* in July 1990. 'His simple sixties designs have been an inspiration to a new generation of designers. Nineties versions of his tunic dresses and A-line shifts were on every catwalk in Paris in March.'

Full circle. It always was one of Cardin's favourite geometric patterns.

PIERRE CARDIN

• • • •

The last time I saw Pierre Cardin was on 23 January 1989. It was collection week, and I was shaky. The crowds had just been expelled from the doors of the Pierre Balmain haute-couture spring/summer fashion show. While there I had been savagely whacked on the back of the head by the two-foot lens of a paparazzo, and then witnessed a brawl between an Italian and French photographer jostling for position. Though a trained business journalist, I could never grow accustomed to this highly combustible atmosphere of fashion fanaticism, this opera buffa.

As we hit the pavement on Avenue Gabriel, lined by the spindly, leafless elm trees of winter, I noticed the heavily made-up mannequins dash from the Balmain stage-door to another stage-door just a few doors down. It was Espace Pierre Cardin. His collection was next.

If I was shaky for Balmain, I was rattled for Cardin. I had press passes to all the major collections of the week, but had not requested tickets for Pierre Cardin for obvious reasons: I was persona non grata at the house. Instead, a colleague of mine wangled an extra invitation. Somehow, I had to show my ticket and pass through the security at the doors undetected.

Some journalists thrive on such ridiculous cloak-and-dagger behaviour. I do not. I would much rather have been up-front, giving Pierre Cardin every chance to respond to his critics, to dispute other people's versions of events. He chose our route, however, and even blocked access to sources who could have argued his case for him. So, here I was, reduced to sneaking into his collection as if behind the glass doors of Espace there was some shocking military secret of international importance.

I picked my moment. A throng of rudely jostling journalists and photographers, licensees and celebrities were attacking the doors. It was a crush of pill-box hats, camel-hair overcoats, steel camera cases. In the midst of this I was swept through the security check and practically on to the feet of Hervé Duquesnoy. He looked straight at me, blinked, and then peered over my head at a face he recognized.

My ticket was for the orchestra. Knowing, however, that that was where Pierre Cardin's staff circulated, I headed instead for the less fashionable balcony where suppliers and marginal licensees were shunted. Up the stairs I climbed and found a suitable spot in the second row.

The show was late, of course. Downstairs in the orchestra hordes were finding their seats. John Fairchild was in the centre of the front row. Next to him was his boyish Paris bureau chief, Dennis Thim. Fairchild was working on his latest book and behind him sat his book editor. The editor appeared to be holding a tape recorder, into which Fairchild was furiously whispering comments about everything he saw. On the other side of Fairchild was Suzy Menkes from the *International Herald Tribune*. Her hair was slightly bouffant, like Julie Christie in the movie *Shampoo*, and she wore a simple purple dress. She chatted easily with the white-haired, stoop-shouldered Bernadine Morris of the *New York Times*. Morris had bifocals that slid to the end of her nose, and she constantly peered over them, inspecting what was going on around her like a high-school biology teacher.

Suddenly, a hawkish, brittle man swooped down on the front row. It was Edouard Saint Bris, making an elaborate show of shaking John Fairchild's hand. He then immediately passed on, ignoring everyone else. I looked at my programme. A card announced that Cardin was going to reaffirm his style, with, among other things, 'les couleurs ecologiques' and 'une nouvelle matière'. The programme also included four black-and-white drawings of pointy-cornered suits and dresses. It was quintessential, cost-conscious Cardin. Other couturiers listed each outfit by order of appearance, with a detailed description of fabrics, and stuffed the programme with glossy coloured photographs of accessories. My mind drifted, and I thought about some of the hilarious comments Cardin has made to journalists over the years. He was still in rare form: later in the year he was to announce, in all earnestness, that 'the woman is like an escargot – when she takes off her big outer shell, she's very slim and sinuous.'

When I looked up the red seats of Espace were nearly filled. Yoshi Takata, Cardin's Japanese licensing director, cruised up and down an aisle in a check poncho and black Diva glasses. Ushering the grand old dames into the theatre, greeting the press, was the slightly bald Bernard Danillon. His contagious laugh managed to rise up over the roar and chatter of the crowd.

Mireille Mathieu, the buck-toothed chansonnier whom Cardin had promoted decades ago, was seating herself in the fourth row where all Cardin's 'front row' ladies sat. Mathieu, her hair bobbed and jet black, was one of the youngest. The wives of French politicians – like the Paris mayor's wife, Bernadette Chirac – sat dutifully in a row and kept one eye roaming for photographers. Most of these women were rather aged, though smart in Chanel-type clothes in primary colours with gold-chain purses. Mme Philippe de Gaulle, wife of an admiral, sat imperiously. Three paparazzi looked around at the women and then zoomed in on Mathieu. Up in the balcony, the row in front of me filled completely with chatty Italians. Italian *Vogue*, I guessed.

Finally the show began. It was all over the place. In the 300 odd-piece marathon there were the vinyl cone-head hats sawn off at an angle. The hula-hoop skirts arrived periodically in various forms – an elegant black dress had a disc covered with fabric, tied with a bow and attached to the rear. Another time a mannequin, her face frozen into a smile, was trying to manoeuvre across the stage with three huge hoops in tow, as if she were drift-netting for cod. Linen-like tunics came out in a pointed hem, folded like a napkin around the body. Trained fashion journalists were undoubtedly spotting interesting technical details that I could not detect. Most of it, I must confess, looked either ridiculous or mundane.

I looked down. John Fairchild was talking the whole time into his tape-recorder; Thim, his Paris bureau chief, was nervously biting the end of a ball-point pen. My photographer, Maggie Steber, was legitimately down in the fray and turned her lens on Fairchild, capturing him in an exquisite moment of pain – eyes squinting as he concentrated on the clothes, his mouth puckered in what looked like an involuntary expression of pure horror and disbelief. Bernadine Morris, meanwhile, had one eye on the show while she talked non-stop into the ear of Suzy Menkes. Suddenly, Morris stopped talking and stood upright. She walked over to the stage, tapped a photographer on the shoulder, and gestured at a costume she wanted shot. Menkes, who had been taking diligent notes throughout, offered Morris a sweet from a round tin.

The music was a surprise. The jolty arrival of mannequins on stage was incongruous to the Brian Eno-like sound that wafted from the speakers, a sort of tinkling, whale-moaning sound that was very soothing. I was anxious for the mannequins, however, who were clearly being shoved on to the stage in a pell-mell order. Some bumped into each other. One even got her foot caught in the hooped taffeta-like train of another and had to contort her body to extricate her foot. After the first half-hour, some fifteen of the Italians sitting in front of me got up en masse and walked out; only three people were left in the entire row. Cardin started sending mannequins on stage in hats that had half a plant attached to them.

By the end of the show, some two hours later, a third of the balcony had left early. Those of us who had persevered had seen everything – everything from silks to wool in purple, aquamarine, a material decorated with blue-and-yellow pointillism. Bizarre lampshade dresses were presented next to simple day dresses that could have come from the pages of a Spiegel catalogue. Columns of rich silk made elegant evening wear. It was a hodgepodge.

At the end, with the audience down, the smattering of applause was decidedly thin. Realizing that bows had to be taken quickly, before the applause died out altogether, Pierre Cardin, André Oliver and a few assistants darted out on to the stage. Oliver momentarily hovered in the back, drawn and white, a few days of beard growth shadowing his face. His hair was greasy, and a friend of his later told me that he was suffering from shingles.

Cardin walked to the front of the stage, his hair tousled, but otherwise looking remarkably well. In his hands he twisted his black-framed glasses. He bobbed his head briefly, twice, acknowledging the crowd. His face was lit up with an enigmatic look – a small, sort of Mona Lisa smile. And then he rushed off stage.

NOTES

Well over 200 people were interviewed for this book. The author tape-recorded 90 per cent of all the core interviews – 117 tapes in total – and in addition took written back-up notes in each and every case. Generally, only a source's firsthand knowledge was printed. Reconstructed conversations, for example, were only used when the source was a participant in the conversation. In the few cases where secondhand knowledge has been used the author makes it clear in the text that the information is hearsay.

Also as a general rule the author did not take one person's claim as sufficient proof for a key controversial fact. Where possible he sought a minimum of one additional confirmation – in many key cases he possesses half a dozen taped confirmations. (In a very few circumstances – incidents where there was only one witness – it was impossible to get independent verification. In such cases the author carefully assessed the source's credibility and motives, and tried to verify the statements by other means, before he made the decision to use his or her stories.)

After the manuscript was written, and to improve further the quality and accuracy of the text, the author again fact-checked major portions of the text. He underlined key claims, anecdotes and accounts in red and sent them to his two researchers. The researchers' job was independently to verify the work by reinterviewing and cross-examining sources. If the source stuck by his or her original story and signed off on the author's written account, the researchers then underlined the red segments in blue – with the date and time in the margin – to prove that the testimony was fact-checked. When sources made objections for reasons of accuracy the author made all the required changes where appropriate.

Occasionally, however, sources tried to deny they had made a previous statement. The fact that their statements were now appearing in cold print startled them and a few tried to retract earlier statements. If their objections were purely face-saving and not about accuracy, then the author overruled their attempts to retract statements and used the original on-the-record, taped quotes. Some sources would talk only on the condition of anonymity. Their identities have been concealed although the same fact-checking, cross-reporting methods were used to ensure accuracy.

The chapter notes listed below indicate some of the sources used by the author in writing each chapter of the book. It is far from being a comprehensive list, but is intended to give the reader an overview of the author's research.

CHAPTER 1

The interview of Pierre Cardin was conducted by the author in March 1988 for a cover story on the designer for *Forbes* magazine.

Information about the previous books published about Pierre Cardin was obtained through interviews with Fanval's publisher, Alexis Ovtchinnikoff; authors Jean Manusardi and Dominique Sirop; Pierre Cardin's press officer, Bernard Danillon de Cazella.

CHAPTER 2

The principal sources for this chapter were a series of interviews with Pierre Cardin's family members, cousin Giuseppe 'Tino' Cardin and brother César Cardin. Other details came from family accounts in Jean Manusardi, *Dix Ans Avec Cardin* (Paris, Éditions de Fanval, 1986). Additional details came from a host of published interviews with Pierre Cardin himself, but most notably a piece in *Combat* (17 December 1961) and the television interview with Claude Lanzmann, first aired in May 1968 as part of the *Dim Dam Dom* French television series.

'Rital. Macaroni' were the taunts César and Pierre suffered as boys as
told to the author in taped interviews with César Cardin. It was to César
that Pierre swore revenge and the author has quoted César Cardin's taped
account verbatim.

Additional information came from the author retracing Pierre Cardin's
route through Sant' Andrea di Barbarana; Firminy; La Tour-du-Pin;
Saint-Clair de la Tour; Saint-Étienne; Vichy; and Paris. The author took
photographs; searched town and factory records; interviewed former neighbours, policemen, journalists and bureaucrats; researched and photocopied
archives in local libraries, museums and exhibitions; and researched standard
history books. Of great help was Vichy's public library and the photographs
of the period.

That Cardin inflicted himself with a wound during the war and hid in the
woods to avoid the STO was told to the author, on tape and reconfirmed, by
his brother César Cardin.

CHAPTER 3

An account of the first post-war couture show was published in *Life* magazine
on 20 November 1944. Information about war and post-war couture and
the couturiers was obtained from several fashion essays, most notably those
published in Ruth Lynam, editor, *Couture: An Illustrated History of the Great
Paris Designers and Their Creations* (Garden City, Doubleday & Co., Inc.,
1972). Other books of particular help were Christian Dior, *Christian Dior
and I* (New York, E.P. Dutton & Co., Inc., 1957); Jane Dorner, *Fashion in
the Forties and Fifties* (London, Ian Allen Ltd, 1975); Bettina Ballard, *In My
Fashion* (New York, David McKay Company, Inc., 1960); Caroline Rennolds
Milbank, *Couture: The great designers* (New York, Stewart, Tabori & Chang,
Inc., 1985); Françoise Giroud, *Dior* (New York, Rizzoli International Pub-
lications, Inc., 1987); Diana Vreeland, *D.V.* (New York, Alfred A. Knopf,
1984); Georgina O'Hara, *The Encyclopaedia of Fashion* (London, Thames and
Hudson Ltd, 1986); Colin McDowell, *McDowell's Directory of 20th Century
Fashion* (London, Muller Blond and White Ltd, 1984); Marilyn Bender,
The Beautiful People (New York, Coward-McCann, 1967); Elsa Schiaparelli,
Shocking Life (London, J.M. Dent & Sons Ltd, 1954); David Bond, *The
Guinness Guide to 20th Century Fashion* (London, David Bond and Guinness
Superlatives Ltd, 1981); Joan Nunn, *Fashion in Costume 1200–1980* (New
York, Shocken Books, 1984); Palmer White, *Schiaparelli* (New York,
Rizzoli, 1986); Edmonde Charles-Roux, *Chanel* (London, Jonathan Cape,

1976); and Jessica Daves, editor, *1947–1967 Fashion Group French Shows* (New York, New York Fashion Group, 1967). Interviews with Thelma Sweetinburgh, Madame Carven, Jacques Rouët and Dominique Sirop were also used, as were photographs of the period.

Information about Jean Cocteau, Christian Bérard and the filming of *La Belle et la Bête* came principally from the following published sources: Francis Steegmuller, *Cocteau* (London, Macmillan & Co. Ltd 1970); Jean Cocteau, *Professional Secrets* (New York, Farrar, Straus & Giroux, 1972); Elizabeth Sprigge and Jean-Jacques Kihm, *Jean Cocteau: The Man and the Mirror* (London, Victor Gollancz, 1968); Jean Cocteau, *Beauty and the Beast: Diary of a Film* (New York, Dover, 1972); Roy Armes, *French Cinema* (London, Secker & Warburg, 1985). Additional information came from the autobiographies of Bettina Ballard, Elsa Schiaparelli and Diana Vreeland listed above. Further information came from interviews with Mila Parély and a source who must remain anonymous, and a written response to questions by Jean Marais.

Information about the house of Dior and Pierre Cardin's tenure was obtained primarily from interviews with Jacques Rouët; information from Maison Dior's archives; published interviews that Cardin himself has given over the years; a number of books already cited above. Cardin has previously given the details of his abrupt departure from Maison Dior on camera with Claude Lanzmann in 1968, and the facts were also published in *Combat* on 17 December 1961.

CHAPTER 4

The scenes of Rue Richepance were recreated by looking at period photographs; visiting Cardin's old rooms which are still in use today as a fashion atelier; and interviews with neighbours. A description of his first atelier appears in the *Sunday News* (24 November 1957) and it has been added to the eyewitness accounts of Thelma Sweetinburgh, Bettina Graziani and Nathalie Mont-Servan. The fact that Dior helped Cardin launch his business has been repeatedly reported before, in places like the *New York Times* (7 August 1958) and a Cardin interview in Jean Manusardi's book, *Dix Ans Avec Cardin*. It has also been confirmed with Jacques Rouët. Further documentary evidence came from the society photographer André Ostier who photographed Cardin fitting Dior with the 'Bal de Rois' costume.

The post-war ball season has been well documented in the writings of Bettina Ballard and other fashion journalists. Of particular help, however, were the society pages of the day: *Time* magazine (17 September 1951); *Life* magazine (29 March 1949, 10 July 1950, 24 September 1951, 28 September 1953, 26 July 1954); *Newsweek* (17 September 1951); the *New York Herald Tribune* (16 January 1949, 2 September 1953). Besides interviews with André Ostier, additional information came from Manusardi's *Dix Ans Avec Cardin* and Suzy Menkes, *The Windsor Style* (London, Grafton Books, 1987).

In an interview published in Manusardi's *Dix Ans Avec Cardin*, Cardin explained how he met Daniel Pérou. In taped interviews with the author three Maison Cardin employees of the 1960s said they believed Pérou helped finance Cardin early on and was rewarded with the top managerial position.

André Oliver's close friendship with Pierre Cardin has been reported before and was discussed at length in interviews with Max Bellest, Andrew Wargo, John Kornblith, Odile Moltzer, S. Miller Harris, Don Robbie, Arnold Linsman, Barbara Ligeti, James Brady, Eleanor Lambert, Daniel Fallot, Mildred Custin, Hiroko and many others, some of whom must remain anonymous. More detailed accounts of Cardin's private life have been discussed and documented at length with several sources but have been left out as they were not germane to the story.

CHAPTER 5

The circumstances of Christian Dior's death were widely reported in many of the fashion books cited in the Chapter 3 notes above, and were further discussed in the author's interviews with Jacques Rouët, Thelma Sweetinburgh, Roland de Vassal and James Brady. The succession to Christian Dior by Yves Saint Laurent has been widely reported in the above-quoted books – in particular the Ruth Lynam edited series of essays called *Couture* – but also in a book published in conjunction with Yves Saint Laurent's exhibit at the costume institute of The Metropolitan Museum of Modern Art in 1984: John P. O'Neill, Editor in Chief, *Yves Saint Laurent* (London, Thames and Hudson Ltd, 1984).

Other articles consulted by the author regarding Cardin's late 1950s period were in the *Sunday News*, *The New York Times*, *International Herald Tribune*, *The Times*, *Le Figaro*, *New York Times Magazine*, *Le Monde* and *New York Herald*.

Cardin's trip to Japan is documented in interviews with Hiroko and Kenzo, and in a series of interviews given by Cardin, such as Suzy Menkes' article, 'A Growing Yen for Luxury Labels', in the *International Herald Tribune* on 20 October 1989. Other background material came from

Cecil Beaton, *Japanese* (New York, The John Day Company, 1959). Oliver's call-up into the Algerian war and subsequent treatment were discussed in the interview with Hiroko and another mannequin, and published in James Brady, *Superchic* (Boston, Little Brown & Co., 1974).

The information about Jeanne Moreau came principally from a taped interview the author had with the actress. Other information came from articles in the *Baltimore Sun, Sunday News, Washington Post, Women's Wear Daily, Vogue, New York Times Magazine, Time, Newsweek, Life, Sunday Times* (London), and various official biographies. Other people interviewed on the subject were Molly Haskell, Florence Malraux, Thelma Sweetinburgh, Robert L. Green, Roland de Vassal, Odile Moltzer, Georges Bril, Raymond Mejat, James Brady, and others. Also consulted were Roy Armes's book on French Cinema, cited in the notes of Chapter 3; Brady's autobiography *Superchic* cited above; and John Fairchild, *The Fashionable Savages* (Garden City, Doubleday & Co, Inc., 1965).

CHAPTER 6

The fact that Cardin has for years been taken advantage of by unethical employees has been published previously – in Brady's *Superchic* and Manusardi's *Dix Ans Avec Cardin* – but was also confirmed and documented in interviews with Henry Berghauer, Odile Moltzer, Jean Manusardi, Charles-Efflam Heidsieck and others.

The structural economic problems of haute couture and retailing during the early 1960s have been discussed and reported at length in many of the fashion books already cited above. The author additionally interviewed Jean-Guy Vermont, François Lesage, André Lemarié, Jacques Rouët, Jean Manigot, Robert Schoettl, Jacques Gourbault, Odile Moltzer, Henry Berghauer and Kurt Barnard. Other sources consulted were *Life, Women's Wear Daily, The New York Times, Guardian, Le Monde, The Times, The Sunday Times*. Also consulted: Daniel J. Boorstin, *The Americans: The Democratic Experience* (New York, Random House, 1973).

Cardin's launch of designer menswear has been published repeatedly in sources cited already. Other publications of particular help were *Le Figaro, Gentlemen's Quarterly, Esquire, The New York Times* and *Newsweek*. Books consulted: O.E. Shoeffler and William Gale, *Esquire's Encyclopedia of 20th Century Men's Fashions* (New York, McGraw-Hill Book Company, 1973); and Joan Nunn, *Fashion in Costume 1200–1980* (New York, Shocken Books, 1984). Other details came from interviews with Jean Manigot,

Georges Bril, Nicholas DeMarco, Michel Bouret, Gilbert Feruch and John Kornblith.

Many publications were consulted about the Kennedy period, most notably, however, the excellent book by Hugh Sidney, *John F. Kennedy: Portrait of a President* (London, Andre Deutsch Ltd, 1964). Hervé Alphand and Odile Moltzer were interviewed for this section as well.

The detail that Cardin wanted his men's perfume to smell like sperm has been previously published in Manusardi's *Dix Ans Avec Cardin* and a *Women's Wear Daily* article. The author obtained additional confirmation from Pierre Cardin's press officer of the day.

CHAPTER 7

Chanel's antipathy towards Pierre Cardin was reported in the fashion press of the day, but has been particularly well documented in James Brady's *Superchic*.

Information about the suppliers to the couture world was obtained by consulting French, British and American publications and books, and also by interviewing suppliers: Jean-Guy Vermont, François Lesage, André Lemarié, Mr and Mrs Jacques Elophe, Claudia Mantegazzi, Claude Coudray, Alexandre, and Jean Barthet. Jacques Mouclier, président de la Fédération Française de la Couture, was also interviewed.

Other books consulted and not quoted above were Jonathan Moor, *Perry Ellis* (New York, St Martin's Press, 1986); Nicholas Coleridge, *The Fashion Conspiracy* (London, William Heinemann Ltd, 1988); Jeffrey A. Trachtenberg, *Ralph Lauren: The Man Behind the Mystique* (Boston, Little, Brown and Co., 1988). General information about Cardin's influence in the fashion world was also obtained by interviews with fashion journalists Suzy Menkes, Bernadine Morris, Thelma Sweetinburgh, Nathalie Mont-Servan, Jacqueline Claude, Robert L. Green, G.Y. Dryansky and James Brady. Also interviewed were Cardin's current employees, André Oliver, Bernard Danillon de Cazella, Edouard Saint Bris, Hervé Duquesnoy, Arnaud de la Motte, Jeff Knipper, Zbigniew Krawczynski and Humbert des Lyons de Feuchin.

Other sources for this chapter: *The New York Times*, *The Times*, *Women's Wear Daily*, *Daily News*, *New York Herald Tribune*, *Time*, *Daily Telegraph*, *L'Express*, The Fashion Group, Inc., *Paris Match*, Agence France Press, *Newsweek*, *Daily Sketch*, *Daily Mirror*, *Penthouse*, *New York Post*, *Christian Science Monitor*, *Daily Express*, *Washington Post*, *Guardian*.

CHAPTER 8

G.Y. Dryansky's scene with Cardin was published in Brady's *Superchic*, but has also been documented and checked in the author's interviews with Dryansky.

Cardin resigned from the Chambre Syndicale in 1966. The resignation letter was published in Manusardi's *Dix Ans Avec Cardin*. This account was further confirmed by Denise Dubois, press officer of the Chambre Syndicale de la Couture Parisienne, who investigated the association's files.

The stories about the hiring of Manusardi and Fallot, their relationship while at Maison Cardin, their various rises and falls, was told to the author in a series of interviews. Both men were interviewed independently, then together. In the joint interview they talked about the cliquish homosexual atmosphere at the house, one reason why they became friends. This was further documented in taped statements of six other employees.

All the stories about penetrating the US market come from interviews, and were reconfirmed in fact-checking sessions with Eleanor Lambert, Mildred Custin, Wilkes Bashford, Marvin Kirsten, Max Bellest, Danny Zarem, Don Robbie, Robert Green and John Kornblith. That Cardin did not sign the Intercontinental Men's Apparel, Inc. contract until the press appeared has been documented in accounts by John Kornblith, Marvin Kirsten and Jean Manusardi.

S. Miller Harris' anecdote about negotiating his contract and subsequent Cardin changes has been confirmed with Jean Manusardi. Another source was Intercontinental's 1970 prospectus.

Jean Manusardi, Mario Sala and Daniel Fallot have all contributed to the story about the start of the 'Environment' business. The fact that Cardin did not design the Pozzi ceramics was confirmed by Sala and Manusardi. Cardin's penchant for moving furniture and decorating has not only been published before, but is repeatedly referred to in interviews with Jean Manusardi, Daniel Fallot, Odile Moltzer, Alain Carré, Arnold Linsman, and S. Miller Harris, among others.

Other sources: *Home Furnishings Daily*, *The New York Times*, *The Times*, *Guardian*, *Washington Post*, *Business Week*, *Daily News*.

CHAPTER 9

Problems with the opening of Espace Pierre Cardin have been previously published in Manusardi's *Dix Ans Avec Cardin*.

The arrival of François-Marie Banier has been published previously. Wrote G.Y. Dryansky on 10 May 1973 in *Women's Wear Daily*: 'He [Cardin] is reputedly a lonely man. Since his affair with Jeanne Moreau in the early 1960s no woman appears to have attracted him. His closeness to Oliver is now a sort of father–son relationship. The last well-known person who caught his sentimental interest was François-Marie Banier, the young novelist who débuted in Paris carrying a soccer ball in a Cardin's menswear show when he was about 15.' Other sources consulted were Jean Manusardi, Max Bellest and Banier himself.

The fact that Cardin had little input into the products that carried his name – although he did have final approval – is repeatedly documented in taped interviews with employees Alain Carré, Jean Manusardi, Max Bellest, Andrew Wargo, Mario Sala, and manufacturers John Kornblith, Marvin Kirsten, S. Miller Harris and Bernard Wachter.

Also consulted was the coverage in *Women's Wear Daily*, *Evening Standard*, *Los Angeles Times*, *L'Express*, *The New York Times*, *Guardian*, *International Herald Tribune*, *New York Post*, *Washington Post*, *Le Point*, *Time*, *After Dark*, *Newsweek*, *New York Times Magazine*, *Connoisseur*, *Daily Express*, *Interiors*, and Espace Pierre Cardin brochures.

Other major writings consulted, besides those of Daniel J. Boorstin quoted above, were Robert L. Heilbroner, *The Quest for Wealth* (London, Eyre & Spottiswoode, 1958). Among others, the following people were interviewed for this chapter: Andrew Wargo, Max Bellest, Mel Reaume, Barbara Ligeti, John Kornblith, Arnold Linsman, Alain Carré, William H. Meyers, Mario Sala, Jean Manusardi, Daniel Fallot, Robert Green, G.Y. Dryansky, S. Miller Harris, Moses Pendelton, Robert Wilson, and Roger Ritchie.

CHAPTER 10

The fact that graft is a part of fashion journalism is not only documented by interviews the author had with journalists who have experienced bribery attempts first-hand, but has also been previously stated in the Perry Ellis biography by Jonathan Moor.

Pierre Cardin's fight with Karl Lagerfeld and Anna Piaggi is the wonderful work of the late Hébé Dorsey as reported in the *International Herald Tribune*.

That Cardin signs all the cheques personally was told to the author by Cardin's press officer, Bernard Danillon, and has been reported numerous times. It was also confirmed by many former employees, including Daniel Fallot, Mario Sala and Max Bellest. The fact that there was no master list itemizing what manufacturers were making what products has been documented repeatedly in interviews with Andrew Wargo, Arnold Linsman, Jean Manusardi, Daniel Fallot, Max Bellest and Mario Sala. It was also the core of the Morse court case.

The account of Cardin signing two wig contracts has been corroborated in interviews with Max Bellest, Andrew Wargo and Jean Manusardi.

The Morse case was documented by complete court documents filed in the United States District Court, Southern District of New York (Marvin S. Morse vs. Pierre Cardin et al., 77 Civ. 5185), and confirmed in interviews with Max Bellest, Jean Manusardi, Andrew Wargo and others.

Other court records used in this book and in the author's possession were: Sheridane Designs Ltd Inc, vs. Société Anonyme Pierre Cardin, 5387/74; Sheridane Designs Ltd, Inc. et al. vs. Société Anonyme Pierre Cardin, 8149–1973; Pierre Cardin et al. vs. Continental Time Corporation et al., 84 Civ. 8070; American Cyanamid Company et al.vs. Picaso-Anstalt et al., 90–1424; Nicholas J. DeMarco et al. vs. Pierre Cardin et al., 15379/90.

The fact that no employee recalls ever seeing a budget or business plan at Maison Cardin has been documented in interviews with Jean Manusardi, Daniel Fallot, Mario Sala, and current employees Hervé Duquesnoy, Bernard Danillon and Edouard Saint Bris.

Cardin's aversion to organization, that he ran the company like a grocery store, that he would not attend meetings – all these assertions are documented in interviews about what the inner sanctum was like with Jean Manusardi, Mario Sala, Daniel Fallot, Alain Carré, Max Bellest, Andrew Wargo, Nicholas DeMarco, and employees who have asked to remain anonymous.

The fact that Cardin bought products and sewed his label into the garments has been documented by three employees.

The 1977 US furniture trip has been documented by dozens of press releases, photographs and monthly clipping-service packets supplied to the author by former press officers of the Cardin organization.

CHAPTER 11

According to interviews with Max Bellest, Jean Manusardi and outside perfume executives, Pierre Cardin in 1966 sold the worldwide rights to his name in perfume, excluding France, to Jacqueline Cochran, a predecessor company of Shulton, Inc. This fact has also been published in *Dix Ans Avec Cardin*. But according to a 1990 court case between American Cyanamid (Shulton's parent company) and Pierre Cardin and one of his holding companies (Picaso-Anstalt), the sale appears to have gone through several flips over the years. According to court records, there was a 'cancellation of the Sales Agreement signed October 10, 1967, between Picaso-Anstalt and Shulton, Inc.' On 26 May 1977, however, Picaso signed another agreement with Shulton for $2 million, this time granting an exclussive licensing contract with a $500,000 option for Shulton to buy the Pierre Cardin name in perfumes, payable prior to the contract termination in December 1991. A dispute over the rights between Pierre Cardin and Shulton in 1990 went to court, but was eventually settled. According to the out-of-court settlement, says American Cyanimid's lawyer, John L. Fricano of Skadden, Arps, Slate, Meagher & Flom, Pierre Cardin has once regained the rights to his name in perfumes under a settlement that was 'good' for his client. Fricano told the author he would try and clarify what happened to the original 1966 sale of the name and the cancellation of the sale in 1967, but after researching the question Fricano's office returned saying such information was 'under protective order and we are not at liberty to divulge it'.

The fact that Cardin sold the rights to his name in writing materials and several other products is documented in interviews with persons involved in the sale, and it was further confirmed with Andrew Wargo and Nicholas DeMarco. Jean Manusardi personally negotiated the sale of Cardin's name in Argentina.

Claims that Cardin has been frequently stolen from by employees have been published in *Dix Ans Avec Cardin* and *Superchic*. The author further confirmed this claim, repeatedly, in interviews with Jean Manusardi, Odile Moltzer, Daniel Fallot, and others who wish to remain anonymous. Cardin's tendency to be suspicious, jealous and distrustful was discussed at length, and verified, in interviews with Robert Green, Bernard Wachter, John Kornblith, Charles-Efflam Heidsieck, Mario Sala, Daniel Fallot, Alain Carré, Max Bellest, Andrew Wargo, Jean Manusardi and Nicholas DeMarco.

The in-house debate – sign more and more licensees for money or cut back and stay focused – was documented repeatedly in interviews with Jean Manusardi, Max Bellest, Andrew Wargo, Mario Sala, Daniel Fallot, Alain Carré, John Kornblith, Morty Spar, Stanley Gillette, Robert Green, and many other PC manufacturers not quoted directly in the book.

The dispute with tie manufacturer Sheridane is documented in court records (quoted above) and in interviews with Jean Manusardi, Max Bellest, Andrew Wargo, S. Miller Harris, John Kornblith and Morty Spar.

Mario Sala's fight with Cardin and his bitter departure is documented through a series of interviews with Sala and further confirmed with Jean Manusardi, who was called as a witness.

That Cardin desired to be rid of Nicole Alphand was a repeated theme in interviews with Robert L. Green, Arnold Linsman, Max Bellest, S. Miller Harris and John Kornblith. Her death – date and circumstances – was confirmed in an interview with her husband, Hervé Alphand.

CHAPTER 12

According to officials responsible for records in the town hall of San Biagio di Callalta, Cardin called asking for an Italian passport so that he could do business in Vietnam. The request for an Italian passport was declined.

Pierre Cardin's 1977 return to La Tour-du-Pin was aired on the local French station, FR3. The author checked further details of his return with the principal of his former school.

Dorothy and John Kornblith stories about the sale of Intercontinental are documented in interviews. Additional sources were the *Daily News*, *The New York Times*, *Wall Street Journal* and *Moodys*.

The importance of Didier Heye to Pierre Cardin was a repeated subject in interviews with Max Bellest, Andrew Wargo, Charles-Efflam Heidsieck, S. Miller Harris, Franco Gentileschi, Arnold Linsman, and others who wish to remain anonymous.

The story about Cardin trying to sew up Chinese manufacturers was told to the author by Bernard Wachter in a series of interviews. Besides interviewing executives at Gruppo GFT and Cardin employee Arnaud de la Motte, the author consulted *International Herald Tribune*, *Elle* (France), *Stern*, *The New York Times*, *Women's Wear Daily*, *Realités*, *L'Express*, *Berliner Morgenpost*, *Welt*, *Abendzeitung*, *Interiors*, *Life*, *Daily Telegraph*, *Time*, *L'Officiel USA*, *Die Weltwoche*, *Bunte*, *Der Spiegel*, *The Times*, *Look*, *Architectural Digest*, *Daily News*, *Toronto Globe & Mail*, and press releases from the Cardin organization.

CHAPTER 13

Information about Maxim's has come from: Maxim's de Paris catalogue, Maxim's magazine, Maxim's des Mers sales kit, Champagne Maxim's de

Paris brochure, Dialog Information Services, Inc., *New York Times Magazine*, *Wall Street Journal*, *International Herald Tribune*, *Time*, *Le Figaro*, *France Amérique*, *Forbes*, *Journal do Brasil*, *Veja*, *Women's Wear Daily*, *Reuters*, *The Times*, *Daily Telegraph*, *The Financial Times*, *People*, *Playboy* (France), *Jour de France*, *New York Post*, *Celebrity News*, and *The Social Pictorial*.

Those interviewed include Humbert des Lyons de Feuchin, Julian Payne, Richard Power, Charles-Efflam Heidsieck, Steve Zapor, William H. Meyers, Franco Gentileschi, François Vaudable, John Strover, Hervé Duquesnoy, Maggi Nolan, and employees who cannot be named.

EPILOGUE

US and North American sales figures are documented by in-house figures audited by DHR International. The analysis of worldwide sales figures is the author's, based on information given him by Pierre Cardin and other executives. The analysis required using comparative valuations for known transactions and making assumptions based on, for example, occupancy rates and average room rates for the Maxim's hotel as supplied by Cardin's executives.

The author has records of the suit filed by Nicholas J. DeMarco, quoted above, and has further interviewed DeMarco on the subject. Other articles consulted were *Wall Street Journal* and *Daily News Record*.

ACKNOWLEDGEMENTS

Heartfelt thanks are due my two hard-working and reliable researchers, Claire Saint-André in Paris and Linda Hirsch in New York. Their dedication, professionalism and thoroughness have contributed greatly to the quality of the reporting. Thanks also to researcher J. Geraldo Soares of New York who untangled many of my special research problems.

Sincere thanks to the publishing world's dynamo agent Arthur Pine. It was his vision and grit that turned an idea into a book. Thanks to all members, blood or not, of Arthur Pine Associates.

Special thanks to Mark Barty-King, publisher of Bantam Press, who exhibited courage and conviction in backing this project through thick and thin. Thanks, too, to the helpful, efficient Bantam staff of Nuala O'Neill, Tom Graves and others. My deepest appreciation and thanks, however, go to Jim Cochrane who in his gentlemanly manner guided me through the panic with firm vision.

Many thanks to Forbes *magazine — the people and institution. Special thanks to Lawrence Minard, managing editor, who first understood that there was a story in Pierre Cardin; and to Richard Stern, who gave me unqualified support when the going was rough.*

The people who have donated their valuable time and energy to help me understand Pierre Cardin are numerous. Many of them have been extremely brave; others extremely generous. Here is a partial list of those who deserve my sincere thanks: Jean Manusardi, Mario Sala, Daniel Fallot, Max Bellest, Andrew Wargo, S. Miller Harris, John Kornblith, Arnold Linsman, André Ostier, Jean-Guy Vermont, Barbara Ligeti, Hiroko, Franco Gentileschi, Odile and Kim Moltzer, Charles-Efflam Heidsieck, and Alain Carré. Thanks to all those who talked to me, and all those who have helped but cannot be named.

Thanks also to the superb fashion pundits who helped educate this rube: Anne Bogart, Suzy Menkes, James Brady, G.Y. Dryansky, Kurt Barnard, Bernadine Morris, Nathalie Mont-Servan and others. But my deepest and most sincere thanks go to the most dignified lady of fashion journalism, Thelma Sweetinburgh.

Lastly, thanks to my parents, Vasco and Jane, who taught me to dream and work; thanks to supportive family, friends and priest.

And thank you, thank you, Susan.

INDEX

develops total environment concept 128; returns to Vichy 132; starts Espace Cardin 135; expands licensed product range 147–50; honours 151; sale of rights 173, 225–7, 250–1; ventures in China 193, 199–200, 204–5, 218–19, 228; and Russia 200–4; joins Maxim's 209; moves into hotels 220; Maison Cardin today 235–40;

finances 171–81; problems 81–2, 89–90, 99, 224; employees' wages 99, 105, 138, 174; finance for Espace 136–8, 142; cost-cutting at Maxim's 214; wealth now 233–5

character and attributes: ambition 47, 61; appearance 2, 79, 175, 197, 221; at home 152–3; compulsive buying 165–6; courtship of media 69, 119, 155–61, 168–9; desire for revenge 10, 17, 133, 141–2; distrust of associates 176–7, 183, 213; economical habits 174; egotism and vanity 1–4, 80, 150, 151–2, 157, 193,

197; *and* occasional humility 151–2; failure to keep appointments 92–3, 103, 126, 131, 153–4, 182–3, 230–1; food 152, 212; frequent office moves 131–2, 164, 214, 235; generosity 177; health 73; lack of organization 4, 54, 115, 118, 124, 129, 161–5; loneliness 150–1, 153; love of property 172–3; money, attitude to 3–4, 171–2, 173, 175–6, 177; politics, scant interest in 21, 110; preoccupation with youth 96, 112; reaction to books about him 6, 235–6; relationships with employees 116–17, 118, 174, 181–6, 186–90, 212–13, 222–3, 225, 236–7; *and* with licensees 166–8; reluctance to delegate 74, 139–40, 182–3; sexuality 61–2, 77–8, 125, 182; shyness and reserve 6–7; social manners 107; technical skill 67; temperament 74, 83, 133; tendency to romanticize 23, 69–70, 158, 194–5; theatre, love of 18, 50;